Evelyn D. M. Scott –
16th March 1944 –

From dear Rene –

=ǀTHE CHANGELINGǀ=

Timothy Faircloud.

EDEN PHILLPOTTS
has also written :

Novels :

REDCLIFF
GEORGE WESTOVER
UP HILL, DOWN DALE
A CORNISH DROLL
THE GREY ROOM
THE JURY
THE RING FENCE
TRYPHENA
THE THREE MAIDENS
STORMBURY
"FOUND DROWNED"
BRED IN THE BONE
WITCH'S CAULDRON
NED OF THE CARIBBEES
A SHADOW PASSES
MR. DIGWEED AND MR. LUMB
THE OLDEST INHABITANT
PORTRAIT OF A GENTLEMAN
THE WIFE OF ELIAS
A VOICE FROM THE DARK
A DEED WITHOUT A NAME
PILGRIMS OF THE NIGHT
A MUSEUM PIECE

Essays :

A WEST COUNTRY SKETCH BOOK
ESSAYS IN LITTLE

Short Stories :

IT HAPPENED LIKE THAT
THE TORCH
CHERRY GAMBOL
THEY COULD DO NO OTHER
PEACOCK HOUSE

THE CHANGELING

By

EDEN PHILLPOTTS

HUTCHINSON & CO. (Publishers) LTD.

LONDON : NEW YORK : MELBOURNE

TO

ADELAIDE

WITH DEAR LOVE FROM HER FATHER

THE FLEET STREET PRESS
EAST HARDING ST.
E.C.4

I.

CRADLED in the Hundred of Clyst there lies a little Devonshire thorp with its own distinctions and historic claims; for Priory dates from the Conqueror and holds a place in Domesday. Ignorant of such honours the hamlet reposes amid miles of arable, pasture and orchard, with an outer circumference of farms and woodlands, where the spacious county wills to lie upon the level for most part and hills only create a far horizon. The homes of Priory cluster close about its perpendicular and embattled church tower, pressing so near upon it that their windows often open above the dormitories of the dead beneath them, where an inner semi-circle of yew trees shrouds the graves in sombre guardianship. At the very core of Priory stands its fane, and the people take their time from the clock tower. Through the village midst there runs a brook making head northward amid water-meadows to join a larger streamlet on her way to sea, and beside it extends an upraised footway, shaded by trees, where passers-by may rest upon seats beneath them. The older dwellings are mostly of white, or lemon-washed cob under thatched roofs; but the central nest of activity, comprising shops and working yards, post-office and main buildings, is of later time and boasts red brick-work, tiles, slates and corrugated iron. Many of the little, road-facing houses are frilled with beds of flowers, their faces brightened by rose and honey-suckle, myrtle and hollyhock. An atmosphere of brisk well-being is created by this comely region—something that none ever thought upon, or strove to fashion. It just happened and, in winter or summer, rain or shine, is ever to be recognised and welcomed. The very breezes blow with tonic freshness; and when, at apple-harvest and cider-making, the breath of Pomorum Patrona thickens the autumn air, only a tang of added sweetness salutes human nostrils. The network of lanes winding in and out of Priory is hedged with thorn and briar, hazel and holly, and crowned with elm and oak, while beneath them, where the water-tables run, trail wild flowers.

A main road travels the eastern fringe of the village and beside it stands an exceptional public house. Once the 'Pen-in-Hand' was a private dwelling and still shows no sign of great publicity; but it has long been the centre of local social life and enjoys substantial patronage, for not only its ancient name but also certain distinctive customs associated with it make the inn unique. The by-gone owner—a retired London tradesman—created new and joyous occupation for Priory's leisure hours, because, loving music above all things and being of genial, generous nature, this vanished worthy drew the people of his day about him and inspired the rising generation with ardour for singing, such as shall be found amid the Wesleyans of Cornwall, and was ever a national endowment of Wales. The practice persisted for, when its founder and his friends were sped, his dwelling turned to a wayside hostelry, it seemed that something of the old spirit refused to depart and folk gathered yet to sing there. The 'Pen-in-Hand' never claimed any man of Letters among its patrons, but music continued to haunt it happily enough and men would

5

sing together at the public bar and hold concerts in the great music-room, now a dining hall, during the winter months. Community singing had long been a precious addition to village life at Priory and still continued with the support and encouragement of William Toozey, the present publican. Combining business with pleasure, Mr. Toozey fostered the art. He felt that it often took the place of unprofitable chatter, and also provoked thirst. Fearing that air-borne music might diminish the existing zest for song, thus far he found broadcasts only tended to stimulate local talent.

Upon one autumn evening, however, there was no music, for men's minds had been stirred by an event which provided much to talk about. Paul Pook, the saddler, a lean, handsome and clean-shaven man with hair turning grey and large brown eyes, smoked his pipe at a seat by the wood fire and spoke in general terms to a companion beside him.

"According as you serve your neighbour, the same most times he'll serve you, Ned. So it comes about that, though Nicholas Withers died a tolerable dreadful death, there's no pity to waste. Some don't care a button one way or another; others are properly thankful to God he's down and out, because he was hard on the humble."

"'Twas his favourite pastime," said Ned Piper, the sexton of the parish.

"In such cases, when a man's swept out of life by fatal accident," continued Mr. Pook, "sympathy flows to the widow and children as a rule; but not this time. Mind you, I understood Nicholas Withers better than most people and was a friend of the family, and I can tell you that if ever a woman felt the joy of living come over her like a restored garment, it was Myra Withers when she heard Nicholas had fallen down the well. And his children likewise. The boy and girl didn't make so much as an effort to pretend about it. All Jonathan wants to know is how his father's left the farm, and all Nora wants to hear, for her mother's sake, is how he's left his money. But that's hid till they open the will after the funeral."

Mr. Piper, a round-backed, solid little man with the build of a beetle, a hairy face and dim blue eyes, nodded.

"He weren't called 'Old Nick' for nothing. A devil of a man without a doubt. I dare say his people feel on edge a bit about his dispensations."

"They do. Meantime, they're like culprits that have gone in chains for years and can't grasp yet the chains are off 'em. They take it for granted he's done evil under his will; but that's nothing against the sense of liberty now he's gone. Nora was singing like a grey bird last time I went up. I grant all that, yet as a sportsman, Nick was all he should be and worthy to be admired."

Elsewhere at the bar, young Jonathan Withers drank beer and talked of his father's death. He was a short, genial, blond youth of eight-and-twenty.

"A straight-forward end," he said, "an ugly accident, but easy to be explained. He'd just had one of his attacks of gout. They keep him up in his bed for a spell when they over-get him—bad for him, and merry hell for everybody else in the house they were. And after 'em, when he got about again, he'd be a bit shaky and uncertain on his feet for a day or two."

"Natural, Jonathan," explained Mr. Toozey from behind the bar. "When burn-gout took him, he had got to go on poor food—milk puddings and white fish and such like—and knock off his beer. Gout serves you that way and weakens the frame, and to a man like your father—a big, powerful man much addicted to red meat and beer same as he was—to knock off 'em and eat pap was bound to make him feeble on his feet till he'd built up again."

"So the coroner said, when he was explaining the death at the inquest," suggested a portly man with a double-chin and old-fashioned whiskers.

"Yes, Mr. Honeywood, he did," agreed Jonathan. "And so it happened. We're re-conditioning our well in the garden and there's a lot of brick-work and such going to it, and Godfrey's men are doing the job. And, up and about again, father went out every evening after five, when they were gone, to cast his eyes over the day's work and see if they'd earned their money. And if he thought they hadn't, he'd have a row with Godfrey next morning. The night he died, he went out on two sticks after tea to poke about, and it's tolerable certain that looking over, or else going down the ladder inside, he slipped in the half light and down he went with nought but the owls to see the last of him."

"You'd think, when he bobbed up after hitting the water, he might have catched the tail end of the ladder down there and saved himself," said Mr. Honeywood.

"It was suggested, but he'd got a terrible blow on his forehead, where he hit the brick-work going down, and doctor reckoned he was unconscious when he reached the water," explained Jonathan. "Death came by drowning. The blow on his brow wouldn't have killed him; so if it wasn't his own work to throw himself in, or the work of a murderer, then there's nought but accident it could be."

"It certainly wasn't his own work, for never a man better loved being alive than your father," said Toozey. "When did you set out to seek for him, Jonathan?"

"Not for a long time, William," answered young Withers. "We knew he liked to poke about alone and mother was very glad to be rid of him for a bit; then the dark came down and night gathered, so she said I'd best to go out and see what he was up to. I thought belike he felt better and had made shift to come down here for a talk; but she said no. So I looked round and couldn't find him. Then I came here to help him home if he was here; and when I found he wasn't, I looked in at Mrs. Faircloud's; but she hadn't seen him neither, so we reckoned something had happened."

A man entered the bar at this moment. It was Inspector Thomas Chard of the police. He did not wear uniform and with his sturdy shoulders and close-cropped, naval beard looked like one who followed the sea.

Jonathan accosted him.

"When was it I came in the station on that night my father died, to tell you we reckoned he was missing and might be in trouble, Inspector?" he asked.

"Round about nine o'clock as near as I can remember," answered Chard. "And I pointed out that nothing could be done till morning, Jonathan."

"Would you say the finding of the inquest was right, Chard?" asked Peter Honeywood.

"Dead right. The usual, William, please. Yes, never was a clearer case of accidental death. My instinct drew me to the well after I went up to Pigslake and heard the story next day and—sure enough—when I sent Joe Palfrey down the ladder, first thing he found was Nick's walking-stick floating on the water.   Then it came over me like a flame of fire that he lay down under himself, and I was right."

"No marks to tell you nothing on the top I suppose ?" asked the sexton, who had come to get his glass re-filled.

"No, Ned.   I went over the ground for any footmarks or clues to suggest there might have been anybody else; but only found a dozen footmarks that Godfrey's workmen had made.   Nothing doing there.   All I recovered was the dead man's cap and his other walking-stick."

"You have never felt it might have been a crime ?" asked the saddler.

"No, Pook.   I come to a case open-minded and only to gather the facts. Joe Palfrey was all for a murder; but 'no' I said.   'Stick to facts, Joe,' I said.   'In this case,' I said, 'everything points to accident'; and so it was. Many had a pretty good hatred of Nicholas Withers—granted; but when it comes to killing, that's a different story.   You want a passionate hate to kill, or else other motives equal strong; and, above all, you've got to be a brave and fearless fashion of man to risk your own neck by doing a capital crime.   But there's not one in Priory I'd go so far as to swear has the gifts for murder.   And thank God for it.   Homicide calls for a different class of man from any to be found round here."

"That's right," agreed Toozey.   "We're the peaceful sort in these parts."

Men came and went.   The old sexton was talking to Mr. Honeywood.

"A whacking grave—near seven foot long it will be.   He stood six feet-four inches in his socks, Withers did."

"Being familiar with the family, I've known the home wasn't a happy one," said Honeywood.   "Not that Myra Withers ever talked about her woes, but her sister, Mrs. Canniford, has oft told me how melancholy it was up there, along of the dead man's filthy temper and cruel hardness of heart.   Where does he go in, Ned ?"

"Along with the Withers people.   There's rows of 'em dating back to the far past.   But he'll be the last, or very near the last.   We're asking for an extension now.   Yard's full.   And where we're going, the ground's clay and I much doubt if I'll have the strength for it."

"I never thought of that," confessed Honeywood.

"'Tis all the point of view," answered Ned.   "If you was a gravedigger, you would have."

"And old Mercy Grepe gone, too, they tell me ?"

"Not gone, but going."

Mr. Piper laughed, but hastened to explain that his amusement was not occasioned by an approaching death.

"The window of our sleeping-chamber looks down on the graves," he said, "and there's dead folk lying within a few yards of our bed—just a natural thing my wife never took no account of till now; because use is second nature.   But Mercy Grepe goes in right under our window—the nearest of the lot—and Alice hates for her to be so parlous near.   Why ?   Because old 'Mother Forty Cats,' as they call her, was a witch !"

"No evil was ever done by the woman, but quite contrary," argued Mr. Honeywood. "A white witch as they say."

"So I told my partner; but she swears for two pins she'll have me out of my house. 'A witch is a witch, whatever her colour,' said Alice to me, 'and along with them mysteries, you never know what they'll be up to after they're dead. 'Tis said their coffins won't hold 'em'."

The sexton chuckled again.

"Her coffin will hold her all right," foretold Peter Honeywood. "Tell your wife that there's no call to fret about a peck of dust, Ned."

At the bar Jonathan Withers was still speaking of his dead father.

"I didn't hold with a lot Dad said and thought," he told them. "He was a 'red' and he often said he knew what he'd do with the quality if he got the chance."

His cousin, Rupert Canniford, a game-keeper, asked a question: "And what would Uncle Nicholas have done with 'em, Jonathan?"

"I'll spare you the details," answered young Withers, "but they were tolerable gory. He said them that owned the land and strutted it for millions of years ought to be shoved under the land, where they'd do more good than ever they did on top of it."

"Nice to think what would hap to the bettermost people if them opinions had their way; but they're tolerable safe for the present," said Inspector Chard, "and seeing your father was a landowner himself, strange he should feel like that, Jonathan."

"So I told him," replied young Withers, "but he said that farm folk was different and only the rich, idle men cumbered the earth and wasted the land, not the farmers."

He turned to his cousin.

"And where would you be if there wasn't no game preserves and no keepers to look after 'em, Rupert?"

"Leave politics to them paid to look after 'em, Rupert," advised Mr. Pook.

"You must aim for what they call 'stability,' Rupert," explained Toozey. "Then you'll take your place with the good citizens and be trustable."

"Cant—just cant and humbug, William," grinned Rupert.

"Well might you be called 'Mother's Misfortune,' Rupert," sighed Chard. "And after the lesson you had and all!"

Young Canniford stood up for himself however.

"When you catch me doing actionable deeds, it will be time to yelp over me, Inspector. I had my lesson, as you say, but nobody's got no bone to pick with me since. I'm all for law and order now. Ask our head keeper, Jacob Townley, to Tudor Manor, if you want my character these days. Townley will tell you what he thinks. And as for what I think, it's a free country and a man may think as he pleases to think."

The talk turned to the policeman himself, who, at five-and-forty, had recently taken a wife.

"And how do marriage suit you, Thomas?" asked Toozey, filling Chard's glass a second time.

"I'm able to answer from growing experience, William. There's nought like a wife to learn you the difference from our outlook and a woman's outlook. Their minds are built on a different pattern from ours seemingly and no doubt any married man would agree with that."

One or two grumbled assent.

"Their minds, to say it kindly, are smaller than ours; but against that, you must grant they are sharper," continued the inspector. "In small things calling for instant action, they are better than us. They go to 'em quicker and tackle 'em more efficient; but when the question is far-reaching and wants looking at all round and presents difficulties that call for a tolerable sized brain, then they are apt to fail. They don't look ahead so far as what we do, but they go to a job sharper and neater handed than us. So you may say they excel at a sudden pinch, or challenge, but in large affairs, the male mind over-tops 'em. They'll jump to conclusions with a desperate courage we wouldn't dare, and they've got less caution and more pluck than most of us when they're up against it; but their conclusions are apt to come out all wrong. Their feelings are prone to get the better of 'em and they find it beyond their power to grasp the niceties of the law. That's how Mrs. Chard seems to me."

"The line they take with their own sex is quite different from the line they take with us," added Mr. Toozey. "They'll give us best on great questions most times, even though at heart they ain't agreeing; but their fearfulest quarrels are between themselves and they find it pretty well impossible to give one another best."

Chard agreed.

"And yet the mind is there and, hate each other as they will, they'll trust each other in the dignity of their motherhood," he explained. "Mothers will trust their babies to the enemy even, well knowing there's an instinct in all mothers to feel that a child's a sacred object. Mothers trust mothers in a way fathers would never trust fathers if they were bitter enemies."

"That's deep, Tom. How d'you figure it out?" asked Honeywood, who was a bachelor.

"I saw it in court not so long since," answered Chard. "Two women, both mothers, fought in the fearful way some low women will fight—all claws and teeth same as savage beasts. They came patched and plastered before the magistrate looking death and poison at each other, and one brought her six-months-old baby to the court-house with her. And when her turn came to testify, though she hated her enemy like hell, she made no bones about handing her infant into the other woman's keeping—just pushed the child into her arms while she took her turn, well knowing it was safe; because a tender infant may safely be said to be a neutral and take no side at all."

"A very clever thought and very smart of you to mark it, Inspector," declared Paul Pook.

"Yes, my intellect works like that," agreed Chard, "and I'd say that marriage throws light on many very fine sides of the female character."

"You're one of the lucky ones, Tom. You've got a winner as everybody knows," suggested Toozey.

"I have, William; but not to say lucky," replied the policeman, whose use of words was always literal. "Luck means chance, and there was no chance about me and Mrs. Chard. A man don't wait to forty-five to wed and leave anything to chance. I've got what I took a darned long time finding—a masterpiece, in my opinion."

"Good looks and good temper and a sweet nature, your Mary Ann—everybody knows that," admitted Toozey.

"But not luck—hard work rewarded, as hard work always should be," summed up the newly-married man.

"Luck, too. The luck was when she took you, Inspector," pointed out Rupert Canniford. "You found just what you wanted; but where would you have been if she hadn't wanted you?"

Chard looked at the younger man thoughtfully yet without annoyance.

"A fair question, Rupert," he said, "but that opens up another side of the subject I'm not prepared to argue upon. When good befalls some men, it's no question of 'luck,' but so oft as not a matter of justice and what they happen to have deserved. Providence don't sleep. I'll say no more except to wish all the bachelors same good fortune as I look to have had myself."

Mr. Piper chipped in from his seat by the fire.

"Wait, Tom! Wait and don't count your chickens before they're hatched. What does a man married two months know of the state? Find how it looks five-and-twenty years hence, my lad, and then decide if you was properly rewarded, or made the mistake of your life."

Chard smiled.

"Give Ned another, William," he said. "He's thirsty along of that outsize grave he's toiling at."

"If there's one thing I envy the rich, it's their gravestones," confessed the sexton. "Nought else; but when I'm took to go under, I'd dearly like to think I'd have a bit of polished Aberdeen granite on top of me."

"Daisies and dandelions more like; and what's the odds to you, Ned?" asked the policeman.

A sturdy, middle-aged and grey-eyed person entered. He was Edmund Naylor, the parish doctor and a man well esteemed.

"A whiskey, Bill," he said. "Been on my legs all day and mighty tired." Toozey hastened to serve him.

"Your car still off the road, Doctor?" he asked.

"Yes, but promised for Monday."

"You've lost a good patient in poor Withers, Doctor," suggested Mr. Honeywood.

"Doc don't think so I'll bet," said the dead man's son.

"He was difficult, Jonathan," agreed the physician. "A man of ferocious temper when the gout got him. Wouldn't bend to it. He might have escaped many an attack if he had been more reasonable between them. But he would fight Nature—a fool's trick always. 'If Nature made me ill, she can damn well cure me again,' he'd say, 'and if she won't, I'll die.' 'You can only die once, but you can be ill a hundred times and yet recover, Nicholas,' I answered him, and he granted that was a bright idea."

"Nick always regarded Nature as a possible enemy, except in the hunting field," said Mr. Pook. "And often there, too."

"Everybody was a possible enemy to him, rather than a possible friend," added the innkeeper.

"And nearly friendless himself in consequence," replied Naylor.

"Us must draw the veil over father and forget the poor man so quick as we can," suggested Jonathan and the physician nodded.

"That's easy, my boy. The best and worst are forgotten equally quick. Great men—good or bad—seldom live more than a few shadowy years in history; the rest of us aren't remembered longer than our own generation—to bless or curse as the case may be. People don't count. Only good deeds are worth remembering; but it matters very little who did them."

The company listened and Jonathan Withers made a curious remark.

"As for father, you'd think once a man was on his back in bed he would be out of mischief for the time being; but my mother always said father hatched his most cruel ideas when he was down with gout—hatched 'em as easy as a broody hen hatches eggs."

The men laughed and Paul Pook turned to Naylor.

"How d'you explain that, Doctor?" he asked.

"Sickness will soften some of us and make others all the harder, Paul. In the case of poor Withers, for some unfortunate reason beyond our power to understand, the poison of his gout got into his brains as well as his body and ministered to his natural failings. He was what they call a misanthrope —felt a hatred of his fellow creatures."

"With the result there won't be many tears shed, nor yet flowers laid on his grave when he's put home." foretold Honeywood. "I've had but one order for a wreath for his funeral."

"And no prophet needed to say where that came from," suggested Inspector Chard.

The arrival of a lad silenced any further conversation on this subject. He was tall, well put together, and built upon more distinguished lines than most of the big-boned men about him. He displayed an odd mixture of the furtive and a sort of arrogance that made him hold his head high. His beautiful but brooding face revealed very perfect, fine-turned features and large grey eyes, that moved quickly to right and left, now placid, now distrustful and anxious. He was a challenging young man and the object of much discussion in his native village, for his story offered elements that put him in a category apart from his neighbours. His countenance might have suggested to cultured beholders a kinship with Greek Antinous in its melancholy cast and combination of physical perfection with a troubled spirit; while in some of his moods, that whimsical magic proper to the Praxitelean Faun would appear.

Timothy Faircloud was the only son of a widowed mother and worked with the foresters at Tudor Manor. None could deny the challenge of his person, but few declared any patience with his self-conscious attitude to existence. Indeed, Timothy's aspirations were ever exasperating and hard to understand and his desire for recognition only awoke laughter, since as yet he could furnish no stable quality to recognise. Some held him a worthless person with a bee in his bonnet; others thought he was unbalanced if not wholly out of his mind. Few cared twopence about him save his mother; bu even she could point to no great reason why Timothy should be much esteemed or endured.

"Just a wilful nature," Nelly Faircloud would explain to neighbours. "A good lad enough and making up to be a good man, but sorry for himself and hungry for friendships he's too timid to win. Not too easy to understand sometimes. Up to-day and so pleased as a dog that's had a pat he didn't expect, and then down to-morrow, like a dog that expects a pat and gets a curse. He thinks too much of what other people think of him and wants to be applauded and don't see that there's nothing to call for any admiration about him except his handsome appearance. But come a few years, he'll grow out of his nonsense and carry on like every other man."

The boy was secretive though none guessed his secrets of much importance; but students of character might have suspected that his combination of qualities was dangerous, since the nature that craves for fame will often sacrifice more important possessions to win it. But none could point to any perils and none ever fathomed the reason for his transitions from cheerfulness to gloom, from arrogance to humility. The general impression that his apparent vanity meant a lack of brain power grew in the village and few troubled about the youth himself, though his doubtful paternity continued a matter of argument among those who enjoy problems concerning the past conduct of other people.

To-night Timothy was in one of his proud moods. He glanced over the company as superior to them all, ordered half a pint of beer and took no part in the conversation round him, though once or twice he smiled at his own thoughts. In truth his sole distinction might have been said to lie in his remarkable face, for more promise than belongs to a lad of nineteen seemed to be shadowed in it. Yet no evidence of any definite ambition or native gift had up to the present appeared to throw any light upon him. He had sung exceptionally well in the church choir until his voice broke, but neither music nor any other form of art attracted him now, though he came and sang at the 'Pen-in-Hand' sometimes. One or two addressed Timothy in friendly fashion, only to find him not receptive and more than usually preoccupied with his own thoughts. He drank his beer, said 'Good night all' as manners demanded and was gone again. It seemed that some being from another world than Priory had looked in to quench his thirst and then vanish.

"My lord's pleased with himself this evening." said Jonathan Withers. "He ain't often that."

"Belike he knows something about what's hid in your father's will," suggested Mr. Honeywood. "It won't be no surprise if Mrs. Faircloud figures there—so a little bird tells me."

"The little bird being my mother—eh Peter?" asked Rupert Canniford.

"No politics, Rupert," advised Mr. Toozey. "Best keep off that subject."

"Don't be squeamish, my dear man. Everybody knows Nelly Faircloud was Uncle's mistress, don't they, Jonathan?"

"Good God, yes—who doubts it?" answered the son of Nicholas Withers.

"And as for Timothy," continued Rupert, "he's soft—the sort that went in with the bread and came out with the cakes—and so like as not he'll end his days in a lunatic asylum. I rather like him. We meet in the woods now and again. He cuts down trees as well as the next man no doubt. In fact a damned fool; and to be a damned fool and make a good job of it, you want plenty of money to cover your nakedness."

"And Tim thinks money is coming his mother's way from Pigslake farm, so he's putting on frills according. Ain't that right, Doctor?" asked Peter Honeywood.

Dr. Naylor shook his head.

"Not quite, but time will show," he said. "I doubt if anything of that sort made Timothy a bit haughty to-night. More likely some inner train of thought or secret purpose that was pleasing him for the minute. He's a queer mixture, that boy—not a damned fool by any means, but a growing intelligence that hasn't won clear from adolescence so far. His unusually beautiful face and the sort of style and bearing which we associate with breeding come from his mother. She was a very lovely woman twenty years ago when she married Bob Faircloud, and Tim's good looks are the male counterpart of hers. But his nature's utterly different, because Nelly is always placid and calm."

"Not to say secretive. A close woman, Doctor?"

"Naturally reserved, Honeywood. Not in the least secretive. A rare good woman. But I'm talking of her son. Sometimes the boy suffers badly from what Science calls an 'inferiority complex'; but he sings small and hates himself because he's unimportant and futile; but something happens, or a word of praise is spoken, and he swings over and treads on air for a bit and thinks himself a fine fellow, till he's crushed again. Morbid and unfortunate, but quite a common condition with the rising generation. He will very likely outgrow it."

"Why should a Priory lad be bitten that silly way, Doctor?" asked Inspector Chard. "I can't mind anybody with a fantastic nature same as that."

"Something in his heredity coming to the surface, Tom," answered Naylor, "something beyond our power to trace back to its sources."

"If you knew who his father was, perhaps you'd get a move on, Doctor," hinted the gamekeeper, and Toozey repeated a caution he often uttered.

"That'll do, Canniford," he said. "I won't have no politics and well you know it."

'Politics' was a comprehensive word in William's vocabulary and appeared to signify everything but what other people understood by it. Discussions on public affairs he welcomed; but by 'politics' he embraced all in the nature of personalities and scandals that pertained to the hamlet and its people. The doctor did not take any notice of Rupert's suggestion and talk turned elsewhere; then a constable entered the bar a minute afterwards the church clock had told the hour.

"Closing time, Mr. Toozey," he said.

It was Constable Palfrey and, seeing his superior officer, he drew up and saluted. Inspector Chard approved.

"Quite right, Joe," he declared. "We must mend our manners, else we'll all get into trouble, myself included."

Drinks were hastily finished and men wished each other good night. Then one and all wandered into the darkness and went their ways.

II

PRIORY, conscious that the son of Nelly Faircloud was developing in an original and not very promising pattern, but quite unable to explain a youth so unlike the recognised run of Priory boys, spoke of him as his mother's 'Changeling,' while those who troubled to think twice on the subject of Timothy agreed with Dr. Naylor that heredity might serve to explain so odd a lad. Concerning that vital matter mystery had always hung thick and theories varied. The charitable saw no reason to doubt that Robert Faircloud was his lawful father, for Timothy came into the world but six months after Robert's death and none could deny that a child often reveals few paternal traits; but others had varied grounds for doubting this humane opinion and pointed to the bygone farmer's unhappy marriage and the tragedy that ended it. Robert Faircloud had rented Valley Farm, five miles from Priory, before he wedded. He was a local man and his parents lived in the village. His married life proved short and clouded, for two years ended it and he died a sudden death. Some believed his gun had exploded by accident as he went through a hedge when rabbiting; others held a darker opinion for his parents openly declared that Bob had destroyed himself to terminate the affliction of his marriage. Accidental death was the verdict, however, and a problem that excited the dead man's neighbours at the time had long ceased to interest Priory.

On her husband's death, after the birth of Timothy, his mother left the farm and dwelt henceforth half a mile from the village in a small and comfortable house. She was believed to be poor but contrived to live well and comfortably, letting lodgings when opportunity offered, as she had already done during her husband's life at Valley Farm. Faircloud's parents had screamed her failure as a wife and proclaimed her infidelity; but while many shared their indignation and would not know the widow, others found Nelly an amiable and kindly neighbour, and only subsequent events chilled their friendship. Near twenty years had passed since then. Those who hated her were gone and now her foremost friend and steadfast supporter, to the shame of the parish, was also sped. Nelly had never married again, but there grew an association to waken violent animus among local women and afford rich entertainment amid Priory men, when time presently revealed the source of her good circumstances and welfare. A very unexpected being was discovered responsible for them and Priory learned that Mrs. Faircloud might be regarded as under the protection of Nicholas Withers. He had known her husband but never pretended any friendship with him, though no open breach was reported between them. Then, after Robert had died and a year passed, Nicholas, contemptuous of public opinion, went on his way, identified himself with Nelly and commanded his wife to divorce him. This Myra Withers declined to do.

Unavailing efforts had been made by the vicar of the parish to cure a situation so contrary to established morals; but now it was becoming a part of social life at Priory and, while some condoned, others marked their disapproval by declining to know either Mrs. Faircloud or Nicholas himself. Her friends grew tired of urging the farmer's wife to divorce him. Myra stayed on resolutely at Pigslake Farm, holding that to be her duty, and a sort of armed neutrality had long existed between husband and wife. It was confirmed that they did not so much as speak to one another save upon the business of the farm. Use had hardened the woman, and, for her children's sake, she lived her painful life under threat. Pigslake was not entailed and the owner would be at liberty to do as he pleased with it after his death; but Nicholas had always exhibited a friendly attitude to his son and even been heard to say that Jonathan was destined to follow him. Few enjoyed his friendship and Paul Pook, the saddler, was the only man in Priory for whom he pretended any regard. He minded his farm well and paid good wages, but numbered few staunch supporters among those whom he employed. He declared that for business and reputation as an outstanding farmer, he lived at home, while for pleasure and affection he turned to 'Lavender Cottage,' the abode of the widow and her son.

As for the paternity of Timothy Faircloud, that vexed problem had long become merely an academic amusement for those with nothing better to talk about. While many believed that Nicholas Withers was his father, others suspected one for ever unknown among the artists who of old had come and gone and occupied lodgings at Valley Farm in bygone days. They argued that the boy in no way resembled Nicholas and said, truly enough, that Withers, with his scorn for propriety of every sort, would not have hesitated to claim him as a son if such had been the case. But Myra Withers felt little doubt. She agreed with Robert Faircloud's parents, that it was the discovery of Nelly's infidelity which prompted her husband to cut his own thread and end a life his spouse had poisoned at the source.

And now Nicholas himself was dead, his wife's long ordeal ended and the question of her future a matter of immediate interest. How the Fairclouds might stand also engaged local attention and some guessed that in his will would be found the buried truth of Timothy. Certain of the more imaginative foretold that Nelly's boy would be found heir to Pigslake; critics of more rational bent pointed out that Nicholas Withers, despite his social record, was an exceptionally good farmer and would have been the last to leave a valuable property in young Faircloud's doubtful and feeble hands. They felt assured that Jonathan must get the farm, for he was capable, well trained and of responsible age. Events thus re-awakened the old mystery and Timothy would doubtless have been gratified to know how often his shadowy origin was matter for speculation while yet the dead man's will remained a secret.

In truth her changeling was a very unknowable child and his mother confessed that she had never reached into the mystery of his young heart. Even her private theories as to the mystery of his body were doubtful; but Nelly's love-hunting days had left no shadow of remorse in a calm and well-balanced mind and her adventures did not serve to unsteady a nature utterly amoral in some directions, yet steadfast and trustworthy upon most social planes of life. She was fond of Timothy, as a beautiful creation for which she had been

directly responsible, and felt concerned for his future and his mental development; but she did not pretend to understand him and knew that many neighbours regarded him as infirm of mind, setting down his odd sayings and bad
manners to that fact. She watched over him closely enough, however, and
felt in no doubt of his sanity.

The desire to be out of the common, challenge his elders and command
their attention had appeared in Timothy at a very early age. As a small boy
he was given to lying on a picturesque scale and would tell how he had seen
and done wonderful things. He talked of fairies and described them in great
detail, while upon the matter of his own childish experiences he reported deeds
of personal courage foreign to his own timid and fearful nature. From his
tales one might perceive the trend of his ambitions and it was easy to note that
his inventions quickly became accepted as facts in his own mind. But there
was another world of dimensions, not to be explained to anybody, in which as
a little boy he moved, a world inhabited by beings with whom none had any
part but himself. He would animate dead things, or breathe imaginary life
into unconscious objects, then make of them his dearest and best friends. For
him these varied choices of affection possessed vital reality: he quickened
them until they understood him, welcomed him and were in close and friendly
associations with his secret existence. They appeared in unexpected situa-
tions, to challenge him and win his regard; they told him their stories and
established bonds of amity that only vanished with his increasing age. At
church a very beautiful, treble voice had won him a place in the choir and he
loved this public function and enjoyed to don his surplice and cassock. From
his seat in the choir stalls a cenotaph to a bygone hero of the Garland family,
who had fallen for his country at Waterloo, confronted him, and one detail
of this massive memorial Timothy held among his most precious secret
associates. It was a winged skull of white marble, grey with dust, and he had
endowed the symbol of mortality with an acute consciousness all its own. He
sang his hymns, anthems and psalms to the winged skull and felt it never
failed to appreciate his efforts. He kept his eyes fixed upon it during the
reading of lessons, or preaching of sermons and read subtle changes in the
skull's expression, indicating whether the object approved or disliked what
was being said from lectern or pulpit. Direct sunshine would waken a grin
on those marble jaws, but Timothy always felt that to see the moon illuminate
them would be a notable experience, though this he had never enjoyed.
Many such like fantasies of youthful invention he kept to himself and they
withered as he grew; but the heart of a wood was ever his favourite haunt and
trees long continued to be his dearest and most precious familiars.

At eighteen, much to his joy, he had joined the foresters of Tudor Manor
and found a fitful measure of happiness and contentment among the woodlands; but when his voice broke and for a time the choir needed him no more,
he abandoned worship, since religion could sound no mandate for him and
though at eighteen his voice was restored, in future he only sang at the
'Pen-in-Hand,' or where there was none to hear him, in the Manor forests.
But there were no nymphs amid the scenes of his daily labour, though he had
reached an age when girls began to interest him. He was not amorous but,
concerning them in their occasional relations with himself, he discovered that

he created a considerable effect upon them and found most of them willing enough to make friends. In their company he generally won a measure of attention and sometimes obvious admiration denied to him by his own sex. On that account he had never cold-shouldered them. Girls would listen to him and apparently give credence to his high-flown assertions of courage and capability. Upon no particular maiden were his thoughts and aspirations supposed to centre, but certain interested persons knew that this was not the case.

Like others of his own family Nelly Faircloud felt no little interest in her dead friend's dispensations. She had been the mistress of Nicholas Withers for many years and his sudden end brought with it a very considerable shock. He had always assured her that her future was well provided for and learning his character at an early date of their intercourse, she was aware that he loved her after his own fashion and that, if she did not lie to him, she might feel assured he would not lie to her. She suffered him and his blunt and brutal nature amused rather than repelled her. She was more faithful to their union than ever she had been as a wife; but she always looked ahead and never failed to save a little yearly from the allowance that Withers made her. She, and she alone, felt some sorrow at her partner's sudden death; indeed she already missed his rough and ready devotion; but her primary interest centred on Timothy. For him Nicholas never pretended much admiration. He always declared that Jonathan was more to him than Timothy, and though he had not informed her of his exact purpose, Mrs. Faircloud felt tolerably assured that Jonathan would inherit Pigslake Farm.

Myra Withers was only concerned for Jonathan, well knowing that her husband would make no provision on her account. But if the farm were left to his rightful heir, then she proposed living with her son until he should marry. Much affection existed between her and her children, and they had supported Myra to the best of their power through long and distressful years. Now the incubus was lifted and with frank thanksgiving she faced freedom and peace in whatsoever shape it might appear. Her sister, Jenny Canniford, felt only interest in the will as it affected Myra. She had always detested Nicholas, not because he practically ignored her existence, but because, as her sons grew to manhood, he had never lifted a finger to help them, or assist their widowed mother, left penniless at John Canniford's death. Nicholas might have found work for the lads at Pigslake and so served his sister-in-law, but no such thing happened and while Harry, her eldest son, now toiled as a hedger and ditcher, whereat he won very small money, Rupert had passed through the tribulations of his former days and was now in steady employment after earlier disgrace. He had been caught poaching and suffered a sentence of one month's hard labour, from which he returned home cowed and repentant. None offered work or a helping hand; and it was the lady of the manor herself who came to the rescue, backed her own benevolent principles and, to the admiration of Priory at so Christian an act, gave Rupert a chance to restore his father's good name in a calling that he had always desired to follow. Not a few, including Lady Garland's head keeper, prophesied failure from her impulsive action; but it seemed that her good heart had not erred, for some saving spirit of grace and sense of gratitude in Rupert responded to this exceptional freak of fortune. Under mighty strict surveillance at the age of twenty-one he donned velveteen, displayed sterling probity and much ability and now, five years later, stood established and in the enjoyment of a healthy reputation. At present he lived at home, while Myra also aided his mother with a little money when she was more than usually straitened; but Harry, the hedger, could not help, though full of filial desires to do so, for he had married while still in his early twenties and lived hard with his wife and four young children. For the rest Jenny earned what she might with her needle and now stood in steadfast hopes of another marriage, for she was comely still, but forty-six years old and with a promising string to her bow. Peter Honeywood, and his attention had long been matter of common attention and approval. No vital word was spoken as yet, though in the widow's opinion a declaration became somewhat overdue. Others shared this conclusion and Honeywood's affairs were the subject of some secret wagering about this time. He was a bachelor—always friendly and amiable, yet of cautious temperament and while greedy of information concerning his neighbours' business, indisposed to any confidences regarding his own. The folk could not quarrel with Peter, but held him vain and too fond of his clothes and personal adornments.

It happened upon the day of the Withers funeral that Jenny discussed her follower with a woman friend, for, when the rites were over, she fell in with Mary Ann Chard, the newly married wife of Inspector Chard, and much in Mrs. Canniford's confidence. Their talk followed the burial, after a small company of spectators and a trifling group of mourners had scattered. It was a ceremony not largely attended; but Nicholas had been a staunch supporter of the local hunt, and the fact furnished one picturesque detail. Two brace of hounds and a huntsman in scarlet splashed the graveside with a spot of colour. Then the small company scattered and Ned Piper, with a young man to help him, filled the grave. Near vanished members of his old family lay Nicholas Withers and completed a row of them. The sexton's aid, who was his nephew and hoped to be a grave-digger himself some day, spoke to Mr. Piper.

"I see on the great monument, lifted to the hero gentleman of the Garland family in the church, that it was erected by his 'mournful relict,' Uncle Ned. Will Mrs. Withers be the mournful relict of Mr. Nicholas Withers?"

"His relict—yes. As to 'mournful,' quite the opposite by all accounts," answered the old man.

"She'll heave up a brave stone to a rich one like him presently no doubt when the earth have sunk?"

"As to that nobody knows but herself. Get on with your job, Jack, and don't chatter," directed the sexton.

Myra Withers did not attend her husband's funeral. For the sake of appearances Mr. Pook urged her to do so, but she was firm.

"He always ordered me away from his sick bed, and he'd order me away from his grave if he could," she said, "and I don't go."

So Paul Pook walked between the dead man's children behind his coffin and Nora showed a little emotion, but Jonathan was stolid and indifferent. Then followed Jenny Canniford with her two sons, Harry and Rupert; while

Mrs. Faircloud made no effort to join the procession. She came alone and mingled with the small congregation in church, then returned home without going to the grave-side. Now the funeral party had scattered and only half-a-dozen among them were returning to the funeral feast at Pigslake. Harry and Rupert Canniford had joined their cousins, Jonathan and Nora, while Pook walked alone and Jenny, falling in with the inspector's wife, asked after Chard and remarked that he was not at the internment.

"Only Joe Palfrey in uniform," she said. "Where's your Thomas to, Mary Ann?"

"Called to a Court case and very vexed he couldn't be here. But he bade me go for respect to the family, Jenny."

"Yes, I was glad to see you there, my dear. And how's your wedded life faring? You was one like to take kindly to your married days."

"So I have then. Very happy so far with Tom."

"There's a feeling of protection I'd say for a woman wed to a policeman," suggested Jenny and her friend laughed.

"I don't get no particular sense of protection along with him," she said. "He's the sort of man, between ourselves, that cries for protection himself. I often wonder how he fared after his mother died. You'll find in the case of sudden disaster—all in the day's work and sure to befall now and again—that women are far better at 'em than men. Tom knows that and leaves 'em to me."

"Not so helpful then?"

"If anything out of the way happens, like the dog being lost, or the cat caught stealing, or a kettle boils over, or crockery breaks, or what not, you may always rely upon Tom to do nothing at all," continued Mary Ann, "and that is helpful in a way, because if he did do anything you can lay your life it would be wrong. 'Woman's work,' he says about anything he's feared to touch, and when he keeps out of a mess, then you know where you are and act according."

"He always seemed a very nice, brave fashion of man to me," said Mrs. Canniford.

"He is a nice, brave fashion of man, else I wouldn't have took him," replied Mrs. Chard. "And, in big things, well able to take the lead. If the house catched afire, or any outstanding misfortune overtook us, I'd so soon trust Tom as another. I'd trust him to call up the fire engine anyhow."

"With your thatched roof and all, I'm sure I hope so!"

"Oh yes. He's got a manly grasp of what they call essentials, same as a policeman high up in the service should have, though what men think are essentials often fall a long way short of what we know essentials to be. . . . He'll get low-spirited about the lack of crime here and says never was such a place for law and order. I'm afraid he half hoped the fearful end of poor Mr. Withers was going to offer something in his line; but then, when he went up over with his superintendent, he saw an accident looking him in the face. And Superintendent Jackson said the same."

"Nicholas went to see how the well was faring each night after the workmen was gone, so as he might report 'em to Godfrey if they were hanging fire," explained Jenny. "Then he got too near in the dimpsey light and he missed his footing and over he went, poor soul. Just one of they fatal mishaps that overtake the just and the unjust alike."

Mary Ann Chard became personal in her turn.

"I see Mr. Honeywood at the funeral, but he didn't sit along with you, Jenny, as one might have expected, things being same as they are."

"He weren't a mourner, so he couldn't come in the mourner's pew," explained Mrs. Canniford. "Too cautious to declare himself like that in any case. Because you expect a man to take a line, and every reason why he should, it don't follow he will take it. Peter's a puzzling item. But he'd dressed in rich black and wore his jet watch-chain he keeps for funerals."

"You can carry caution too far in my opinion," declared Mrs. Chard, "and I'd go so far as to say he does. A woman like you don't want to be approached with caution and somebody ought to tell the man, that it looks a pretty bad blot on his affection, if not his manners, to bring caution to work on you."

"The affection's there," answered Jenny, "but caution's Peter's second name and he fetches it to work on everything. I've thought myself that some women, with a record of facing life so brave as what I have done, might feel it a bit of an insult to be approached as if I was a doubtful bargain; but then I've looked at it from Peter's side and can't but see there's things have passed through his mind to my disadvantage."

"What things?" asked Mary Ann. "Lord love us! What things? You're religious and healthy and got good looks yet for all your misfortunes. You're a widow and understand the male as only widows can. A godsend to an old bachelor lucky enough to get you. And him ugly and too fat and ten years older than you at that."

"Seven years older. He's fifty-three. And you've got to remember he's a business man and though he don't know nothing of marriage, might well reckon that he was getting the losing end along with me. He's stout, granted, but I wouldn't say he was ugly—just ordinary."

"Well, 'tisn't for nobody to rush in," admitted the inspector's wife. "There's a lot don't see their good luck till it's given 'em the go by. I hope he'll come to his senses before you feel you've changed your mind about him. But I hate to think of an angel like you, Jenny, going begging to a market gardener."

Mrs. Canniford smiled wanly.

"I'm an angel with encumbrances," she said, "you've got to mind that, my dear girl, and though Peter might be slow to see the advantages of a tidy good wife, he'd find himself mighty quick to spot the snags. No snags in me myself, I grant you, and no secrets and nought to fright him; but there's my sons, near my heart, and both not offering much hope for anybody else."

"A man marries a woman, not her family," declared Mary Ann. "Tom always said the brightest blessing about me was I'd got no family and stood pretty much alone in the world."

"Them elderly bachelors know a lot more about marriage than you'd think for," answered Jenny. "They've looked on at the game from outside and got a bird's eye view of it. Peter's dealing with a woman and her two grown-up sons: that's one reason no doubt why he treads so careful, because caution costs nothing, but may save a lot."

"Well, what about your sons ?" asked the younger.

"They're as God made 'em and I'm satisfied with 'em, though not to say blessed in 'em," answered Mrs. Canniford. "Harry's like his father—good as gold and stands to work and never catched out in a crooked deed. A good husband and a good father and a good neighbour. Bursting with generosity if he'd got anything to be generous with. But never a pinch of luck. Too unselfish a man ever to have any luck. They say God helps them that helps themselves; but I say He did ought to help them that help other people. And He don't always help them that help themselves for that matter, because when my other boy, Rupert, helped himself to them pheasants back along, all he got for it was a month in the lock-up."

"But it made an honest man of him ever after—so Tom says. He says Mr. Townley, the head keeper to Tudor Manor, thinks very highly of your younger one," replied Mrs. Chard.

"Yes—Rupert stands well now, thanks to Lady Garland, who gave him his chance. But Honeywood don't like Rupert and he dreads poor Harry's poverty and went so far as to tell him once that, in his opinion, Harry didn't ought to have any more children."

"That's your son's business, not Mr. Honeywood's," said Mary Ann.

The widow smiled at a recollection.

"You don't often see Harry up in the air, but the worm will turn now and again. When Honeywood aired his views on that subject, my son let loose, if you can imagine him doing such a thing, and told Peter that the number of his family was for God to decide, not a damned market gardener ! Yes, swore and all he did. I could hardly believe my ears. More could Peter, and when he went off, Harry cried out that, for indecency and blasted impudence combined, he'd never heard his equal. I was proud of Harry in a way, because he's used to go under and give other people best if they look at him; but he rose in rebellion that time."

"Quite right, too," agreed Mrs. Chard. "A nice world if people was to run about telling husbands how many children they was to get."

They parted then and the policeman's wife went home, while Jenny followed the road to Pigslake. Before her walked Harry and his wife, while ahead of them, Mr. Pook now accompanied Jonathan and Nora Withers and Rupert. The parties joined together, coming through a trim but uneventful garden that separated the house from the high road. . . . It consisted mostly of green plots, enlivened by clumps of pampas grass and reigned over by one massive auracaria—a tree very suited in local opinion to stand for a symbol of the vanished farmer. The dwelling was of red brick under russet tiles upon which a golden lichen flourished. It faced south and behind it extended the farm-yard, byres, barns and main outbuildings, while the land surrounded all and flowed out for half a mile over the high road to the south and west.

Under the great 'monkey-puzzle' stood Myra Withers with a man, half a foot shorter than herself, for she was a tall woman, slightly built but upright and strong. Her hair was grey, her face handsome, but impress of suffering and the bitterness of a life's misery had stamped itself upon her expression.

Her malady was of the mind and her body knew no ill. Her countenance suggested strength and purpose, yet the fact that these qualities were ever denied fruition had stamped Myra's features. Frustration looked out of her careworn, blue eyes and sounded in her voice; but to-day, in the company of the family lawyer, it seemed that the barriers imposed by unhappy married life were down. There rang a cheerfulness and resolution in her speech, far different from the smouldering indifference usually marked to accompany any utterance.

Mr. Morris Mallaby was known to his present companion and, in secret, he had often sympathised with her when constrained to do the will of Nicholas during past years. But she had never revealed her inner sentiments to him on the occasions when he came to the farm and he apprehended little pleasure from his forthcoming duties. He was a small, unpretentious person attired in black, clean-shaven and weak-eyed. He concealed a strong vein of sentiment, that ill became his profession, and often found himself bewildered before the challenges that human nature brings to a country lawyer. Mr. Mallaby had missed an omnibus, which passed twice a day through Priory from the neighbouring market town, and he had been called to hire a taxi-cab in consequence. Even so he arrived too late for the funeral and suffered another painful shock to find that Myra was not attending it. The fact impressed him and confirmed many of his fears respecting her relations with Nicholas; but in the matter of a husband's burial, he felt that convention and the respect for propriety and custom, so dear to himself, should have taken his late client's widow to the grave-side. While she talked to him and he drank a glass of milk, he was conscious that, despite the occasion, he had never seen or heard Mrs. Withers in better spirits; indeed she startled him by the frankness of her general opinions and satisfaction at the errand which had brought him to the farm.

"You will forgive me for being late," he said. "Out of no disrespect for the dead, be sure of that, Mrs. Withers. Be sure of that."

"You're in plenty of time for the funeral meal, my dear man," she answered. "That's more important than the funeral. They'll be back-along in half an hour. Nice autumn weather we're having. If you'd like to see the well where Nicholas Withers fell in and died, I'll show it to you, Mr. Mallaby."

"No, no, indeed. I read the sad particulars. I wrote to you, remember; and now I can say again what a sorrow it was and how much I felt for the family."

"Come in the garden and smoke if you're a smoker," suggested Myra, and he followed her out of doors.

"I don't smoke, but I should like to feel the sunshine," he said and talked on in his gentle little voice.

"Events such as these—tragical and wholly unexpected—always reveal to me a most pathetic side," he told her. "For what do they mean ? What can we imagine when they happen and some strong, virile being vanishes like the morning dew ? To me they signify something from which law and order and decorum are lacking. Not really, of course, but on the surface. Sudden death reveals all the secrets of the dead, strips his private affairs bare, brings to the light his inner plans and preparations for going on living and, under the soulless operations of the law, leaves naked any sacred secrets he may possess, his private affairs open to public scrutiny for those who knew him not; or perhaps thought they knew him and failed to do so. Painful reflections to a sensitive mind, Mrs. Withers."

"Are they?" she asked. "I've never been called to feel sentimental in all my life, my dear man. Not built that way. As for Nicholas Withers, you may fancy you've got some surprises in his will to shake me up; but you needn't to fret about anything like that. The only surprise would be to find he'd made an honest will and I lay my life he hasn't done that."

"It was always a great grief to me that he couldn't see eye to eye with you, Ma'am."

"Why a grief?" she asked. "Why were you sorry to find I wasn't a cruel devil of a woman, same as he was a cruel devil of a man? If you'd got any grief to spare, better to have shed it on them weak folk he cheated and mis-handled all his life. But don't waste no pity on me. He's left me nought save what I stand up in—that I very well know; but even at that I'm happier than any time in my life these thirty years past. That I'll swear to and couldn't hide if I wanted to. I hear it myself—in my own voice—and feel it in my bones. You've got to be chained up body and soul, like I was, to know what freedom means, Mr. Mallaby."

"Yet you might have divorced him had you wished," he suggested.

"I might. He tried everything a cruel heart could think upon to bully me into it. He was set on that woman—that whore—Faircloud's widow and badly wanted to marry her. And that's where I had him. I wasn't going to see Pigslake took away from Jonathan in the future by any act of mine. He liked Jonathan well—always did—but if I'd quit and took the children, that would have been the end of their chances hereafter. However, you'll read the will come presently."

But Mr. Mallaby continued to concern himself with the past.

"I wish you'd come to me in those days. The law can often convince reasonable people and help them to do their duty both to themselves and their neighbours," he said. "Had you put the position before me, or any skilled attorney, we might have showed you a course to satisfy you both."

"Not the law, nor yet the prophets, could have showed any such a course," she said. "That's what I know and you don't, Mr. Mallaby."

He shook his head.

"There was the opening for a reasonable and just compromise if you think a minute, my dear. That is assuming, of course, that you feel no re-ligious objection to divorce."

"None whatever; but how would divorcement have served me better than holding the man?"

"Why, you could have driven a fair bargain and promised to free him on the condition, all signed and sealed, that in that event, Pigslake should be left to your son and nobody else."

Myra stared.

"What a fool I was," she murmured. "I never hit on that!"

The lawyer changed the subject.

"Time cures all," he said. "You settle down and reach a contented frame of mind now."

"It'll take a few weeks to grasp he's gone for good," she answered. "I know now he can never issue no more orders, nor ring his bell and bawl for attention when he's got the gout. He won't wake up and curse me and the doctor and all eternity no more. Not a living man or beast will ever see him, or smart at his bitter tongue again. There's nothing to snatch up and heave at my head, or his daughter's, where he is now. Nobody to hear him down there. In the churchyard once for all and never to leave it. I wake of a morning light-headed and wonder why. But it takes time to realise a great blessing like that and let it be part of your life."

"Very sad—terribly sad," sighed Mr. Mallaby. "You must struggle with yourself to avoid thought of the past and envisage the happier future of your children and yourself."

He was glad to see the mourners returning at this moment and hastened forward to meet them. An elaborate cold luncheon awaited their attention with the food and drink proper to such an occasion. Mrs. Withers sat at the top of the table with Paul Pook on one side of her and Mr. Mallaby upon the other; while, when he had carved the cold ham and chickens and heaped the plates, Jonathan sat opposite his mother at the bottom of the table, with his Aunt Jenny on his right hand and his cousin, Rupert, upon his left. Harry Canniford sat beside his wife and there remained Nora, who came and went to help two serving maids. The company was unusually silent, speaking only on casual subjects and devoting most attention to their meal. Mr. Mallaby chatted to Nora when she took her seat and ventured to hope that her chickens were doing well, while Mr. Pook, conscious that, as the deceased's only friend, he should devote attention to the memory of Nicholas, discussed him with the widow.

"All went very suent, Myra, and the weather held fine and sunny. A bit of beat smoke blew over from Best's plough-land, where they are burning up the stubble now, but it was no odds. Barrows, the huntsman, brought hounds to the grave-side and blew his horn at the end. And, thinking upon your late husband and the doubts in some minds, I couldn't help wondering. You'll hear some hints that an enemy might have took advantage of him—a nasty thought the Coroner didn't hold with for a moment; while others again guessed he might have took his own life, and that's more fantastic still in my opinion."

"A score might have done it and no shame to them, Paul," replied Myra; "but he'd never have killed himself—he'd just got over a gout attack and was on his feet again. Too fond of his own way of life and too fond of his body to maltreat it."

"So I should have agreed."

"Oh yes. I ain't going to pretend any nonsense about Nicholas. He was a savage, heartless, God-forsaken manner of man as all the world knows; but what I've suffered at his hands nobody knows except myself and my children. He knocked five and twenty years off my age and now, please God, I shall get some of them back."

Mr. Pook's eyes grew round. He made no answer, but picked up his knife and fork and went on with his dinner, while Myra filled his wine-glass again with brown sherry and then poured some more for the lawyer.

When the saddler felt that further conversation must be made, he left Nicholas Withers alone and spoke of his private affairs.

"Have you heard tell about Ivy ?" he asked, and Myra nodded.

"Met her in the village two days ago. She's leaving Tudor Manor and coming home."

"That's her intention and I'm a thought put about," answered Pook.

"She's been there fifteen years she tells me and only going now because her ladyship don't want a lady's maid, being past the need for one and in the nurses' hands and don't know anybody even by sight no more. She's a bed-lier now and not long for this world, so Ivy says."

"Yes, only the nurses and the doctor between her and death. She's long forgot to recognise Ivy, and my daughter, who's got her own bleak wisdom, says that when anybody's gone out of their mind, the sooner they go out of their body the better."

"No doubt," agreed the widow. "So she'll come back and look after you ?"

Paul, somewhat gloomily, surveyed his situation.

"As a widower, with Mrs. Beer and her daughter to look after me, I've settled down comfortably and got used to the single life. When my wife would ride that hoss, and broke her neck and my heart simultaneous, then I felt a lost man for a bit. But religion and common sense, working together, righted my balance. I brought up Ivy and, as you know, she's a rare good woman and very highly thought upon. Lady Garland was a wonderful mistress to her and, such were Ivy's parts, that she was took into her ladyship's confidence and rose to be much more than just a lady's maid. That was quite all right; but it's a very ill-convenient thing for her to want to come back to me."

Mrs. Withers nodded.

"I dare say it might be," she said.

"Not a word against her; but she's one of them remorseless well-doers that get on your nerves now and again," he confessed. "Very high principles and so on. She's thirty-two now and assures me that she intends to marry and have a home of her own presently, if the right man haps to turn up. I hadn't the heart to tell her he never will, because she's not the fashion of woman to win any affection in a general way. Respect, yes; affection, no."

Myra made a suggestion.

"It's doubtful whether Ivy can count upon a husband," she admitted, "because them looking for a wife round about thirty wouldn't feel that she was their meat I'm afraid; but there's nought to prevent you from taking another wife yourself, Paul, and it might be a very clever thing to do. A kindly, comfortable woman who would keep Ivy in her place."

But he shook his head.

"I don't marry no more, Myra. No wish to try again. I'm getting on, and if I was to make a mistake, it would hurry me. No, the problem has got to be solved different. Some marriageable women might reckon that having to live with Ivy would be a greater snag than having to live with me, and, even if I did take another, that wouldn't be dead certain to get my daughter out of the house. As for her, she's always felt very keen after a husband for the last ten years, and I hoped up at the Manor, in her excellent and honourable employment, she'd find one; but she didn't get a bite I'm afraid. She ain't comely and though there's men would forgive her that for her sense and high principles, she's apt to take a sad view of things in general, and nought casts a man down quicker than a sad view of life."

"Men are more hopeful than what we are, as a rule," admitted Myra. "It ain't so much what Ivy says as the mourner's voice in which she says it. But a high sense of her duty, as you say."

"Very high indeed," agreed Ivy's father. "And her duty, as she sees it for the present, is to come home and watch over me."

"If she thinks so, then you're for it, Paul. But if it was known that she had your leavings behind her, some self-seeking man might come forward. Such a man might forgive her poor value to the eye; but he wouldn't over-look her financial advantages if you was to name them."

"Ivy's a hook that would call for a proper tempting bait," he admitted, "but between ourselves, Myra, I haven't got such a lot of money. Saddler's business ain't what it used to be. And if the impossible was to happen and I thought of another, then I'd want a tempting bait myself. A female would demand to know all mine was hers, and I shouldn't blame her for making sure neither."

"You speak of a situation as you find it," she replied, "and I'm not one to praise marriage, God He knows; but——"

Nora interrupted and thrust a junket in a large dish under her mother's nose.

"Will you take the afters, Mother?" she asked. "Everybody's finished his meat but you and Mr. Pook."

Their meal proceeded in leisurely fashion until Mr. Mallaby mentioned that he hoped to be on his way ere long.

"I want to catch the half after three from Honiton," he explained, "so if we may turn to business now, Mrs. Withers."

Thereupon Paul departed as the will was no concern of his, and Jenny Canniford also offered to leave Pigslake with her sons.

"Me and mine being what we were to Nicholas, there's nought that calls for us to bide, Myra," she said; but Mrs. Withers bade her stay.

"I'd like for you to hear," she answered. "It will save us coming round to tell you. There's but one vital thing to us and that's how Jonathan stands. The rest will only interest one that won't hear it to-day."

Her sister nodded.

"The Faircloud woman you're aiming at no doubt."

"Yes—that's all the question—her and her son."

"Everybody has long known what she was," said Jenny, "but as to Timothy, most hold that Nicholas had no hand in him."

"Anyway you best all stop and listen to how it's to be."

They left the house-place then and assembled in the parlour, while Mr. Mallaby arranged his papers and addressed them. The will was a short one and took him less than five minutes to read. Nicholas Withers had named but four persons in it.

To Jonathan he had bequeated Pigslake and all pertaining to the Farm. He was also residuary legatee.

To Nelly Faircloud he had left ten thousand pounds free of all taxation, and 'Lavender Cottage.'

To Paul Pook he bequeathed his hunter—a valuable gelding.

Lastly he directed that an old hind—Adam Merry—who had worked as shepherd for him and his father before him, should be allowed to dwell in a cottage on the farm as long as he lived and continue to receive one pound a week.

All were silent when the reader had finished, but Myra extended a hand to her son who sat beside her, and pressed his fingers.

"Incisive, brief and definite according to the habit and custom of the dead," summed up Mr. Mallaby, "and you must permit me to express much relief that the crowning impropriety, which you had only too good reason to fear, was not committed. Your father's capital, Jonathan, was roughly somewhere in the region of fifteen thousand pounds and when we consider what remains after his estate is wound up, there should be ample to see your farm safe till the harvests of next year. Should your plans embrace selling the farm, that of course will be in your power; but I trust you may continue your life here and carry on a concern that has been in your family for nearly two hundred years."

Jonathan looked at Myra.

"We bide, Mother?" he asked.

"Sure we bide, my son," she answered. "Nought wrong with Pigslake."

Mr. Mallaby hastened into his taxi-cab and the Cannifords strolled back to Priory together. Harry sighed at the iniquity of the world, but his wife declared a hopeful factor.

"Jonathan will take our George to work at the farm presently—he promised me," said Susan Canniford.

"I thought to the last moment we should hear that scarlet woman was going to have Pigslake," declared Jenny. "It's something to thank the Lord for she didn't."

"She's got what's a darned sight better than Pigslake," said Rupert. "Ten thousand quid and freedom to do what she fancies for evermore."

"And nought but her poor, weak-minded boy to hoard that hugeous mass of money up for," added Harry's wife.

"He'll lord it over the parish now, Susan," laughed Rupert. "His mother's money would go to his head like drink—if she let him touch it. But she won't."

"In his life-time your uncle gave Mrs. Faircloud a lot of money," said Jenny, "and I'd go so far as to say he didn't only keep her—he kept her straight, if you can talk of straightness along with such a woman. She knew she'd have to watch her step with Nicholas and, if he'd catched her deceiving him, that would have been the end of the goose with the golden eggs."

"They suited each other mighty well if you ask me, Mother," declared Rupert. "Birds of a feather; and now she's free, she'll lay her nets for another man I shouldn't wonder and won't take long to find him. But he'll have to be a good few years younger than she is herself to suit Nelly. Perhaps I'll try my luck."

"Shame on you, Rupert !" cried his parent. "How often have I blushed for your evil sayings."

"Mark me, that woman will vanish away from Priory now," Harry told them. He was an indeterminate, middle-sized man with a wrinkled brow, a thatch of yellow hair and a thin yellow beard which did not conceal his full lips and trifling chin. Nothing more unlike his brother could have been imagined.

"And as for Tim," concluded Rupert, "he'll be a gentleman at large. He likes the girls, so maybe we shall hear he's up to some May games along with them. They'll listen to him now I shouldn't wonder."

"He'll aim for something higher than woodman's work no doubt," thought Harry.

"You bet !" answered his brother. "He weren't called 'Changeling' for nought."

III

TIMOTHY sat with his mother upon an evening one week after she knew her fate. The great legacy had created a tornado of mingled emotions in his mind and even Mrs. Faircloud, who knew him better than anybody, felt somewhat mystified at her son's excitement. For it appeared to be streaked with a network of thoughts that wound black and ugly threads through the fabric of this triumph. One moment he was full of the event, picturing his mother's affluence and future freedom and contentment, the next he would sigh, fall silent and allow an expression of melancholy to cloud his animation. Anon from gloom he would emerge again, and she noticed that he dwelt upon her liberty as the paramount pleasure in their new situation. Timothy did not speak of any alteration in his own future, or identify himself as a factor in coming plans that Nelly might be pleased to make.

He had long since comprehended her relationship with the dead man and often mused upon it as irregular and exceptional. He had hated Nicholas cordially, but never felt need to protest at any bad treatment of his mother, for with her the farmer appeared to live a life in absolute opposition to that he conducted among other people. With her Nicholas was gentle, considerate, almost affectionate in his rough fashion. He cared much for her, found her companionship all sufficing, was jealous for her well-being, even kind to Timothy himself when disposed to be amiable. How his mother, without any apparent effort, had tamed this bellicose and brutal man, the boy could not guess, and his efforts to find out failed; for his parent would never discuss Nicholas but to express her devotion.

"He's difficult to understand, Tim," she would say in her pleasant subdued voice, "but I understand Mr. Withers, and when he got to find I did, we grew to be very close friends, and have so remained; because he understands me, too, and I'm not too easy neither."

Thus, in varied words, Nelly would reply to his puzzlement. She had once been beautiful and was a very pretty woman still. Unimpeded by any moral views, naturally sensual but intensely practical and long-sighted, Mrs. Faircloud was drawn to Nicholas from the first by his virility and a certain quality of rough sense and shrewdness that kept him safe, despite the aversion that his method of life created in other people. They were drawn together in a mutual bond of utter indifference to the reactions of the world at large. His will had not surprised Nelly, for Withers promised long ago that she should be left well provided. But she had kept her bargain faithfully and been true to him. Neither ever lied to the other. She was going to miss Nicholas and she knew it, but no ideas as to the future were yet formulated in her mind. She proposed to wait awhile and find how life felt without him. She believed that physical passion had died with Nicholas and could not imagine the man capable of bringing it to life again. Perhaps no nobler emotion had ever quickened her. She as yet had not considered any new suggestions for Timothy's future, but explained to him that their lives were now secure.

"I shall have about the same as I always had under his protection," she told her son, "but not a lot more if I don't touch the capital. And I don't ordain to meddle with that."

"Will you leave it to me when you go ?" he asked.

"If you're a good boy I most like shall," she promised and changed the subject.

"I'd thought to lose two friends back along, Timothy," she told him; "but one's spared to me, Mercy Grepe's going to live, though Dr. Naylor gave her up. Just her will power battled against nature, and nature yielded and let her bide."

"Her they call 'Mother Forty Cats'," said Timothy. "She's counted a witch. What d'you fancy so much about that queer old bird, Mother ?"

Nelly laughed out of her grey sleepy eyes, which still made a wonder of her face behind their long lashes.

"Anybody with her mort of sense would seem a witch to everyday people," she said. "Wisdom like old Mercy's always looks to be witchery to us common-place folk. Cats granted. She loves 'em and understands 'em far deeper than we can. And they understand her and will neighbour with her, whether she wants 'em or not. They tell each other about her I believe. She says them that understand cats understand women, and how parlous few do that ! Not many of us ourselves I'm sure."

"She's done some wondrous cures, and now she's wiped the doctor's eyes by curing herself," admitted Timothy.

"Yes, wondrous cures. She never harmed a fly, though she granted to me it lay in her power to hurt if she minded," answered his mother. "And parson is on her side, too. He never saw no harm in her. Along of his bulldog that was. The dog took parlous ill, and vet. said best to put him out of his misery as he couldn't do a thing for the creature. And Mercy heard tell and went to his reverence and asked to see the dog before he was slain. 'If everybody was put out of their misery, just because they happened to be miserable, there wouldn't be a soul left alive,' said she. ' 'Tis a monstrous thing to kill a dear dog because he's sick and the vet's too big a fool to know what ails him.'

So parson showed her the dog and she's well nigh so skilled in dogs as cats; and the dog knew it. She talked to him and he grunted back, and she felt him over and stroked him and physicked him and ended by saving him. And for her reward, which was all she asked, she's been promised to lie where she wants to lie in the churchyard."

"It's a good thing she isn't going under for a bit yet, then," said Timothy.

"It is then—I'd miss her."

Mrs. Faircloud resembled her aged friend, for, while still regarded with a certain amount of suspicion in some quarters, none save the Withers family could declare any personal cause of animosity against her. She was peaceable and nobody had ever heard her speak with lack of charity against another; she was always friendly and willing to pleasure man or woman when it lay in her power to do so. Most deplored her way of life and not a few refused to know her, but none could furnish a personal grievance, or cite any unneighbourly action. Some, not ungrateful for deeds of kindness, supported her, but she went her way absolutely indifferent to the attitude that other people might be pleased to take. Praise did not elate her, or reports of censure and condemnation cast her down. Nor was she curious, finding her own affairs amply sufficient to interest and occupy her mind and body.

"Now Lavender Cottage is yours, shall you sell it and buy a bigger house?" asked Timothy.

"The house has been mine a good few years," she answered. "Mr. Withers gave it to me for a Christmas present a long time ago. Quite big enough for you and me, and if I stop at Priory, I shall stay in it."

"Sometimes I hope you'll bide and sometimes I hope you won't," he said. "It would be wonderful to find myself among different things and different people; but then again I might hate them and hanker after the woods again. I don't want to go."

"I don't much want to go myself, Tim. I'm so well content here as I'm like to be any place. I'd say it depends on you more than me in a way, because if you was to feel you'd like higher education and work up to a black-coated trade, then it would be better fit we went to Honiton, or some such market town, where you could be taught what fashion of book-learning you'd like to master. For any high purpose such as that I'd spare money, of course."

"I've got a lot of ambition," declared Timothy. "Some days it overmasters me, Mother, and I feel I could pretty near reach up to the stars; then, other days, it's gone and I fear I'm properly doomed to sing small. Learning from books might help; but I reckon there's something in me that's bound to come out and astonish you and everybody one day. Books might help: I like 'em. I know I've got secret powers. I read that old poetry book in the parlour and I like it—especially about trees. The man says just what's right about trees. He didn't know 'em so well as I do; but he knew 'em pretty well. Then there's deeds. I often say I'll surprise you; but I've done more than that in a manner of speaking, because I've surprised myself in the matter of deeds."

"'Tis a very cheerful thing to find yourself cleverer than you thought, Tim," agreed Nelly, who had marked his fitful elation through the past month. "It learns you to rely upon yourself. If you can't trust yourself, nobody else will."

"That's right," he said. "I can trust myself, and only nineteen, too."

"What have you done to please yourself so well ?" she asked. "I thought it was the money."

"Not only that, but that pleased me for your sake, not my own. As to what I've done, perhaps I'll tell you one day; but I doubt it."

"Who have you told ?"

"Not a one. And, mind you, that's a big thing in itself. I'm witty enough to know that. If you do a fine deed, it may be a finer one still to keep dumb and deny yourself the pleasure of blazing it out."

"You're getting too deep for me, Tim," she answered smiling. "You've got surprises hid from me yet, I see. If anybody had told me you'd do a fine thing and not let the world pat you on the back for it, I'd have said that never was you."

He regarded her doubtfully and returned to the starting point.

"I know it's fine; perhaps other people might think it wasn't. Perhaps you mightn't. But don't you go anyway. You stop here, Mother, and let me carry on my work with the woodmen."

"I'll do nought till another Spring be it as it will," she promised. "And you go on doing fine things, my treasure. Some day perhaps I'll hear tell about 'em from somebody else than yourself. Then they'll come back to me."

He laughed at that.

"I'll hit on a fine deed to please you sooner than you think perhaps. I've done another deed for that matter everybody's welcome to hear. I've got ideas. I sing in the woods now my voice is steady again. I sing the rhymes from the poetry book and I can make new rhymes ! I've catched myself making a rhyme easy as easy. Who's here could do that but me ?"

"Do you talk to the trees same as you used to when you were a little chap, or have you given that up ?" asked his mother.

"I catch myself talking to them sometimes yet; but I've lost the old feeling that they were my private friends. I'm not grand enough yet to be the friend of a tree."

"You came home crying two years ago, because you'd found the wood-man's cross on one of your beech-tree friends and knew he was doomed to be thrown."

Timothy laughed again.

"I did then, and called the head man—Enoch Thorpe—a murderer and said I'd dearly like to hang him. But he didn't see the fun of it and told me if I dared to speak to him like that again, he'd cast me out. But I'd rather be planting than felling. Planting young trees will always be the work I like best, and watching 'em grow after."

Timothy, at the command of Nicholas, had never failed to give his mother half the weekly wages he earned at forestry; but now she allowed him to save and put by—a course that made no great appeal to him. But he enjoyed this increase of pocket money, for it raised his status and enabled him to stand drinks occasionally, like elder men, and thus increase the scant attention usually devoted to him. He left his mother now, lighted a cigarette and strolled off to the 'Pen-in-Hand.' The usual company was assembled there and Nicholas Withers—his death and his will—continued to form a topic for interesting discussion. Every detail of the dead farmer's dispensations was now common knowledge and before young Faircloud arrived, Mr. Toozey expressed a general opinion that they were more just than might have been expected.

"For my part," he said, "I'd got a fore-token that we'd see the family out of Pigslake and Mrs. Faircloud lifted up. And lifted up she surely has been; but blood is thicker than water and land's sacred, and though Nick spurned his wife, he clove to his son, so Jonathan carries on. Young to be master in big place like that; but he's keeping his headman, Christopher Banks, and ordains to follow in the old roads and not do anything his father wouldn't have held with."

"It goes to show Nick doubted of Nelly Faircloud," said Piper, the sexton. "He knew she could never stand up to Pigslake, though the woman was all the world to him."

"He cared a lot for her, little for the boy," explained Toozey, "and he knew Tim was no farmer and she hated farming. She'd had all the farming she wanted at Valley Farm, when her husband was alive. She'd only have sold. But now the old name will run on and Jonathan's trustable to carry it."

"Will Mrs. Faircloud bide here, or take herself and her fortune off I wonder?" asked Rupert Canniford. "Timothy says he don't know. I catched him mooning in the forest on my rounds a day or two since. Not doing a hand's turn of work—just feeling he was a big man now with ten thousand pounds behind him—lucky toad !"

"And goes so high and mighty as if he'd earned it himself," laughed the inn-keeper. "I've heard nothing as to his mother's intentions; but he told me last time he was in here he didn't want to leave Priory—'for his own reasons'," he told me.

Rupert agreed.

"His own reasons being Katey Wish, the baker's daughter," he said. "Master Tim's had his eye on Katey ever since she used to blow his nose for him in Sunday School. However, there's more than Timothy after Kate. She's a pretty piece if you like 'em small."

"A very clever child," declared Toozey, "and young Faircloud, for all he's odd and uncertain, has got a mind, though you can't see much promise to it yet."

"He's an ambitious chap with more will to do something out of the common than wits to do it with," explained Rupert. "Just vain."

"He's that mysterious !" said Ned Piper. "He puts it on a purpose and smiles at nothing. He came with a bunch of flowers from his mother for the new grave a bit ago and took pains to tell me they weren't no gift from him. Very superior he was and put on his quality face."

"He often looks like a race-horse got among plough-horses," admitted Toozey. "Which makes you feel your Uncle Nicholas never got him, Rupert. Or so I see it; but that's politics and no affair of ours."

As often happened at the 'Pen-in-Hand' the object of passing discussion himself appeared at this moment and Timothy sauntered in for a drink. He was amiable and friendly.

"Good evening all," he said. "My usual half pint, Mr. Toozey. Any singing to-night?"

"Feel like singing these days I dare say, Tim," suggested Rupert.

"Not particular. I sing a bit in the woods. Sometimes I've got a fancy to have my voice tried out in a town and find if it is tip-top, or just ordinary."

"Luxuries in your reach now," admitted Rupert. "We were wondering whether you and your mother was going to stop at Priory. I reckoned not."

"You reckoned wrong then. We stop till the turn of the year anyway."

"You stop," advised Mr. Piper. "Let your money circulate in your native village, boy."

"Stand us a drink for a start," suggested the game-keeper.

"I was going to," declared the boy. "Name it, Rupert, and you chaps. Drinks on me, Mr. Toozey."

In the cheerful spirit thus created, the dead man's nephew returned to a topic that always attracted him.

"We needn't pretend no sorrows for the late Mr. Withers and I dare say you hated him like everybody else including his family," said Rupert to Timothy; "but I've often wondered about the man's end and if they got the truth of it. Did you ever hear your mother pass any opinion on that point, Faircloud?"

"No, I never did. You couldn't say much about him to her, because he was her very faithful friend; but she took the verdict for granted," replied Timothy.

"And did you—knowing what sort of man my Uncle Nicholas happed to be?"

The younger considered. Then he smiled to himself, but explained the reason for his amusement.

"I was only laughing at Inspector Chard and that ape, Joe Palfrey," he said. "If there'd been anything dark about the old man's death, they wouldn't have found it out."

"They looked for clues, but the ground was covered with the workmen's boot-marks and nothing to go by," said Piper. "And Constable Palfrey isn't an ape—he's a very clever man and my wife's nephew."

"I thought for a bit there might have been a murder," confessed Timothy, "for there was a lot had a bone to pick with Mr. Withers and few to speak in his favour round here."

"True," answered Peter Honeywood, who had just entered, "but you've got to mind the difference between just hating a man and hating him bad enough to slay him. You've got to look all round a murder before you commit one. All right so far as the enemy is concerned no doubt: you can best him once for all if you kill him: but unless you've got to such a pitch that you don't care what happens to yourself after, there's a lot more to think about. You're playing with your own life when you do a murder, and pitting your wits and craft against the might of law and order and the skilled men let loose like hounds on your track to hunt you down."

"That's right," seconded Rupert. "It takes a brave chap to commit murder and a mighty bright one—man or woman—to cheat the police after and hide his own tracks and leave nought to catch him by.   There's a good many might have wanted to put paid to Uncle Nicholas, but where's the one of 'em could have escaped after?   No—his game foot went back on him and over he went."

"A clever murder—if it was one," said Toozey, "but 'tis little likely. And Chard a good bit disappointed, for he'd hoped to shine.   But Tom Chard's like you, Rupert: he says there's nobody round here could have finished off Withers without leaving a clue."

"An easy murder come to think of it all the same," argued Ned Piper. "Anybody who knew the man's ways and how he'd go to the well after dusk, when the workers were gone, might have hid handy and give him a jolt from behind and sped away.   Not that any man did."

"How's the Withers family looking up?" asked Honeywood.

"They're all right.   They know their luck by now and the change that's come in their lives," replied the game-keeper.   "Aunt Myra looks ten years younger and Nora sings like a grey bird.   She'll be worth catching now, Nora will, because Jonathan's very fond of her."

"He'll carry on pretty safe," prophesied Honeywood.   "He's got a good brain, and whatever else Nick didn't teach him, he taught him farming."

Timothy departed at this juncture and when he was offered another drink in exchange for his round, he looked at a new wrist watch and said he must be off.

"Another time," he said, "and if there's no singing here, I'll go for a song somewhere else."

"She'll like your voice better than what we do," laughed young Canniford, but the boy did not respond, lighted another cigarette and was gone.

"Got a date!" grinned Honeywood.   "Beginning early.   His mother's son was likely to!"

They talked of Nelly's legacy and debated her future.

"There's them that will let the past bury the past," foretold old Piper. "Men's going to be after her again now she's free and well to do."

They considered the probability and found it an entertaining topic until William Toozey stopped them.

"No more on that subject, gentlemen, if you please," he said.   " 'Tis the sort of politics well known to be forbid here."

"You have a dash, Bill," suggested Peter Honeywood, but Mr. Toozey thought otherwise.

"If you was to ask me, I'd say Paul Pook was the man might be best like to fill her eye," he said, "though the last to want to."

"Not him.   It won't be no fossil when she picks up another," declared Rupert.

"She likes 'em fierce seemingly," pointed out the sexton.   "Pook would be like a tabby cat after she'd had a Bengal tiger."

Then the talk turned to business and Peter's market garden.

He praised the yield of the year, but spoke bitterly of those to whom he sold his produce.

"Thank God round here we don't have much truck with greengrocers—

no need to," he said. "And them too poor to own a yard of land can count upon good neighbours to help them. But it's my fate to deal with the traders and a bigger lot of rogues you won't find. The public pays fancy money for green stuff and the growers get shameful rewards for their labours; but they blasted middle-men fatten like the dishonest pigs they are from both sides. They rob rich and poor alike, and if you was to go to hell, I lay every second lost soul you met would be a greengrocer."

"Strong," commented Toozey. "Uncommonly strong for you, Peter."

"If your feelings are probed to the roots, you speak accordingly," explained Honeywood, "and that's the ugly truth about greengrocers, William."

Elsewhere young Faircloud had gone his way to do what Rupert guessed. Beyond Priory stretched a water-meadow girdled with trees and cottages and known as the village green. It was considerably larger than such centres as a rule and to-night lay shrouded in darkness, with no more than a sickle moon and stars above and a twinkle of little lights round about. The stream ran through the midst and, at a hand-bridge over it, a pathway cut the grassy and reed-grown waste at right angles. Here and there opened marshy hollows and pools, where children fished for minnows, and in spring the verdure sparkled with cuckoo flowers, yellow irises and kingcups. Now the ragwort lighted it and round about upon the elms there hung snow-white clusters of 'travellers' joy.' The bridge was a familiar tryst and, trusting that one only might be upon it to-night, Timothy approached, to see a solitary figure awaiting him. Katey Wish, the baker's daughter, had arrived. She was a little, cheerful soul, a year younger than the boy, and for six months she had renewed their infant acquaintance and succeeded in winning his affection. To enter his life had proved difficult, but at last Katey achieved her purpose. Returning home in the omnibus from their market town, she had found herself beside Timothy and reminded him of their Sunday School days. They fell into talk and there proved to be something about the girl that appealed to him. Future attachment grew upon that meeting for Kate was frank and when, presently, she confessed that she had longed to know him and loved his face for many hopeless years, Timothy found himself much gratified at discovery of an admirer so staunch and herself attractive. He glorified Kate into a girl quite out of the common and greatly enjoyed the secret which they proposed to keep between them: an understanding to be married some day when they were older and Timothy equal to providing a home. Katey pretended nothing. Her admiration was genuine and the fact of secret betrothal to the best-looking and most wonderful boy in Priory gave her unbounded delight. But she kept their understanding close, met Timothy when it was possible and proceeded happily with her business: to help her mother in the baker's shop.

Katey knew all about what had happened to Mrs. Faircloud and came now inspired with an idea to be laid before her sweetheart. It was the self-same thought that occupied his mind when last he had spoken to his mother.

Timothy put his arms round Katey and kissed her, while she kissed him back. She was a neat, bright-eyed and pretty little person, always pleasant to see, with added beauty of expression and complexion won from perfect health and good temper, keen love of life and some sense of humour, which often mystified Timothy, who lacked in that matter.

"I always know when you're up and when you're down," she said. "I know it in your tone of voice no matter what you say, and when I heard you singing, after I'd been listening to nought but the night birds, I knew you was up. And that's good because I've had an exciting thought."

"Let's go in Chorley Woods," he said. "Them they say are haunted, though nobody ever saw the ghost."

"He was the man who had the bakery before father," she reminded him. "He hanged himself there after he'd failed. He died on an oak and swung three days before they found him."

They discussed the dead, but Timothy was cheerful to-night and turned to himself.

"You're right. The going's good with me. I've just stood a round at Toozey's. I went to sing, but they were all for talk and I heard things. They don't understand me, but I understand them easy enough."

"I understand you."

"You do so; but you're different. Rupert Withers is the cleverest of 'em. D'you know why ? Because he's like me and spends his life with the trees."

"He ain't like you in no other way," said Katey, "but if you think well of him, then he's got his good points no doubt. Mother says he's mean over money."

"I don't think well nor yet ill of him. He's just a killer, like any other game-keeper. But he granted that——"

He broke off.

"No matter for him. No matter for anybody else but you. And I'll tell you something I've found out. If you want to be on good terms with yourself, you mustn't look to others to help you. You must do it yourself. Other people ain't going to try to make you feel pleased with yourself—quite the contrary."

"Most folk find it easy enough to be," said Katey. "But there's times when you can't be pleased with yourself try as you will. I used to feel full of wonder when you praised me and got up in the air about me. I'd puzzle to think however a little go-by-the-ground like me could have made you in love with her. But other days, when you wriggled full of woe, like a worm on a hook, and said you was worthless dust and so on, then I wondered how ever such a meek and hopeless chap had got up enough pluck to speak even to me. You're a rum mixture, darling."

"I have been," he admitted, "but no more of that. I've found out a lot of things about myself worth knowing—tolerable deep things but not such as to cast me down. And one was that if you want pleasure and success and to be well thought upon, you must come by 'em single-handed. I know it. If I hadn't got to know you yourself same as I did, I'd never have known you at all. Think of that ! When you scraped acquaintance in the bus that day, I wished you away at first, but I was civil and see how I was rewarded. I've known a few girls off and on, but never one to understand me nor make me think twice about 'em till I got you.   And now you're the best thing I have got, or ever shall get."

Katey purred.

"You'll learn me a lot you'd be wishful for me to know in time," she said.   "I fell in love with your face long since; but you've got to pay for loving a man and going to do my part."

"No girl could say fairer.   We'll learn together.   There's a lot more in life I want to know about when I've mastered it, Katey."

"You'll master it with a brain like yours I expect," she answered.   "I never felt life to be particular mysterious myself till you showed me that mysteries was harbouring in everything, down to the tree in the hedge, or a bird on a bough.   But trees mean some queer things to you I shall never grasp home."

"Because you don't look at 'em right."

"How should I look at 'em ?" she asked.   "A tree is just a tree to me, same as it is to everybody else but you.   Other woodmen count a tree their daily job;   you seem as if it was your neighbour and better worth than you are yourself."

"I thought you knew more about 'em by now," grumbled Timothy.   "You cast your eyes over a big tree as a lump of wood, to make tables and chairs and ships and house-frames, or to burn for fuelling.   That's wrong.   I see it as a great solemn creature that was standing up to life years before I was born and most likely to live years after I am dead."

"Lor what a thought !" cried Katey.   "I'll catch myself curtseying to 'em next."

"I'd sooner see a girl curtsey to 'em than to the quality.   I'd often touch my cap to a whacking tree when I was a kid.   Something about 'em seemed to call for it.   They do more for me than any human can—even you, or mother."

"What do they do ?"

"I don't know exactly."

"Well, you can't do more for them than make up rhymes about 'em—or try to."

"Only try.   I tore up that one I showed you about the big spruce.   I'm very clever to get rhymes and tell about trees, but I can't tell about 'em right. They're too deep for me as yet, but I'll master 'em some day."

"You ought to write a rhyme telling about me," begged Katey.   "You give the trees a miss and write about me, Tim."

"I haven't rose to you yet, any more than I've rose to the trees."

"If trying to turn rhymes and failing at 'em casts you down, I should chuck it," suggested Katey.   "I'd say you was poetry in yourself.   You are to me anyway and that ought to be enough."

"Trees are grander than anything even proper poets can say about 'em," he decided.   "What was it you wanted to tell me ?"

"Us.   You and me.   Would you say your mother's fortune brought our marriage any nearer, or made no difference ?"

He considered the point.

"Of course I can see you've took it very favourable," added Katey, "but that was just for her sake and not your own.   If she was to marry again, for instance——?   You'd hate that I reckon."

"I took it favourable for a lot of different reasons," he explained.   "And, of course, it got a move on for me as well as mother.   Money's money and money's power.   It isn't the best sort of power they say, but few folk can show any power more powerful.   And I think it does bring our marriage a good bit closer.   As to Mother's marrying again, I don't say it's very likely; but you never know.   She wouldn't ask me anyway."

"No business of ours.   But now I'm coming to what I was going to say. How would it be if you was to find out Mrs. Faircloud's opinion of me, Timothy ?   I feel a fearful lot would turn on that; but I'm always hopeful myself and she's a very kind woman.   There's a lot likes her very much. Mother likes her very much and Miss Grepe—her they call 'Mother Forty Cats'—she likes her.   And you can see in a minute, if I satisfied Mrs. Faircloud, it would be a tower of strength to me."

"I don't care a farthing dam who likes you and who don't," said Timothy. "I'm a man now and I'm a brave man and a clever one and sure to be dead right in such a thing as choosing my future wife.   All the same I wouldn't say but we've reached a stage to let out what we ordain to mother.   And not only her, but everybody else.   I had the thought myself not an hour ago when I left home.   To win you was a very fine deed on my part—a big thing. We've kept so dumb about it that I doubt a soul knows, though some may very likely guess.   I might tell mother we're tokened and I don't see no more reasons to keep it hid.   Then most likely she'll ask you to come to tea and figure you up and find I've done a pretty smart thing.   And you can tell your father and mother; then they'll ask me to tea I expect."

Katey approved the plan.

"Sounds just such a sharp thought as you was likely to get," she said. "They'll all agree we're too young for the minute; but that's no odds if they don't try and choke us off each other."

"God help any who'd dare to try that," he said and fell silent pursuing his own thoughts.   They were sitting on a fallen tree with his arm round her, and Timothy's reflections now led to some general opinions from him.

"I'm tolerable excited and tolerable content to-night," he said, "and when I'm in a way like that, I generally get a jolt to bring me down again.   Looking forward to what you would like to happen is a harmless sort of amusement, though you mostly know it never will happen; but you get the pleasure of picturing it if it did.   Now I've got the feeling I'm strong enough to make things happen.   And them that feel so, show they've got power.   I've made things happen in my time and I shall again, and let the people see them happen."

"So they will then; but you'll never be like Nicholas Withers and make hateful things happen—never.   If you were such a man as him I'd run away from you; but you was never built to do ought but good."

"Mother tells how folk call me a changeling," he answered, "and I am a changeling compared to them that call me so.   I'll change again and yet again if I please; but never to you."

"So long as you don't change into something horrid and fright me, I don't care for no changes," promised Kate.   "But I pray you'll bide a woodman, because you're at your best and happiest along with the trees. Some girls might be jealous of 'em, but I won't be."

The boy's mind was still largely occupied with subconscious thoughts.

"The trees teach you one great thing anyhow," he said, "and that's to keep your mouth shut. They do miracles of growing over your head and under your feet, but never a word about their wonders. 'Tis enough that them with eyes can see. And for humans it's a great wonder, still to do great things and keep 'em to yourself after."

"If they are good wonders, why shouldn't everybody hear about 'em ?" she asked, but did not wait for an answer as the church clock struck ten.

"There ! Time's up. Come along and see me home, Tim."

As they walked back together, hand in hand, Katey indicated the position.

"Now we'll go the whole hog, as father says, and I'll tell him and mother we're tokened and properly living for each other, and you'll break it to Mrs. Faircloud. Then you and me can sit back and see how it strikes 'em."

"Yes, that's right. And we must be firm. Nothing like showing firmness. We ain't asking permission, or any such thing. We're telling what's happened and what we're going to do about it at some future time. When a couple choose to be married, they're the big noise, not other people."

Katey laughed.

"'Tis a good bit out of the common for a girl to be the big noise with her father and mother," she said, "especially if they've got a parcel of other children, like Dad and Mum. But I'll do my best. To-morrow then."

"They've all been in love in their time," he pointed out, "and though most like they never felt so grand about it as we do, they'll know the danger of trying to baulk such as me."

Her father was in the bakery at the rear of the shop when the girl got home at a quarter past ten; but Mrs. Wish, a hard-worked, somewhat nervous woman waited up for her.

"I won't have you so late of a night, Katey," she said. "Half after nine's the time for you to be home."

"Something interesting happened and I'll tell you to-morrow, Mother. I'm sorry, but you'll well understand when I explain. A very nice thing, to please you and father above a bit I hope."

"That's as may be, my dear. Now go to bed."

"Have father finished Captain Mason's wedding cake, I wonder ?"

"Not to my knowledge, but he may have."

"It's offering to be a champion when I saw it, Mother."

"No doubt of that; but little them that eats a wedding cake think on the master hand that made it," said Mrs. Wish.

"Got something better to think of most like," suggested Katey. "And I'll tell you my news to-morrow, Mother."

But what she was to learn promised no surprise for the baker's wife. When man and maid walk out together in village circles, the fact is very widely apprehended and Milly Wish knew her daughter's companion. She had already been disposed to investigate Timothy's romance; but then came the news of his mother's legacy and Mrs. Wish held her hand, being among those who cherished no ill-feelings against the widow.

IV

THOUGH he had long been dead to her, the eternal departure of her husband's personality, came for Myra Withers as a mighty release and blessing. A slave had received her liberty and felt the weight of her chains no more. She was free to develop her own instincts and follow her own bent, while her children, fearfully at first and slower to realise the immense change in their outlook upon life, responded with increasing zest to a freedom and a sense of security beyond their experience. Peace gladdened the air of Pigslake and, in varied measure, all experienced it. The spirit of the farm was changed and the head man, Christopher Banks, sounded a warning.

He admired Jonathan and was ready and willing to support him; but he felt an element of danger in the sudden loosening of the old, harsh discipline and remorseless drive. The year had been a prosperous one; hay and corn were both above the average and roots promised well. Much work was in hand and sales of stock occupied the new farmer's mind; while his mother served him with her long experience and helped him to appreciate a little world in which he was now his own master and the master of his own farm. He desired to justify the new responsibilities and faced them bravely and sturdily; he showed good sense and foresight and inspired confidence in his neighbours. All indeed approved, and Dr. Naylor, who was a keen student of heredity and its problems, pointed out at the bar of the 'Pen-in-Hand' that Jonathan promised to be a happy example of inherited virtues.

'He's got the best of his father without the worst," he said. "That's remarkable and encouraging. He has a strong will and determination and he's not afraid of work; but there's no love of cruelty and brutality for their own sake that made his father such a human failure."

Many beside those most involved welcomed the disappearance of Nicholas Withers, for not a few small people had suffered at his hands when it fell in his power to afflict them and, in some cases, Jonathan was able to right certain outstanding grievances. Indeed his eyes were opened to various of his father's deeds that shocked him and he marvelled to his mother how one man had found it fall in his reach to torment so many.

Nothing astonished Myra, however.

"It was your father's pleasure to hurt them around him and he'd have crucified his enemies if he could," she said. "He used all the strength he had to give himself that sort of pleasure, because there was a close time for the other creatures he hunted, but none for his fellow humans."

Jonathan did not lack reflective instincts.

"Beastly in a way to think your own dad was such a man," he had said to his mother after the discovery of further revelations.

"Yes, sure it is, boy," she had answered, "but you mustn't let beastly things breed beastly thoughts no more. Forget him, same as I'm trying to do."

Jenny Canniford found herself a considerable gainer by her brother-in-aw's end. Myra was fond of her and had always helped by strategy to assist Jenny's meagre support with farm produce when possible. Now these things could be given openly and luxuries enriched the widow's table. Cream, butter and eggs were at her service and thus she shared Myra's content and increased happiness in the new dispensation. Harry Canniford found himself a gainer, too, for food came to his family from his mother and Jonathan had definitely promised Harry's wife that her first-born should be employed at Pigslake when he reached school-leaving age. George himself wanted to be a policeman and Constable Joe Palfrey was the ideal of what he aspired some day to become; but his parents attached no importance to his dream and their eldest was well aware that he must begin life as a farmer's boy.

Autumn followed its ancient uses and the folk pursued the pattern woven from immemorial time. At Mr. Toozey's bar men gathered and he always found that singing won more supporters as the day grew shorter, the hours of darkness longer. Customers would bring in a bit of news, good or bad; while others listened and commented. An item, trivial in itself, might be found to possess racy significance when examined from some new standpoint. Possibilities also presented themselves and were canvassed. On one occasion, when they were drinking together, Peter Honeywood raised such a problem with Jonathan Withers and asked him a question.

"When are you going to take a wife?" he inquired. "Time you thought about it now."

The market gardener received an unexpected answer.

"Some say it's more than time you did, Peter," replied young Withers. "As for me you're right. I want a wife to help my mother nowadays. I shan't waste no time when I've got the luck to find her."

"That's one for you, Peter," sniggered the sexton, for Mr. Honeywood's long dalliance was common knowledge. Somewhat disconcerted Peter turned to his glass and Toozey murmured, "No politics gentlemen, please."

Then Ned Piper proceeded and spoke to Jonathan.

"Have you turned your thoughts to your father's memorial stone as yet, my lad?" he asked. "Too soon to lift it till another Spring I grant you; but not too soon to think upon it and set it in order. If Stokes is to cut it, he'll take months and months of time."

Jonathan looked at the old man.

"That's for my mother to decide, not me, Ned," he answered. "I asked her that self-same question a night or two since and what d'you think she said?"

"Couldn't hazard no guess, things being what they were," replied Piper.

"She said: "Your father turned my heart to stone, Jonathan, and that's all the stone he'll ever get from me.' She may change her mind, or she may leave me to do what I will about it. Plenty of time anyway."

"A fearful thing to say," ventured Toozey.

"And not true neither," replied Myra's son. "Nothing would ever turn my mother's heart to stone, William."

They talked of the wonderful recovery of 'Mother Forty Cats,' the white witch.

"Doctor took no credit. He said it was just amazing exercise of will power," explained Toozey. "She was dead for all practical purposes and then she made what you might call an expiring effort and be blessed if she didn't turn the corner ! When Dr. Naylor went in next morning, tolerable sure he'd find all over, there she was sitting up, like a ghost, all eyes, taking a spot of warm milk and wishing the man good luck !"

"It shows how one thing hangs upon another," said the sexton, "because if she'd a died, she'd have gone in to the appointed spot promised her by parson; and then my wife would have left my house; because she wasn't going to have that deep and doubtful creature lying within six yards of her pillow by night."

"There won't be no nicer bones in the yard when she do go," declared Honeywood. "That woman never did a mite of harm in her life, but quite a lot of usefulness."

An ironical observer, empowered to link Peter's praise with subsequent incidents, had won some entertainment from this remark; but no man may surely join present with future and none ever saw that amusing connection, or guessed it.

A startling event heralded what was to happen and Jenny Canniford, trotting through the village one afternoon about her own affairs, was accosted, to her amazement, by another woman with whom she had long ceased to be on speaking terms. Mrs. Faircloud, of all sinister spirits, stopped her, smiled upon her, and asked if she might have a word.

Jenny felt the colour rush to her round face and her heart quicken before a challenge so extraordinary; but Nelly was calm, spoke in her usually subdued and amiable voice and revealed no hint of grievance or vexation.

The elder stood still and cast her eyes about her as though seeking support.

"I wouldn't say there's anything that calls for a word between you and me," she murmured.

"Perhaps there isn't and no harm done," answered the other; "but you know two things, Mrs. Canniford; you know how other people's business is the stock in trade of talk to Priory and I'm sure you know I'm well intending and always willing to pleasure the folk when I may."

"Granted and what then ?" asked Jenny, still gazing with hunted eyes but calming down.

"Then it follows I was sure to hear about you and Mr. Honeywood—no business of the parish nor yet of mine; but I'd say just one word in friendship and you mustn't take it ill."

Jenny gasped, but found herself incapable of replying.

"Take it or leave it," hurried on the other; "but I'd beg you to put that matter before my old friend, Mercy Grepe. And don't bear me ill will for giving you what I'm dead sure is mortal good advice."

She nodded and smiled and was gone, leaving Jenny transfixed upon the side-walk of the little street. Here some trees overhung the roadway and there stood a seat for any tired traveller set beneath them. It was empty, and now Mrs. Canniford took her emotion and indignation to rest awhile. She panted, looked with unseeing eyes at the streamlet running below and considered this outrage on good manners and decorum. Such an affront at first bewildered her and she felt in a mind to hasten with it to Pigslake and invite Myra's opinion. Then came second thoughts and deeper reflections. For half an hour the widow sat quite motionless and her brain pondered the information and advice thrust upon her from this preposterous source. That people spoke of Peter's Fabian policy was no news to Jenny for she had herself protested at his tactics in several ears and received considerable sympathy; but any suggestion that it might be possible to do something definite in such a delicate business had never as yet occurred to anybody. And now was come a hint from one always regarded as an enemy: that Mercy Grepe, a woman granted exceptional wisdom, might be of practical assistance ! Jenny knew not a few who had consulted Mercy on their private affairs and many who gladly gave her credit for admirable counsel; she liked the wise woman and was glad to hear of her recovery; but she had never taken any of her personal problems to Mercy, feeling that questions of finance must lie beyond her aid. Now admittedly the case was altered and the thinker conceded to herself that, assuming anybody competent to advise on such a subject, Miss Grepe might best be approached.

There she left the matter and went about her business; but in the evening she spoke of the adventure to Rupert. He owned to have considered the market gardener's delay.

"I've had it in my mind," he said, "to give Peter a prog or two about you. You ain't getting any younger and no more is he. But I'd say that 'Mother Forty Cats' might very likely give you a tip. She's a downy bird and have helped a lot of lame dogs over stiles, so it's said."

"I was overcome by the sauce of the woman to dare to speak to me at all; but, on thinking it over, I couldn't in honesty condemn her," confessed Rupert's mother.

"Nelly's all right," he said. "She's pretty clever herself—must be to have carried on all those years with Uncle Nicholas and not got tortured for it. I'll bet you might do worse than take her tip, Mother. And no call to feel sour with her anyway, because she had nothing to gain."

"I've always took your aunt's part and always shall do," said Jenny.

"That's all right. We were all for Aunt Myra against the old devil, but a little thing like that don't trouble Nelly, nor yet hurt her. She knows your fix, same as the rest of the parish, and she's got a nature to help folk where they'll let her. So I'd try what she advises. If old Grepe can't rise to it no harm done, but so like as not she will."

For once Rupert displayed a spark of generosity. Very occasionally he had been known to do a friendly action entailing loss to himself. Jenny remembered to this day how her son had once given his father an ounce of tobacco; but that was an outstanding incident.

"I'll let you have your half-crown for 'Mother Forty Cats,'" he said, "if she helps the good cause. If she can't, then give her nothing and let me have my half-crown back. You will be the judge if she earns it."

He produced the money and, after further consideration, Mrs. Canniford decided for the experiment.

"I wouldn't say it put me under an obligation," she argued, "because 'tis contrary to reason I should offer friendship to that loose woman whatever betides."

"She won't mind whether you're friendly or not," replied Rupert. "You don't matter a flip of her finger to Nelly. A woman worth ten thousand pounds have took the trouble to give you a useful hint—that's all there is to her. And mind I have my money back if Mercy Grepe don't earn it."

Thus advised Jenny proceeded. She had thought more than once to congratulate the old woman on her recovery and now she resolved to do so. Mercy lived in a two-roomed cottage and was now, as usual, strong enough to minister to herself and look after her tiny dwelling and garden. She was a great herbalist and, among her dark opinions, lurked the conviction that not a weed grew which lacked precious properties had man the wit to discover them.

She was with her plants when the visitor came to see her and helped to weed for a while before they went indoors together. Jenny had brought a gift; a tin of clotted cream. This came from her sister; but concerning the present business Mrs. Canniford had spoken to nobody save her son.

"'Tis a brave sight to find you on your legs again, Mercy," she said, "and your well-wishers should do all they know to build you up now. A most triumphant battle you've fought by all accounts and Doctor says it weren't him that saved you alive, but your own fine fighting qualities."

"No," answered the wise woman. "I was at a pass when I couldn't have saved myself, Jenny. My case had got too parlous for that; but I always said to Naylor and the parish nurse, Miss Martin—I always said, 'Three heads are better than one, my dears,' and we all worked together on my perishing carcase. Yes, we worked together with but a single thought: to save it; and we did save it. But never you take no credit that's due to others, Jenny, because that's little better than thieving. We was all very clever and our goodwill kept me above ground and a very fine joke arose out of it, because Alice Piper, the sexton's wife, hearing I was to lie under her bedroom window, ordained to leave the house for fear I might rise up and look in upon her by night."

Mercy chuckled and took the tin of cream. A dozen cats were circling round her with tails erect.

"They know what's in it," she said. "I've let down a tidy lot of cream from kind people lately, including the vicar, and Naylor tells I can't eat too much. What don't a cat know that interests 'em? But they can't hide their little secrets from me. I've got a nice brood of kitlings from old 'Ginger.' She's borne eighty-four kitlings since she came to me and counts to carry a hundred before past bearing."

"You've filled Priory with cats, and some go so far as to say we're a thought over-catted nowadays," said Jenny.

Miss Grepe was very thin, but the old, keen fire had returned to her eyes and the energy to her voice. She was bald and always covered her head with a close-fitting cloth cap and a scarf. She wore good, yellow, false teeth in her lipless mouth and on her body short skirts which revealed the extreme tenuity of her legs. A plaid shawl was drawn tightly about her and fastened over her middle with a large safety pin. A neat and trim woman, whose dwelling room defied those who expected to find sinister signs of mystery, for it lacked any hint of the occult. The place was poverty-stricken yet not uncheerful and scrupulously clean. Almanacs adorned the walls, brass utensils shone upon the mantelshelf and a cactus with red tassels stood on the window-ledge and glowed ruby-bright in the afternoon sun. The cats followed, but Miss Grepe drove most of them out, shut the door and offered Jenny a chair beside a peat fire.

"Sit you down," she said. "A lot have happened since I saw you, and Nicholas Withers gone untimely, too."

"Yes, he's gone and oh, the difference to Pigslake, Mercy ! You might say they breathe another air up there now."

"I'll make you a pot of tea if you're minded," said the old woman, "but I won't offer you none of your own cream, because to give back what you've received as a gift brings bad luck. And it ain't manners anyway."

She put on the kettle and brought some plates from a little Welsh dresser against the wall opposite the fire. Then she went to a hatch under the staircase, that led out of the kitchen to her bedroom above, and produced a seed cake.

"Yes," she said. "Myra and her children will give God the praise without a doubt, and not only them."

"Who wouldn't, my dear ?"

"When people asked me what I thought of Nicholas Withers, as they often did," replied Miss Grepe, "I always answered the same thing. Such ugly customers as him are the outposts of desolation, stuck up by the Almighty for warnings, or as you might say danger signals. They learn you what to fly from and 'tis idle to hate them, or curse them. They do their dirty work for the Lord's purpose—to show other people what to avoid—and they'll often come to a sudden and shameful end when their Maker's done with them. To see a man like your brother-in-law grinding the face of the poor and going his way and using his strength to wrong the weak and outrage the innocent, is to say, 'By God's mercy I won't never be like that.' A nice question where such sad characters go hereafter; but if I'm right and they're put here for a purpose, then there's hope for 'em."

These subtleties did not interest Jenny.

"So long as my family ban't called to meet the man again in eternity, that's all any of 'em would ask," she said. "None of us deserves to be faced with Nicholas in the heavenly mansions, and he didn't ought to be there."

"A difficult subject I grant you," conceded Miss Grepe, and changed it.

"And how's Honeywood fetching along," she asked. "Cast away as I have been, I've missed the news, my dear. Are things forwarder ?"

Thus Mercy led straight to the point and soon learned that no forward movement could be recorded.

"He comes and goes and looks ripe for the definite word; but no. He leaves me as I was. He'll bring a basket of fresh vegetables off and on—to pay for his tea no doubt. He's nice minded like that; but nothing doing. He dropped in a bit ago—in his nigger-brown suit dripping with jewellery— and I thought the accepted time was come at last. He took a good tea and smoked his pipe and praised the weather and said his carrots were a wonder and cast his eyes over me smiling and confident. And then off he went. 'Tis troublesome and calls for patience. I've got a queer feeling, Mercy, that

I'm in his cold storage, same as a leg of New Zealand mutton or what not, waiting the man's time and pleasure."

"Like the butcher-birds, that catch their prey and stick the things on thorn bushes till they want them," said Mercy. "I know the sort. Tell on."

Jenny explained the complications and the indecent amusement awakened by them in the parish; then she summed up with an appeal.

"If you, with your deep knowledge of human nature, could give me a wrinkle, I'd willingly pay for it, I'm sure. 'Tis a baffling problem and I can't for my life see what a nice woman, as I claim to be, can do about it. I don't want to lose him and stand a laughing-stock and I'm pretty sure he don't want to lose me. I expect he's weighing my sons in the balance; but a man marries his wife, not her family. I've heard Peter say so himself—to keep his heart up perhaps."

"A like question has come before me once and again," said the wise woman, "mostly when there was very good reasons why the man should get on with it; and then the way out for the woman is a lot harder. In your case, Jenny, if you've got a trustable friend, there's a tolerable simple plan to open Honeywood's eyes and fetch on the climax."

She revealed an age-long remedy which had neither occurred nor been as yet suggested to the other, and grasping its huge significance, Jenny debated whether such a counter move lay in her power. She felt a measure of fear, however.

"Peter's Irish on his mother's side," she said, "and it flashes out now and again. In a way he's proud of it; and, if he got wind of such a thing, I might have more of his Irish blood on my hands than I'd cope with."

"Irish blood is prone to wrath, I grant you," replied the old woman. "The Irish won't forgive, nor yet forget, nor yet learn. They hate learning like the plague, so fall easy meat for the Pope of Rome. I've heard parson say so. But, if you do as I tell and use your woman's wits, there's no reason why he should know a thing about it. The devotion's there, else he wouldn't be on your doorstep so often; but you've got to remember Peter's a bachelor and very ignorant. You've spoilt him I expect."

Jenny fumbled for her purse and produced Rupert's half-crown.

"I'll make bold to offer you this spot of money, Mercy," she said, "because such advice as you've rendered me is worth it and I mustn't pick your brains for nought. You live by 'em and I'd say nobody earns your small money better than you do."

But the other stroked a big black cat now on her lap, with his green eyes looking thoughtfully at Jenny, and shook her head.

"We can tell about that after. If it's a failure, I won't ask for anything; but if it's a success, that's different and you can give me what you feel like when the time comes, if it do, and you find what my counsel is worth."

"I shan't hang back I'm sure," promised Jenny. "I'll just call home exactly how Peter stands to me now and proceed according. At our last meeting I fell in with him coming out of church and praised the sermon very heartily. It was a good chance, because the text was 'Now is the accepted time'—a fine performance and pat to my affairs. 'Time don't stand still with the youngest', I said, 'and never runs faster than along with the middle-aged'. And 'nothing venture, nothing have' is another of them true sayings too often neglected', I said. 'Twas dark by then and I couldn't see how he took it; but he answered that he didn't know but what I might be right. 'There's not your equal for sense in Priory,' he went on, and I answered that I was glad he thought so and believed he weren't the only one that did. Then he said 'good evening' and went his way—to the 'Pen-in-Hand' I expect."

"A very fair starting-off place for what I advise," declared Miss Grepe. "You show him, Jenny, and if I know the man, he'll come to heel. If he don't, then no loss."

Mrs. Canniford returned home after expressing considerable gratitude. A somewhat difficult and delicate task now awaited her, but she felt in a mood to undertake it while her spirit was high, knowing from experience that resolution is apt to falter when too deep reflection intervenes. It was Saturday and, aware that his shop would have been closed at mid-day, Jenny repaired to the saddler's, and expected to find him at home. She did not intend to stay, but invite Paul Pook to visit her at his convenience as soon as he could do so. She proposed to suggest tea on the following day and hoped that the family friend might be able to accept; in which event the coast must be kept clear and Harry directed not to call and bring his children. For Sunday was an occasion when he often came to see her.

Jenny knocked at the side door of Paul's establishment, and it was Ivy Pook who answered the door.

"Evening, my dear girl," she said. "I've come for a word or two with your father, counting to find him home and his tea drunk by now."

"His tea's drunk and he's gone out," answered the young woman, "but if you've got the time to spare, come in and wait for him, Mrs. Canniford. He's only run out on an errand for me."

Ivy Pook was a woman of thirty-two. 'Girl' Jenny had called her, but she looked old for her age, with lustreless hair and eyes, a large, well-formed body, a prim mouth and an assertive nose. The suggestion of sadness created by her face seemed to centre in this organ which was thin and pointed and stood as a mournful apex to her features. She lacked all interest for the male, yet the only person surprised to find it so was herself. She knew Jenny very well and had once told her in confidence that not a man had ever offered for her.

"Shall I hot a cup of tea ?" asked Ivy in her dreary voice, but the other declined.

"No; I've took my tea thank you. And how is it with you ? A proper upheaval I'd say—to leave the Manor and come to be your dear father's right hand. I never thought her ladyship would part with you so long as she lived."

"More did I," said Ivy, "but so it was through no fault of mine, nor yet hers. When Lady Garland's intellects went 'twas decided that professional nurses would be better than me—her in bed all the time and calling to be handled. So I resigned, and I missed her a good bit at first; but not so much as you might have thought, because she hadn't recognised me about her for some time. However there's no immediate fear of death. She may live for so much as a year yet if not longer. The nurse tells me she's just about the same trouble as a baby in arms and nothing fatal to carry her off in sight so far."

"Very sad—such a good, kind creature and so generous and well loved by everyone."

"That's right. You couldn't but love her, Jenny. And nobody knew her better, or valued her more than what I did."

"Or served her better," said Mrs. Canniford.

"She was well alive to my devotion," declared Ivy. "I had a touch to anticipate her every thought. Those were her own words. Once when I found a precious jewel, that had got lost in the moss beside her favourite garden seat and everybody thought a new housemaid had stole—when I found it, she said I was the joy of her life. I'll never forget that."

"And now you'll be the joy of your father's life," declared Jenny.

"My duty as I see it now is father," admitted Paul's daughter. "There's a lot calling in his life to establish and tighten up. He's got in a careless way as widowers will do. But I'm used to have everything just so about me and I'm opening his eyes gradual to a slovenly spirit that's creeping over him. Not in his business nor yet in his sport; but in the home. His idea of comfort isn't mine. He hates changing his underclothes."

"The men get careless about little things that be very apt to offend us women."

"They do, and it's for us to check 'em. We go before them spick and span and spotless and properly furnished in every respect, and they ought to serve us the same. I always thought to have a home of my own some day and still count upon it now I'm free of service."

"Why not, my dear ? Plenty of time."

"No," confessed Ivy, "there ain't plenty of time and you know that very well. But I'll often wonder. It isn't as if I was one of they women that shun the male by instinct and plan to go through life without a partner—far from it. What I know of nice men, I find myself to like. I neighboured with the male servants at the Manor very friendly; but they held off and now I'm running pretty near the limit. And a child lover I am, too."

"You wait," said Jenny. "All things come to them that wait. Men who marry to please the eye often find they're mistook and, with your homely looks, Ivy, you've got the satisfaction that no man would snatch at you same as he would at a pretty flower. You was never one for a very young man I'd say; but when the right one comes along, he'll look beneath the surface, and there he'll find what's better than pink cheeks and the glad eye. He'll be a man round about forty I shouldn't wonder, a chap long past the silly stage and all for a nice home and a loving heart and a good cook and so on, and a wise woman apt to look both sides of a sixpence before she casts it away."

Jenny meant well but was unfortunate, as the well-meaning are so apt to be. The younger coloured up and stared out of her faded eyes. For a passing moment in the candle-light there came a frosty glint in them, like the sun on a dead fish. Meantime her bosom rose.

"I didn't know I was all that hideous," she said. "But we live and learn no doubt. There's uglier than me in the village, unless I can't see straight and, whether or no, when I marry, Jenny Canniford, it won't be to count my husband's sixpences."

"May he have more than you know how to count when he do come, my dear," replied Jenny, who was famous for her soft answers; but Ivy champed on the bit moodily and made no reply for some time.

Then she spoke again.

"And another thing might interest you. To Honiton Fair I crossed a gipsy's hand with silver and she told me I'd live to see my grandchildren, so now then."

"What I say is——" began Jenny once more, and then Miss Pook rose from her chair and interrupted.

"You'd best to go," she said. "Something has kept my father, so if you won't leave no message, I'll ask you to go, please."

At this moment, however, Paul himself arrived and Mrs. Canniford, feeling her visit a failure, made all haste to be gone.

"Waiting for you, my dear man," she said, "and feared I was just going to miss you. But I'm wishful to speak a few words when you can find time to hear 'em and if you could make it convenient to take your tea with me to-morrow, or when you please, I'd be ever so glad."

"Certainly," agreed Pook. "Certainly, Jenny. I'll drop in round five o'clock to-morrow for a dish of tea."

"And I'll have a nice egg on toast for you," replied the woman. "Thank you very much."

Sincerely hoping that Paul's daughter might not accuse her when she was gone, Jenny hastened away. Much—indeed all—would now depend upon the saddler's response, but she could not guess how he might view Mercy Grepe's inspiration.

Elsewhere Timothy's news had already reached those most likely to be interested in it, for he had told his mother that he proposed to marry Kate Wish, the baker's daughter, and the girl's parents learned his determination from Katey herself. All those concerned listened calmly and the boy felt almost disappointed to find Mrs. Faircloud not unamiable. He had prepared forcible reasons and a resounding expostulation if she opposed him; but no display of masculine will-power was called for.

"Very interesting, Tim," said Nelly. "A question for the future, of course, and I'd be most pleased for my part if something was to come of it in a few years time. I've seen Katey along with her mother now and again and thought she was a very pretty, nice-spoken child. Come she grows to her full body, she'll be a fine girl. But I wouldn't say I knew her. Bright, clever eyes she's gotten. Do she seem clever to you?"

"Outstanding," replied Timothy. "A very quick mind, else she wouldn't have interested me. As a rule, Mother, you don't feel much for them you've grown up with; but since I came to manhood, though I'd known who she was since Sunday School days, I didn't know her nature. But when we got acquaint, I found her well suited to me and me to her. And comparing notes, I find she'd always felt a lot drawn to me."

"Very interesting," repeated Nelly. "Ask her to tea Sunday, Tim. Then she and I will have a tell. Does her mother know anything about it? But I'll wager she does. It ain't a very great astonishment to me neither. Friendships like that are marked lightning quick in little places. I must see Milly Wish and I hope I'll find her and Samuel content."

"Kate was going to tell her people to-day, same as I've told you," answered Timothy. "And I don't see no reason why they should be discontent I'm sure. And it won't signify if they are. You can't come between true lovers. She's a lot more than pretty. She's beautiful, and nicely spoken as you say, and I'll have her to tea Sunday, Mother, and thank you for asking her. Quick as you are, you'll soon see she's one in a thousand, and she's often told me that Mrs. Wish thinks a lot of your goodness and upholds you."

Nelly laughed.

"I don't want no upholding, you funny boy," she answered. "But I've pleasured Milly now and again, and she's pleasured me. This is a big thing about you young people and I'll like to hear her views, and she'll like to hear mine I expect."

In the baker's home Katey had made a similar announcement and gathered from her parents that they judged any such alliance very improbable.

"Don't you bank on nothing like that Kate," advised her father. "You're both a lot too young to know your own minds in my opinion, and you can lay your life that will be his mother's opinion also."

"We're not against it, nor yet for it, Katey," added Mrs. Wish. "Father and me will keep an open mind and turn it over and hear what Mrs. Faircloud's got to say; but you have to think of a good few things when you consider joining up with Timothy some day. There's different opinions regarding him 'mongst them who've thought upon him at all. He's very unlike the general order of young men: there's agreement about him so far, but no further."

"That's why we were drawn, Mother," explained Kate. "Just because I found him unlike other chaps and a head and shoulders above 'em in mind and body; and he found me, in his opinion, so unlike other girls that he couldn't but fall in love with me. That's the grand thing about it and shows 'tis a living affection."

"Listen and don't interrupt, Katey," continued Mrs. Wish. She patted the baby in her arms, who was crying, and continued while Samuel Wish, lighted his breakfast pipe and also listened.

"There's divided opinions touching Timothy," continued Milly, "else he wouldn't never have been called a changeling, same as he is."

"He's proud of it," declared Katey, and her father rebuked her.

"Shut your mouth, girl, and let your mother talk," he said.

"Some hold him just at the awkward age, when boys think it manly to be rude to their betters, and guess he'll mend in that matter," proceeded Mrs. Wish. "They consider there is nothing wrong with his intellects but only his behaviour. Some say he's proud, while others think he's vain, with nothing to be vain about but his face. They just reckon he's what you call a sealed book and only God knows what's inside of it till the pages open."

"Like the pie," said Katey." 'When the pie was opened, the birds began to sing,' Mother !"

"Quiet, fool !" ordered Samuel.

"Others again," went on Milly, "don't hold any such thing. They count that the boy's wanting and so all's said. They grant that he's a very fine object, but have got a screw loose; which is to say his mind's clouded. So there you are."

"And what do you think, Mother?" asked Katey. "I don't think myself, because I know. I know he's got a big brain and more in his little finger than all the idiots who find him too deep for their wits to understand. But what do you and father think?"

"I've never thought on the subject myself," said Samuel. "Far too busy to weigh the weight of every labouring man's brains in this parish, him included. I wouldn't say I knew him but to nod to. What do you value him at, Milly?"

"He's a pleasant sight to see," admitted Mrs. Wish. "And you'll rarely come on a more beautiful face. He's out of the ordinary there, same as his mother's out of the ordinary, and there's a mystery in that quarter which ain't nobody's business but Mrs. Faircloud's. I speak of people as I find them, and a kinder, friendlier woman than her I don't know. She's done me a service many times. As for the boy, I never thought to measure him up, and I don't know what his mother's views on that subject may hap to be. But this I know: if she thought he was wanting, she'd take very good care he didn't marry and hand it on."

"Tim says there's a screw loose in most everybody, only we're all in the same fix and don't notice it, Mother."

"If he knows he's queer, then I'd say it couldn't be and I'd put my foot down, Kate," decided Samuel.

"He's queer in comparison with other men, Father, but that's because he's better than them, not worse," explained Katey. "You can drop that rubbish out of your heads for keeps. He's a very clever man and he told me in so many words that I was the first to find it out; which I did do; and I'm also clever enough myself to agree to this without a murmur. If Mrs. Faircloud tells you that Timothy's addled and didn't ought to marry, then I'll take her word for it, because I'll trust her; but I'm dead sure she won't do any such thing. And mind this: Schoolmaster always told Timothy the brains was in his head if he felt minded to use them."

"That's a fair offer, Father?" asked Milly, and the baker admitted it, though doubtfully.

"It sounds fair," he said, "but I'd need to satisfy my own judgment where your future life's concerned, Kate. His mother might not see quite straight in the matter of her own child. But I may tell you this, since we're on the subject. At the 'Pen-in-Hand' the identical question once rose and Dr. Naylor, who never burks the truth, said from a long understanding of young Faircloud, he considered he was as sane as anybody, but given to too much thought upon himself and morbid as to how he struck other people. 'Morbid' is the word. So we'll leave it at that. If his mother agrees he's all right, then I'll see how he strikes me. But this understand. I don't countenance any thought of marriage till you're both a good few years older than at present, and until I know his money and prospects and intentions."

Milly nodded.

"There you are then—wise words, Katey," she said. "I'll see Mrs. Faircloud."

"She'll know what you're come for, Mother, because Tim is going to tell her to-day," answered the girl.

"So that's that," agreed Mrs. Wish, "and now you'd best look after Dora and Teddy. I hear 'em fighting in the garden."

Katey hastened to her duties.

"I'm happy now," she told them, "because I well know what the day will bring forth, Father."

"First that ever did, then, to my knowledge," he answered.

V

BEFORE the mothers met, Nelly tended a little to misdoubt her easy surrender, yet feeling it was idle to go back without sufficient and strong reasons, decided to see Dr. Naylor, who had brought Timothy into the world and always declared a friendly interest for mother and child. She chose a time when the boy was at work and the doctor at home, and he welcomed her and declared himself pleased to see her.

"You look as well and as pretty as ever, my dear," he said. "Nothing wrong, I hope?"

"I'm all right, Doctor; though a thought put about over Tim. I ought to have come before. I agreed to something yesterday, but I'll tell you about that, and it's not too late to go back on what I said if you so advise me."

"Talk away, Nelly. I'm idle this afternoon."

"Never was you idle, I'm sure. Well, there's a common thing has over-got the boy. He's in love; but that's a sort of stepping-stone in his life and I want to take stock of him and size him up. Which I have done; yet still there's points that nobody can answer for me wiser than you. You know him and you understand him best of all and, next to you, I do. Granted he's unusual in his outlook and his ideas; but is he weak-headed, and do his odd ways and thoughts and ups and downs signify anything to put him off the rails? That's the plain question."

"Before I answer it," he said, "go on and tell me exactly how Tim strikes you yourself nowadays. How your good fortune appealed to him I can guess, but I should like to hear his reaction. He thinks independently for a youngster and that's a very good fact in my opinion, because a boy who can think independently will probably be able to shift for himself in the future. But now you talk."

"Schoolmaster always said the brain was there, though Timothy would be wool-gathering instead of learning," began Nelly. "The foresters hold him a good workman, when he's minded to be, and he mostly stands to work; but now and again he'll take a day off and be no use at all. He likes planting, but don't cotton to the axe, whereas the axe is what they mostly want from him. And since I came into my legacy I mark a change. His dreams are cheerfuller; but he's up in the air oftener. And still full of secrets, same as he always was as a child. And one he let out yesterday which explains a lot to my mind. He's glad for me about the money; but he's gladder still for himself, because his courting has gone to please him. I knew he was a lot took by a young girl, yet he never named her to me, or thought I knew anything about it, and I never named her to him. It's Katey Wish he's in love with, and now I hear she accepted him a good bit ago. But he couldn't hold the secret no longer and he's very high and mighty about it. He says he's got other successes, but won't name them."

"Not other girls?" asked Dr. Naylor.

"Oh no, nothing like that. He's not that sort at all. Other fine secrets known only to himself, but giving him a better opinion of himself."

The physician loved to talk, nor did he often pause to consider if his listener was sufficiently educated to understand him."

"We must look at this in a proper spirit, Nelly," he began. "The last thing you said was the most interesting, because if Timothy has been up to any achievements that tend to restore his self-respcet, that is very good news. Such enterprises, if they produced that result, were laudable since he knows right from wrong very well, and they would not have made him proud of himself if they had been wrong. At least I am old-fashioned enough to think so. The will to be noteworthy and win praise is an everyday matter and none would be found quite free of it. That is hardly a defect, though it takes pathetic shapes in the old as well as the young. It is a weakness of our common nature always to feel that we are a little better than our neighbours— above them and superior to them. To be a little better bred, a little richer, a little more important, a little wiser—which we invariably feel ourselves to be —and a little more significant in the scheme of things. Some pride themselves on being older than we are, some on being younger; some are gratified to stand a little taller, or on having better teeth, or better eyesight, or more hair on their heads. To such nonsense even quite intelligent people will sink. They win subconscious pleasure from these trivialities, forgetting that life is all a question of values, not possessions, and that probably the person they judge inferior would care nothing for their superiority even if he recognises it. In his turn, very probably, the supposed inferior person cherishes other standards and other inner gifts, superior to your own, that would stagger you if they came to your ears. Timothy is not vain of his appearance, though one might have expected such an exceedingly good-looking boy to pride himself on it."

"No, Doctor; he doesn't care a straw for his looks I'd say."

"That's to the good. I don't think he compares himself unfavourably with others, or is jealous of others: what he wants is to excel and become outstanding himself; but as yet he has not found his medium. He may never find it; there may be nothing in him awaiting development, in which case his vague ambitions will probably peter out and he'll settle down to be a thoughtful sort of working man, content with his business. He may have no creative faculty and he is not to be pitied in that respect, because the genuine, creative instinct brings plenty of sorrow, disappointment, and stress that we everyday people escape. He may have a morsel of art in him— enough to colour his thoughts and awaken his interests, but not enough to demand self-expression. All that is beyond our guess. Nobody can trace the genesis of an artist: they appear to defy heredity and nurture alike. The artist is often a changeling, just as Timothy is a changeling; but in your boy's case, if he had any driving force in such a direction, one might have expected it to have given signs ere now. His beautiful appearance, for example, would have been a valuable asset in one direction, had he shown any liking for the stage."

Nelly laughed.

"I always know when he's putting it on and acting," she said, "but I wouldn't say he's very good at it. He hates towns, so he'd never fare well at play-acting. All for the open-air so far."

"Does he read much?"

"Not much, Doctor. There's an old poetry book he'll read now and again, and funny you should name the theatres, because, only a bit ago, I found something that Timothy dearly liked. I was going over a lot of odds and ends—books and magazines, ever so old, left by lodgers in my Valley Farm days. I was going over 'em and turning 'em out for the rag-and-bone-man. And among 'em was a play in good bold print I thought might please Tim, because seemingly it happened in a wood. So I told him and he promised to read it, which he did do a few nights since, and said it was the finest thing ever he had read and he'd treasure it and read it many times. Somebody by the name of William Shakespeare wrote it in bygone days, and I was glad to think I'd chanced on a tale to please him."

"Good!" exclaimed Naylor. "If we can get Timothy to fasten on Shakespeare, much might come of it. A man who knows his Shakespeare is well furnished. I'll remember that. Plenty of forests and moors and haunts of wild Nature in Shakespeare. But for the minute there's his engagement. We can't have him taking a wife at eighteen, but it's a nice question whether the fact of his being 'tokened' at that tender age is going to make him or mar him."

"Nineteen next month, Doctor, and I've already told him I wouldn't stand for it a moment till he was over one-and-twenty."

"No, no; but though childish nonsense in most cases, an attachment of this sort is by no means out of the question for Timothy. You couldn't prevent him from regarding himself as definitely committed if you were to try, and I'm glad you didn't try for this reason. To be in love is to find some-body in the world more precious to you than yourself; somebody more com-pelling; a goal to strive for; a priceless object to attain. Real love ought to banish egotism and switch your thoughts off yourself to something better; and though Timothy naturally feels very proud of himself for winning this young person, his pride won't lessen the fact that he is now united by promise and betrothed to a kindred spirit who must ever come first in his thoughts. In fact, 'keeping company' ought to do him good if he really loves her, and I'd say he was just the boy who would love on a decent, honourable plane."

Nelly considered this.

"I'd like to think that, too," she said, "and I don't see why I shouldn't think it. He ain't the love-hunting sort—not yet anyway. I'd say, as to that, a lot depends on the girl. There's some girls can keep a man in order, and some can't, and some don't want to."

"You speak what you know," answered Naylor drily. "See her and figure her up, as you would be able to do exceedingly well no doubt. The Wish folk are Wesleyans and highly self-respecting."

"More than that—good friends of mine."

"Like most of us are, Nelly. You see Kate. She may mean a deuce of a lot to Timothy and be a very good influence. If he puts her at the centre of his little stage and she has the wits to stop there, then I'd say the result ought to be quite sound. The unselfish, altruistic people—like yourself— are always the most contented and often the happiest. It's preoccupation with Number One that makes us miserable nine times out of ten."

"Easier to pleasure folk than not—so I've found," she said.

Naylor rose to show the interview was at an end.

"There we are then. We'll pin our hopes to the girl and William Shakespeare, Nelly; and if Katey Wish fails him; the poet can't. He never failed a sane Englishman yet."

"Thank you very much, Doctor. I didn't know books could serve a young chap so well, never being no reader myself," confessed Mrs. Faircloud; "but if you'll put the old gentleman's stories in train and order what else he's wrote to be sent to Timothy, I'll gladly pay for 'em."

"It shall be done, my dear," he promised.

Thus fortified the mothers met and the boy's parent was able to take a definite line.

"I've got Dr. Naylor behind me, Milly," she said to Mrs. Wish, "and if you like Timothy and if Samuel likes Timothy, when you see him close and have a tell, and if I likewise approve of Katey, when I see her close and have a tell, then, so far as I can see, there's no harm in them being tokened. My boy's just on nineteen, and I've made it clear I wouldn't suffer no marriage till he's past twenty-one. And by that time they'd know if they was still of a mind."

"Much what I was going to say to you, Nelly; and much what Sam said to me," answered the other. "You figure up Katey next Sunday and we'll figure up Timothy and compare notes and ordain according. God knows I wouldn't put a snag into the works of true love; but they're very young and may change their minds. And it's the best kindness to give 'em a chance to do so."

"If we reckon 'tis workable, then a good few years must certainly pass," agreed Tim's mother. "He'll have to be earning a lot more money for one thing, and I've offered him the higher education to do so; but he don't want to leave Priory, nor yet his work in the Manor woods. As to that, we can see by next Spring if all goes well. But, if Samuel and you turn him down, then I reckon I'll take him some place else as soon as I can move."

"I don't think we'll turn him down any more than I think you'll turn Katey down," said Mrs. Wish, and the issue proved her correct.

Timothy's sweetheart duly came to tea attired in her best. She was somewhat self-conscious and had little to say during the meal; but Nelly felt no objection to a certain wariness and reserve in the presence of Timothy. After the meal was finished, however, she dismissed her son and invited Katey to help her clear away and wash up.

"I'm going to have a talk with Kate now, Tim," said Mrs. Faircloud, "so you can push off for half an hour and then see her to chapel, because I know her father and mother like her to go with them of a Sunday evening."

So the boy disappeared and, in the atmosphere of familiar duties, the girl became more talkative. She had taken to Nelly and felt pleased with her friendly reception; while the elder found her not difficult to read and devoid of much guile. Two things Katey made no effort to conceal; her admiration for Timothy, and her possession of intelligence. She was small and not of exceptional good looks, but her animation and obvious happiness appealed to Nelly, and she like her unconscious display of will power and humour combined. Katey's hostess travelled a good deal of ground and asked certain personal questions, receiving direct answers. Small things pleased Nelly. She liked the girl's voice and views, won of the younger's large personal experience among growing children. Katey indeed proved intensely practical and old for her age; but youth and the joy of youth sparkled in her eyes and her laugh was happy. They attained to an amiable understanding and when Timothy came for her, the visitor received a kiss at parting and bade good-bye in her downright fashion.

"And I dearly hope," she concluded, "I'll make you feel to like me, Mrs. Faircloud, so well as you've made me like you."

"That's a promise then," said Nelly. "And you work to make Tim laugh now and then, same as you've made me. We don't laugh enough in this house."

On the following Sunday it was the changeling's turn. He went for a walk with his sweetheart during the afternoon and came back to take his tea with her parents. He made himself talk and behaved well. Samuel Wish was didactic and said several things that did not appeal to Timothy, but he received them thoughtfully and in silence. The baker spoke without reserve before his family and indicated hopes that any future son-in-law would be ambitious to prove his worth.

"I'm looking to hear, Faircloud," he said, "that with your mind fixed on marriage in the time to come, you'll grasp how you must rise above the open air to the indoor ranks of labour. In a few years, you'll be husband-high and Kate wife-old; and before that, while your brain is young and active, you must see if you can't turn it to some higher sphere than cutting down trees. I ain't against tolerable early marriages, you understand, if a young man's got the wherewithal behind him; but no big results was ever known from cutting down trees for them who did the cutting. The estate gets the money, not the forest men. So I hope, by the time you've reached to full age, and Mrs. Wish and I welcome you as a son-in-law, you'll find yourself heading for a good position in trade or what not."

"I hope so, too, Mr. Wish," agreed Timothy. "I've got it in me to stand high and I will stand high one day."

"That's the right spirit," declared Samuel, "and I shall watch your endeavours and advise you when you find yourself wanting advice. To stand high is a very good aim and, even if you don't hit the mark, you can always get the comfort of knowing you tried. But there's only one organ can promise a fine position in life and that is the brains in your head. You must fix on a calling that demands brain power and must cultivate your brain, from whence cometh your help under God."

"Do you say your prayers morning and night, Timothy?" asked Mrs. Wish.

"Yes, I say 'em," he answered.

Samuel placed the advantages of a baker's life before his visitor, but the hideous thought of working at an oven through the small hours of night prompted Katey's lover to some expression of his own instincts.

"I don't reckon I'd shine at any such craft as that," he said. "I've got a feeling, Mr. Wish, that I'd do my best in the open air. I don't fear the darkness, or anything like that. I'm fearless by night so well as by day; but an open air life would suit me better than a shop, or sitting at a desk. I'd sooner go for a soldier, or a sailor, than be fastened down in a room."

"Would you be brave enough for a soldier?" asked Milly.

"I'm braver than folk seem to think for," he answered. "I laugh to myself when I hear I'm not brave. A lot braver than anybody round here if the truth was known."

"So he is," supported Kate. "He'd love danger if it offered, wouldn't you, Tim?"

"I've been in danger and come well out of it," he assured them. "And danger tunes you to be strong and show you what you can do if you're put to it."

"He loves to be alone in moonlight," continued Katey, "and he'd sit in the churchyard all night without turning a hair if there was any call to do so. Moonlight's well known to make some people creepy if they haven't got any company; but not Timothy."

" 'Tis Hunter's Moon next week," added the boy, "and if a fine night I shall most like walk out and poke about and mark the woods."

Samuel shook his head.

"You mustn't be silly," he said. "I don't doubt a smart young man like you has got his share of pluck and can stand up for himself, else Heaven help any future wife he may find to take him. Courage ain't a matter of fearing nightfall nor any other natural thing that happens. You must have the courage to face the ups and downs of life, and the courage to do that comes from trust in your Maker and the dead certainty the Divine Eye is watching your every step. If you properly understand that, then it follows you'll be brave without an effort and find no need to brag about it. But if you've got gifts worth talking about, my boy, you must give 'em a chance to appear, and if, as I say, they're worth talking about, then Manor Woods didn't ought to be the place for 'em."

"You mustn't hide your light under a bushel, Timothy," explained Mrs. Wish. "You must let it blaze out for all men to see."

"Just what I've told him time and again, Mother," cried Katey. "He knows he's got gifts, but can't put a name to 'em yet. That right, Tim?"

"Yes," he replied. "I'd say that's right. I wouldn't be happy to bide a nobody all my days, because there's gifts moving in me I can't put a name to. And when I find what they are, Mrs. Wish, I won't hide 'em. And so like as not, Katey will be the first to find 'em, with all her cleverness."

"Love's very apt to be mistaken on that subject," said the baker, "and see in the loved object a darned sight more than is there. But if you've got gifts, then it's high time you began to know what they're good for and how they promise to help you take your place in the world."

"You and mother will be the first to know when they come out into the open and show themselves," said Katey. "Tim's nineteen next June—on the first day of the month, and that's time for the gifts to show up if not sooner."

"You bring 'em to us so soon as you've caught 'em, Tim," said Milly while her daughter laughed and even the lad smiled.

"They may be like the grey squirrels—perishing hard to catch," he said, "but once found, I won't let them go."

"A lot turns on this," pointed out Samuel. "A lot turns on the value of what you count to be hid in you. It's a fanciful notion and I don't think much of it myself, because proof by trial and error is the only way to find out what you can do and what you can't do. I had no clear gift for my business; but it was there only waiting the chance to blossom out, and after I'd tried to be a carpenter and failed, and tried to be a plumber and failed, and my father, in his haste, said I was wanting and the first in his family to be so, I turned to baking, and there I was—a master in three years ! And only round about your age when I kneaded my first dough. So gifts may wait opportunity to show 'em, and, again, they may be bad gifts as well as good gifts. If there's no religious foundations in a young youth, he may welcome a wicked gift and not say 'Get thee behind me, Satan,' but put it in practice and be pleased to find the results hopeful and fail to see the primrose path is really the brimstone road to hell. So you've got to look into your gifts pretty careful and satisfy yourself that they are no temptation of the Devil before you launch out to use them."

Timothy cast his eyes about uneasily and twitched a little around the mouth, but he nodded and spoke of Kate.

"My girl will know all about that," he said, "and if she was to think I'd got on a wrong track, I lay she'd show me where. I ain't frightened of the Devil any more than I'm feared of anybody else."

Samuel uttered a few further warnings, but summed up on a friendly note and agreed to countenance the betrothal.

"I believe you're a good boy," he said, "and I know Kate's a good girl and time tries all, so we'll leave it at that and trust you to do your duty in that state of life to which God may call you."

Then the Wish family, as represented by the baker and three children, went to chapel, and Milly stayed at home with her two youngest; while Timothy, relieved to be free, returned and related his experiences to his mother.

"Very good sense and quite worth remembering," said Mrs. Faircloud. "Samuel's a great one for high opinions, and time tries all, as he truly told you."

The engagement excited wide comment, mostly unfavourable, when it became known, but this did not trouble those most concerned. Her own generation of friends, of whom she had many, congratulated Katey very heartily, while other men, to his face, could not but declare that Timothy was a lucky lad. Both lovers found the passing attention agreeable and while the girl's happiness concerned itself only with her devotion and her triumph, the boy enjoyed the notice his engagement occasioned and considered that he now claimed greater respect than of old. All was open and the need for secrecy existed no longer. Something Timothy missed, for a sense of power had accompanied the thought of hood-winking the people; but Katey much valued her new status. She indeed was very percipient and had guessed that more neighbours were familiar with the situation than her sweetheart imagined. Now they came together without subterfuge and, as a precious concession for which her parents had to be thanked, Katey was allowed once a week to take his dinner to Timothy in the forest and spend an hour with him while he ate it. The generosity of her father provided this meal and she generally brought him a meat pie and a thermos flask of hot tea on such occasions.

Upon their second meeting thus, at the fringe of uplifted woodland, they sat together and Katey quickly perceived that it could not be counted one of her lover's good hours. She therefore set about to lift him from a somewhat petulant and moody frame of mind. It was early November—a day of bright sunshine and east wind, and the vast scene beneath them Timothy had always declared to be the most splendid that he knew. The outspread vales below were for the moment set in a golden frame, where, to right and left of their view point, rose great beeches ablaze with light. Their leaves had not yet turned to burnished copper, but shone lustrous yellow in noon-day sunshine; while a receding foreground glimmered under blue plantations of young conifer that swept the shoulders of the hill. Though the wind struck cold at this height, its magic beautified the subtending lands, and while distance was dim, middle distance gleamed with genial illumination as miles of foliage ripened to the fall and offered rare theatres for the play of Eurus. A dagger he carried, yet brought his own sorceries of tender colour along with it, to clothe the earth in luminous and milky mists, in opal hazes of rose and azure, in loveliness of half hidden horizons that turned the scene to fairyland upon his passing. High lights there were that twinkled and came and went. Steam of a railway train threaded the valley with fleeting pearls and the more steadfast reaches of little rivers, or the walls and windows of men's houses, flashed like white stars upon the sunset glory of a departing year.

Katey opened her bag and displayed attractive food. Then suddenly, in his usual abrupt fashion, Timothy voiced a grievance more preposterous than usual.

"There's mornings when even my clothes turn against me," he said, "and struggle not to go on my body. The very buttons won't slip into the button-holes and I know everything's hating me. And I damn my shirt and cuss my pants like the born fool I am. And other days they welcome me. Same with trees, same with everything else. I always know in my bones if the trees are glad to see me, or turned against me; but I never know the reason. And to-day's one of the unfriendly days, and this time I guess for why. Everything knows I'm set on seeing the Hunter's Moon to-night and the day things are jealous of the night things."

Kate was accustomed to these wild assertions and they had long ceased to trouble her, for, as a rule, at her touch, Tim was accustomed to emerge from any unpropitious dream quickly enough.

"No matter for that nonsense," she said. "The sun's always friendly and he'll make the moon as bright for you to-night as he can. Be cheerful because I'm cheerful. Time enough for you to get moped when you find me moped. All's well and we're tokened before the nation and you ought to get me a nice finger-ring, so mother says."

"I'm going to," promised Timothy. "My mother has told me the same, and when I do, it will be a pretty fine thing."

"That's better," she said. "I don't want anything to cost a lot of money all the same. Father says it will be the real test of how much you love me to hear how much you've saved by this time next year. And he's going to pay me proper wages now—half-a-crown a week—for me to put by."

"I'll try for a ring with an opal stone in it same as mother's got in a ring she'll wear sometimes. She can't remember where it came from, but it's a lovely jewel with all the colours of the rainbow packed into a raindrop. They say an opal brings bad luck, but be damned to that."

Instantly he changed his mind.

"All the same it may be true. Very likely I've had the best luck I ever shall have when you took me. That's better luck than most men get in all their lives."

"Same here, darling," declared Katey. "I ain't afraid of a bit of pretty stone whether or no."

"A stone's a stone. Some loves a grave-stone better than any other stone on earth. Some gets their comfort by keeping a stone in a churchyard clean and smart; some by hanging bright stones round their necks, or in their ears, or on their fingers. Mrs. Withers said that her heart was all the stone she'd got for old Nicholas. And the stone-cutter, Jack Travers, told me once that the time for his business was just after a death. 'Strike while the iron's hot and the grief fierce,' he said. 'The longer time passes, the cheaper the grave-stone's like to be.'"

"A beastly thing to say," decided Kate.

"Business makes you beastly," he answered. "I wouldn't go in business for a fortune."

"Father's cooked a lovely batch of sausage rolls this morning," announced the girl, "and I've fetched along three beauties for you and a slice of cake. A proper feast. So start on 'em."

As usual she cheered his spirit and he ate with excellent appetite, praised the food and told her of a good thing.

"I've read a very fine tale since I saw you. I'm not one for tales, but my mother found it tidying up a lot of litter. It's a stage play and, being about a forest where the people lived, I read it and it was a wonder. '*As you like it*' the play is called, and you must find time to read it, because it's full of love-making and a wondrous girl, who dressed up like a man and went in the woods. What they call enchantment I'd say, but the people are just so much alive as real people and you can't believe there never was such folk really, nor yet such a forest. And now, in the glens and goyles round about the Manor Woods, or moving under the trees, I can see 'em—yes, I can see 'em and hear their talk. There's a fool, too—a comic chap—and a gloomy son of a gun that yarns away and takes a tolerable dark view of things, same as I do myself. But the wonder is they are all alive—so much alive that after you've read about their doings, you want to read it all over again. I've read it through three times already."

"Lor, Tim! What a thing to find!"

He nodded.

"I can see 'em," he said again.

It was true enough: a great adventure had borne fruit in this virgin soil, echoing what Timothy already felt about love and enlarging his narrow outlook on many other subjects. He did not exaggerate when he declared that he could see his new acquaintances. His mind was of an order swiftly to clothe the dream figures, transfer his ancient devotion from the trees to the living shades that moved among them, see Rosalind in her doublet and hose, mark her lover set his rhymes within her reach, listen to melancholy Jacques, prick his ears at the tinkle of Touchstone's cap and bauble. They came as strangers to his theatre of daily work—fellow beings more seductive than fox or squirrel, his earlier friends, realities for Timothy so long as their magic lasted. The time was coming when he would read more and find in Shakespeare light upon his own young life; but for him that first tremendous experience of human creation waned slowly and just now no creatures in the quick created keener sense of reality, save Kate herself.

"I've heard of theatres," he told her, "and no doubt in such places everyday folk would dress up and speak the words; but I don't want to hear live people do it. All I want is in the words, and I can see and hear the rest for myself."

"What matters is that they do you good and make you feel happy along with them," she said. "And I'll read the tale and feel happy along with them, too, because you do."

"You must; then we can talk about them together and see if we think the same about them. I doubt town folk would make much of it; but if you know the woods, then it all seems as if it must have fallen out just so, though you know it never did."

"Fancy inventing a lot of men and women and making 'em come alive!" said Katey; and the nature of such a bewildering feat kept the young people silent for a moment. Then, invigorated in mind and body, Timothy kissed Kate and went back to work, while she trotted home considering the things he had told her.

She fell in with a horseman upon her way to Priory and met Paul Pook returning from a morning of sport, for cub-hunting had begun and the saddler was once again upon one of his own saddles. He had made it for Nicholas Withers and now, together with the fine hunter left him under the dead man's will, it had returned to him. Katey knew Paul very well, for he esteemed the baker and was on terms of friendship with Samuel's family.

"Good morning, Mr. Pook," said the girl. "You look fine on your lovely new horse, sir. Do he suit you comfortable?"

"He's took to me, Katey," declared the rider. "At first I went in doubt. A horse knows his rider and he understood the old master wasn't on his back. Very clever they are in that respect. I'm three to four stone lighter than Mr. Withers was and it puzzled the horse a bit; but now he finds he's a gainer by that, and he's learned I can ride and know what he can do and what he can't do. And now we're very good friends."

"You won't drive him so hard as what Mr. Withers did I expect," suggested Katey.

"I shan't ask so much from him. I'm not the wonder my dead friend used to be on a horse. When he looked to be taking risks, he wasn't really, along of his marvellous judgment. If I took risks, they would be risks and the hoss would know in a moment the master mind weren't behind him. Then, very like, he would lose heart, and if a hoss loses heart, he's apt to make mistakes and bring you to grief. There's some things you can do many times if you don't over-do 'em, Katey. You can ride to hounds many times and rejoice in the sport same as I do. But you can only break your neck once, so I keep in bounds."

"At your age you didn't ought to be so venturesome as when you were young, Mr. Pook," she suggested.

"I never was, my dear. Doing dangerous things never appealed to my fashion of mind."

Katey remembered the death of Paul's wife and said no more on the subject.

At his fireside that evening Paul Pook informed Ivy that he should be out to tea on Sunday.

"I take tea with my old friend, Mrs. Canniford," he said. "She's wishful to talk and I haven't had much speech with her since the changes at Pigslake. I'd hoped that Nicholas Withers might have remembered Jenny in his will perchance, but I didn't much expect it and it didn't happen. However, she's got Mrs. Withers behind her now and will benefit no doubt here and there."

"That'll suit me very well, Father," answered his daughter. "I'll go up to the Manor and drink my tea with Mr. Bodkin and the others and hear how her ladyship's faring. And as for Mrs. Canniford, I'd be careful if I was you. She talks too much and says silly things better not said."

This unfavourable criticism did not surprise Ivy's father for she seldom praised a neighbour and was naturally censorious.

"Jenny's all right," he answered. "She talks I grant you; but you'll seldom hear an unfriendly speech against another woman on her lips, and she's had a hard life. Talking costs nothing if you don't talk evil."

"I shall always take my stand with truth," replied Ivy. "Truth may give pain to weak people, but it never gives pain to me."

"You're lucky then."

"I know truth from falsehood, be it as it will, and whatever mouth it comes from," declared his daughter, and Mr. Pook congratulated her again.

"A tower of strength for you. Few have got such a gift," he told her. "I wish I had."

"I expect you'll find Mrs. Canniford's after something for one of her son Harry's children," suggested Ivy. "She's always trying to better his case, and there's people very ready to fasten on a well-to-do man with no encumbrances, like you, and try to interest him and get to his pocket for themselves, or their relations."

"A natural thing," he answered. "A well-to-do man without any outside calls expects it. But I can't help Harry there. His eldest boy, George, is going to Pigslake so soon as he's old enough; the others are too young to help yet. I'd like to see everybody rewarded who's done their duty well and faithfully, same as you have yourself; but Harry's duty, no matter how well and faithfully it's done, don't bring home much bacon."

"Yes," agreed Ivy, "I've done my duty well and faithfully as you say, Father; and shall so continue."

Sunday came and Paul kept his appointment. Mrs. Canniford had advertised the fact of his visit to her family and warned them off; but to Rupert she did not mention the matter, because he was apt to spend Sunday morning, when not on duty, in bed, then rise and disappear for the rest of the day. He often went to Pigslake now on Sundays and was welcome.

Jenny had her house to herself therefore and made unusual preparations for an exceptional meal. She knew her friend's tastes, purred over him while he ate good things from Myra and seated him in her most comfortable chair. Then, after he had finished, he praised the fare, lighted his pipe and bade her speak.

"It's like this, dear Paul," began Jenny frankly. "I haven't got no secrets from you and never shall have, and you've always been a true friend, so far as lay in your power, to Myra and me and our families. I often said you was the only one to find the little good hid in poor Nicholas."

"Yes; you like to look for the good in a man," agreed Paul. "Not much to admire in Nick, but as a rider to hounds he was worthy of all praise. A grand horseman. Fine sport him and me have seen, and the hunt will miss him more than his home do."

"For certain. But it ain't him. It's me—me and Peter Honeywood. And now I'm wishful to set Peter before you—in strict confidence."

"As you see him," suggested the saddler.

"Exactly so. You know, like everybody else knows, he's after me; but he's pushing delay to such extremes, as they bachelors will, that I can't think he's treating me so gentlemanly as he might. And now the coast's clear and the sun shining and the goal in sight, why don't he get on with it?"

"You've left no doubt in his mind that you're willing?"

"Not a spot, Paul. He knows all about me and how I'm situate. No discredit to me in any fair-minded ear. There's me—poor as a mouse and widowed; there's my eldest—married and got a family. A very good man Harry is, but simple and awful poor, as them that be apt to breed freely often are. A glutton for work, but not one to do it with any lasting fame. I wouldn't say I was proud of him, but he does his best. And Susan, his wife, is such another—the salt of the earth in a manner of speaking, but no knack to make her mark, or hold her own, or catch the eye. In fact a very godly, unnoticeable, unlucky fashion of woman. They'll be rewarded some day, where brains are but dust in the balance; but not here. Then there's Rupert, flourishing and turned a new leaf now and well thought upon as third gamekeeper at Tudor Manor. I never see none of his earnings and more didn't his father in his life-time. Close as the grave he is, but putting money away I expect and always fond of it from childhood. I've often hinted a few shillings a week would be a tower of strength, and he says 'some day.' He's waiting, of course, for Peter to speak. So there it is—Harry with a heart of gold and no intellects and Rupert with no heart at all, I'm fearing, but sharp as a needle. And neither a mite of use to me."

"Have you put these facts before Honeywood, Jenny?" asked Mr. Pook.

"Certainly I have. Peter knew my first and would often come in and pass the news when John was bed-ridden and wanted to see a friend now and again. But, there again, Honeywood's caution always held the man back and you'd seldom hear anything from him that wasn't well known a month before. Very interested he was in my dear husband's pangs and often said 'twas wonderful what the human frame could stand. Bring a pinch of tobacco for John sometimes he would, or a fresh lettuce, or an old illustrated paper."

"And now he's hanging fire," summed up Paul, "and you wonder what to do about it?"

"That's right. And I've got a thought and I'm wishful to see if you'll help to bring things to a climax, my dear man."

"What can an outsider do, Jenny? I can't tell Peter to offer for you and stop playing about."

"No, you can't do that—far from it; only I want you to fall in with a little plot—quite honest and seemly I'd say, but a plot notwithstanding. There's nothing quickens a man like Peter so fast as to find he ain't the only pebble on the beach, nor gives a defenceless woman more power over him than to let him think he isn't."

"A false scent—eh?" asked Paul.

"That's right. If he was to discover I'd got a possible besides him and hear my praises on—well, on your lips, Paul, or drop in some day and find you drinking a cup of tea along with me, I'm tolerable sure it would spur him into action. If Peter found out that your mind looked to be occupied with me now and again, it would darn soon be a match to the powder; and I should never forget your goodness and bless your name."

Pook took a considerable time to reflect on this proposition and regarded Jenny in a somewhat searching manner; while she, feeling that she might have gone too far, displayed nervousness and felt a quickening of pulse. Presently he smiled and relieved her, but did not as yet reply.

"For dear John's sake," pleaded Jenny, to which the visitor made answer.

"As for John, I never heard he was particular anxious for you to take another, and many husbands feel strong on that subject," he replied. "You can see that in the wills men leave behind. But, as John had nothing to leave, the question don't arise in your case."

"He never rose to making a will and where he is now, he'd put safety first for me beyond a little thing like that," she assured him.

"I expect he might," admitted Paul. "In a word then, you want for me to sting the market-gardener and see if I can make him jealous."

"It sounds to be asking a lot put that way I'm afraid."

"It is; and there mustn't be any reflections on me, Jenny. I wouldn't marry again for a woman's weight in gold."

"And right to say so I'm sure, after losing your priceless girl. Nobody

c

knows that better than me; but Peter doesn't know, and if he don't rise to it instanter, then you can drop it again."

The other nodded.

"I'd pleasure you sooner than most and I think you're heading for an honest, prosperous man, else I'd warn against. Honeywood's all right. But he ain't the only cautious one. I'd have to ask for you to sign a paper, Jenny, setting down our secret, and I'd keep that paper till the prize was won; then I'd give it back to you and let you burn it."

"For you I'd be very willing to sign anything," she promised. "God's my judge, Paul, I'd never have asked any living man but you for such a hugeous favour."

"Fetch out pens and ink," he said, "and I'll write for you to sign. There can't be a witness, but your hand-writing's good enough."

The document was swiftly composed and attested. It recorded the exact nature of the secret understanding and made Mr. Pook safe against any future aspersions in the event of failure; while Paul promised increased displays of guarded but unconcealed friendship. Jenny then expressed undying thanks and supreme confidence that success was now a matter of days at most.

"I know him well enough to be dead sure the moment he fancies you're on the track, he'll rush to his victory," she said. "And you'll get your reward some day, my dear, when the Books are opened, if not sooner."

Feeling that one good turn deserved another, she asked after Ivy and hoped her advent was giving him satisfaction; but Paul reported on his daughter in no fatherly fashion.

"She's getting into the saddle," he said. "A melancholy addition to the house, but women will be melancholy at her age if their hopes are baulked. Terrible wishful to find a husband—so set on it as yourself—but with no chance whatsoever. As a rule, Ivy's pattern of women have got sense enough to give up hope and take what Nature sends 'em in a patient spirit; but not her. Hope won't die. She's got a tongue, too—a lot sharper than I thought —and when I grow too old to hold my own against her middle-age, she's like to give me hell."

Jenny sighed at this grim picture.

"Why don't she go into one of them institutions?" she asked. "There's plenty of places where good work is being done by dogged, obstinate Christians like Ivy. Looking after unwanted children and the weak-minded paupers and so on. Then she'd be helping the world and forget herself and lay up treasure where moth and rust don't corrupt."

"You ask her," answered the man. "You give her a hint where she might shine. I'd pay good money if anything could tempt Ivy away from looking after me. And if she thought I was seeking another partner myself, I'd soon get the edge of her tongue. So I'll need to watch out over this caper very careful indeed."

"Then don't you whisper our secret in that quarter for mercy's sake," urged Jenny, "else she might well spoil all."

"Fear nothing," he said. "I can take her measure."

"Some women have a hideous craft to make you dislike people they dislike," explained Mrs. Canniford. "They wake a feeling in your heart that there must be something deadly wrong with any creature they hate themselves, and so make enemies where no such thing ought to be. I don't say Ivy is that sort, but she doesn't care for me I'm sorry to find and she might try to influence you against me, Paul, if she had a whisper you was befriending me on account of Honeywood."

"Fear nothing," he said again. "I'm my own master and not prepared to stand any dictation from her, nor yet fall in with her manners and customs where they threat to shatter mine. This affair is between us alone and we needn't make a mountain out of a molehill in any case. It's quite simple and orderly and the object of it is well within reason. We're out to open the eyes of a well-meaning man, who's prone to treat time as if it was eternity— quite a common thing, but misfortunate where a woman's concerned and marriage the goal. I shall just give more thought to you, and I can be seen at your door now and again, and you can come to tea with me, or look into my shop and so on. Then any such departure from the usual will be fastened upon double quick and get to Peter's ears first of all, if he don't hap to notice it himself."

"He's that self-confident I doubt if he'll notice it or think twice about it if he does," answered Jenny; "but others will notice it sharp enough and open his eyes, or so I hope."

Mr. Pook considered.

"I'd be disposed to think one firm stroke would save time and trouble," he said. "I'd little fancy the thought of half the parish chittering about you and me and making fun of Peter or anything like that. We might find we'd made a mistake and failed altogether if he took it wrong."

"There's nobody like an Irishman for taking it wrong I grant you," she agreed. "Now you've frightened me, Paul."

"No case for fear. Only I'd say one stroke to the root would be better than a lot of fiddling blows. And it might save time. I've got a pretty good thought already; but I'll turn it over and let you know what's in my mind."

"Ah !" said Mrs. Canniford, "there's no friend like an old friend; and them that have got you for a friend have got what's better than riches, Paul."

But the man was too busy with his reflections to value this high compliment.

"I'm no plotter and little likely to shine at anything devious," he assured her; "but in this matter and for your future peace and security I'd do what I could. I've got an idea flash to my mind, Jenny. How would it fall out if you was to ask us both to tea the same evening ? I'd drop in first, and when Peter arrived, he'd find me in your best chair very comfortable and you toasting a plate of muffins, which I'll bring you on the day. Then I'd show I weren't none too pleased to see him, and you can lay your life he wouldn't feel no better pleased to see me. That's what they call direct action; and presently I'd clear out with a few warm words of farewell from you. Then, seeing his danger, he might take the floor the minute I was gone and not go himself till he was caught and landed."

Jenny stared.

"A bold stroke sure enough," she said. "I was all for keeping you apart;

but you look deeper than what I can. I knew he wouldn't come to-day, because he's gone to see another market-gardener at Honiton."

"So he said at the 'Pen-in-Hand' last night. He's interested in some pickling cabbages."

Mrs. Canniford tittered.

"And us behind his back pickling his cabbage I shouldn't wonder ! But God send he don't pickle ours if he comes to hear about it."

"He never must hear about it and no chance that he should, because nobody's going to hear about it on this earth but you and me," concluded Paul. "The fewer in a plot, the better it's like to prosper. You ask him for the day to serve you best and let me know. That's the idea and no niggling."

But it was Jenny's turn to reflect.

"A woman likes to niggle and get her way so," she said, "while a man's less patient and wants to win out short and sharp. I'll sleep on it. I wouldn't say you're wrong, Paul; but it might turn out a ugly blank for me if you was to frighten Peter away once for all. Besides, if he thought you was in the field, he might lose heart before a man like you."

The saddler grew impatient.

"Well, that's what you want, isn't it ?" he asked. "You can't have it both ways. Where there's plotting, there's danger on both sides, but if you do your part, it ought to work out with a kill in the open after a brisk run."

VI

THERE dawned upon Myra Withers about this season the fact that her sister's son was spending most of his scanty leisure at Pigslake and, having a fairly accurate estimate of Rupert's character, she judged his purpose when the young man committed one of those very unusual actions that, at rare intervals, marked his career. For if a mean, not to say stingy, person makes a gift, involving the least sacrifice to himself, then attention is awakened and reason sought. Rupert went to Honiton on an errand for the head keeper of Tudor Manor, and in that market town spent twenty shillings upon an attractive chalcedony necklace. Next Sunday he came to dinner at Pigslake and presented his gift to Nora in the presence of her family. He made no secret of it, but declared that a condition attached to the necklace.

"I saw it in a watch-maker's window," he explained, "and I thought it just the very article to suit you, Nora, and I said: 'I'll buy it for her if I've got enough money.' But there's a snag to it. Can't spend capital for no return. And I must have a spot of interest on the deal."

"And what was the deal ?" asked Nora, taking the little parcel into her hands, "and what hard bargain are you going to drive for it ? We all know you, my lad. You don't do anything for nothing."

She and the game-keeper were on friendly terms and of late she had bettered her knowledge of him and found him cheerful company; but her father had always detested Rupert and he never showed himself at Pigslake while Nicholas lived.

Nora was delighted with the necklace though surprise dominated her gratitude. "Fancy you chucking your money about like that !" she said, handing the gift to her mother. "Wonders never cease I'm sure."

"You wait till you hear what I want for it," he answered.

"And what might that be, Rupert ?" asked Myra. "A pretty trinket and solid and good. What did you pay for it ?"

"Two pounds I gave for that necklace," said Rupert, who felt the lie lent additional distinction to his present. "And what I want for it is to take a walk with Nora and come back and have my tea along with you all before I go to work. I'm on night duty just now. Our big shoot is due in a fortnight and there's a few in Priory want watching at present. Never was such pheasants."

"There's a lot about," agreed Jonathan.

"It's a bargain, Rupert," agreed the girl. "I'll fetch my hat and jacket and walk out over along with you to Crab Tree Common. That'll do very nice."

"And you can come back to tea if you mind to," added Myra.

"Thus without mystery, Rupert laid direct siege to Nora—from policy rather than affection. She was heart-whole as yet and at no time had wakened into admiration for any man, while the spectacle of marriage, as witnessed in her home, had long decided Nora never to take a husband. This Rupert knew, but hoped that he might exercise enough art and attraction to change her mind. She possessed small acquaintance of young men, but he guessed that under the new conditions of liberty, her experience would swiftly increase, and his ambition was to win her if possible: an impulsive idea inspired entirely by ultimate hope of gain and exceedingly unlike Rupert; but since expediency alone prompted him, he felt there would be plenty of time to come to conclusions when he learned more about her prospects.

"Fancy you wanting to take a walk on Sunday," she said, "with a night's work waiting for you and all ! I'd have guessed you'd have spent half the day in bed for choice, as you mostly do when you can."

"Chance of a walk along with you might fetch the laziest out of bed," he declared. "I've often had it in mind, but was too humble to ask."

"So you thought you'd buy a walk with me and reckoned you'd run to two pounds ?"

"When I saw that necklace, I said 'That's going to be Nora's whatever it costs.' I felt somehow it was dead right for your pretty face. And it is. If you look in the glass when you get home, you'll see how well it favours you."

For Nora was wearing the necklace.

"And now I shall have to think up a gift for you. You rich bachelors look after yourselves too well ever to want anything."

"I may be tolerable well off some day," he answered. "I'm the saving sort; but money don't goody very quick if it's safe and I'm not one to run risks."

"You live rent free with Aunt Jenny anyway. That saves your pocket."

"Oh no I don't. I help. She wouldn't be without me. Some day, if Tubby picks up his courage and offers for her, she'll go to him : then I'll need to look around."

"By 'Tubby' you mean Mr. Honeywood, I suppose ?"

"Him, yes. As for me, I'm due for one of the lodges. It's my turn to get one when our second keeper gives up; but there's a rule at the Manor and always was, that a keeper at a lodge must be married—a tiresome complication and a bit of old-fashioned tyranny, but that's how it is."

"Well, a bright lad like you ought to be able to look around and find a girl with a spot of money coming to her and pluck enough to take you."

"I might, no doubt; but I'm not the cold-blooded sort that puts the main chance before all else. People seem to think so, but it's a lie. I wouldn't run after any girl unless I'd woke into proper love and respect for her, and money hasn't got anything to do with proper love."

Nora was rather impressed.

"Dear me !" she said. "Who'd have thought to hear such fine ideas from you, Rupert ?"

"I'm like the Changeling," he assured her. "Living alone in the woods most of my time, I get ideas. But, unlike Timothy—his ideas are moonshine most times—unlike him I think pretty sensible thoughts now and again."

"Fancy him being allowed to token himself to Katey Wish ! She's a dear friend of mine and I think a lot of her and she's amazing happy about it; but I don't know. Of course, to hate his mother is in my blood. I was brought up to hate her; but I never felt no hate for Timothy, only sorrow for him having such a wicked mother."

"We don't choose our parents, nor yet decide if we're to be born in wedlock or wrong side o' the blanket. Some day, when I know you better and you know me better, I'll tell you what I think about him."

"He's a lovely young man, whoever his father was," said Nora.

"What did Mr. Withers think of him ?"

"Nought. He wasn't father's sort. Father despised him I'd say. Thought him a weak straw of a boy."

"In his head, yes. Not in his body. He's strong and stands to work."

"We'll see how it goes for them then. Katey says she understands him and that he tells her amazing things and reads books. He may be full of surprises —like you are seemingly. He tells Kate it's the woods have taught him."

"No—it's love that's taught him," declared Rupert. "He isn't too young to fall in love. But, we'll see how it goes for them, as you say, and whether it turns out the real thing."

"Proof of the pudding's in the eating, no doubt. She's very wishful for me to know him, but mother wouldn't like that over-much. She forbids for his name to be named among us, of course."

"She would, no doubt. Talk of something pleasanter. How's Jonathan standing up to his job ?"

"All farmer now. Him and Christopher Banks are going to set the Thames afire next Spring."

"Your brother will have to find a partner presently and keep the famous name of Withers to the front."

"Much too busy to go courting yet awhile I'd say. I've never heard him name a girl," she answered.

Rupert tried a different line of approach.

"You'll be his hen-wife same as you were your father's, no doubt ?"

"Oh yes, and paid for it now, which father never thought to do. We're running high class table birds, and layers also, and getting rid of the mixed stuff and carrying on proper. Mother's market woman and she much likes the idea of going to Honiton once a week."

"I hope Jonathan has been open-handed about your money? He ought. There's a lot of skill goes to keeping poultry on a good scale."

"Oh yes, I'm saving."

"Wise girl."

"Lucky girl to be able to."

"A pound a week I shouldn't wonder."

But Nora was not prepared to name the figure.

"Go on wondering," she said and grinned at him.

"It's a fine thing for a clever, understanding chap like Jonathan to have money to his hand and firm ground to jump off from," Rupert told her. "In most cases an ambitious man has to build up his money first before he can do all he wants, and that takes time—years most likely. In my case, to save up the necessary is hard, slow work, because, even when I come to be head keeper, it isn't big money and not enough for what I'd like to do."

"Against that you're living how you best like to live," suggested Nora. "To be a game-keeper is worth more than money to you, because of the life. You'd sooner be in Manor Woods than in a shop drawing twice the money. I've heard you say so."

"That's all right; but a time will come, if it hasn't already, when I'll find myself putting somebody else's comforts and pleasures above my own," prophesied Rupert. "Then, when that happened to me, all would be changed. A wife couldn't get no satisfaction out of me being a game-keeper; and for his wife's sake, if he's the sort I am, a man wouldn't think it a hardship to give up his work and take on something more likely to give her a better time."

"Very large-hearted I'm sure," replied Nora. "What they call 'noble sentiments.' Perhaps we'll hear you've found her some day."

"You'll be the first to hear it if I do," promised the young man, and then, feeling that he had given Nora enough to think upon and made a tidy start, he abandoned personalities and spoke of his own work.

"Our big shoot comes soon now. In the old days her ladyship would always join the guns on the first day, together with such other ladies as were in the house party, and all have lunch together in the open if the weather was right for it. But not of late years—too ill. But her nephew—him that inherits everything when she drops—has ordered the shoot as usual. We keepers wait on 'em at the lunch interval. Very amusing and tips flying about after the week's ended. I'll get you a brace of pheasants presently."

"Jonathan shoots now and again. He shot a hare last week—thought it was an out-sized rabbit—so he said."

"Not him! He knows a hare from a rabbit all right. Don't you let the Harriers hear that, else he'd have a black mark to his name."

"The hunt folk all thought the world of father," answered Nora. "He was a master at hunting himself. Jonathan don't ride to hounds, but he'll keep in with them that do. Nobody wants to quarrel with sport."

"See your birds are safe of a night time," he advised. "Foxes are very clever to get to 'em in a hard winter and the Hunt's tolerable mean when it comes to paying for 'em."

"What's the new man like—her nephew who will follow her?" asked Nora.

"Very different from what she was," he answered. "We shan't hear so much about the rights of man and a lot more about the rights of property when he comes to reign. A rank Tory he is."

Thus passed an hour and a half and presently the couple returned to tea. They fell in with none they knew and both regretted it for different reasons: Rupert because he would have liked to be seen taking a private walk with his cousin, and Nora because nobody had seen and applauded her new, chalcedony necklace.

When the visitor was gone they discussed him and Jonathan asked his sister what they had talked about.

"All manner of things," she said. "And I can tell you this much: there's more in Rupert than meets your eye."

"Nobody ever doubted that," agreed the young farmer. "So long as he didn't make love to you it's all right. I wouldn't like him for a brother-in-law."

"No, he didn't make love to me, or if he did, I didn't notice it; but he talked about love in a general way—very respectable and copy-book. He said you'd be marrying before long he thought—to keep the famous old name of Withers going."

"He's a liar anyway," said her mother, who had been looking at Rupert's gift. "They may be chalcedonys, or they may not—I know nothing as to that—but he never paid two pounds for 'em. He's got his faults," she added. "He's passing mean to your Aunt Jenny and don't give her half so much as he ought."

"She'll escape from him if she takes Peter Honeywood," suggested Jonathan.

"And then I believe he'll marry himself," declared Nora. "He's due for the next Manor Lodge that falls vacant; but only the married men get the lodges."

"I don't see you at a Manor Lodge, Nora."

"I don't see myself in one—not with Rupert," she answered; "but he was rather great on true love and he said, if such a thing happened to him, he'd put the girl's welfare high above his own, or something like that. And he also said that it looked to be happening to him and, if it did, I'd be the first to hear tell of it."

"You zany!" said her mother. "What was that but making love to you? Next time he's up here, you can drop casual to the young man that I don't hold with cousins marrying. That'll give him a hint. It's a very common opinion they should not."

"But a wrong one, Mother," explained Jonathan. "I heard Naylor in the pub. on that very subject answering Toozey, and he said there's no reason against if both come of healthy stock."

"Right or wrong, it will serve for Rupert," decided Myra.

And on his way home, to change his clothes and go to work, the game-keeper also considered where he stood. Nora's flippant attitude did not trouble him and he was tolerably sure that it lay in his power to win her. He decided that she was an average, cheerful, healthy girl and likely to make a good wife; but it would be necessary to know much more about her interest in Pigslake and her future chances of money. Indeed, Rupert already felt somewhat impatient with himself for taking so much trouble before he was better informed. Precipitation had never been an error with him and he determined that time must elapse and inquiries be made before he proceeded further. He judged that it might be in his mother's power to find out if Nora could claim any interest in her late father's property. A sense of irritation with himself was, however, the principal emotion Rupert derived from his Sunday labours.

At the 'Pen-in-Hand' that evening, after church hours, there was singing and it happened that swift-footed rumour already chronicled Rupert's recent operations. Christopher Banks, the head man at Pigslake, joined the company. He had taken tea as usual with the Withers family, learned of Nora's gift and guessed at young Canniford's purpose; but he was not in Priory for that subject and explained his unusual appearance on the Seventh Day.

Christopher was a square-built, sturdy man. His eyes were black, his hair grizzled, and while his tanned and heavily-lined face was clean-shaved, he wore a thick Newgate fringe of hair beneath his chin to keep his throat warm.

"Come down after Doctor," he said, "and you can give me an unsweetened, William. Poor old Adam Merry's parlous ill and his granddaughter, who dwells with him, came in an hour since and said she wouldn't be responsible if doctor didn't see him before night. Jonathan was out, so missis asked me to summon Naylor, which, of course, I have done. We're put about, because none of us would have any evil overtake Adam."

"A wonder how the old chap kept the dish upright with Nicholas for all those years," said Toozey.

"It was, and a lesson, too. Nobody knew how he done it. He just opposed his Christian spirit to Nick's heathen one and carried on, and, short of killing Merry, the master couldn't do a thing about it. But it was all in the day's work for Adam. No fighting and no effort on his part. He just followed what was the Bible rule in his opinion and never took no notice of Nicholas nor his rages. Farmer tried every sort of trick to get an ugly answer from him sometimes. An old game of his that was. If he took a dislike to a man, he'd egg him on till the victim lost his temper, and then he'd sack him. Very fond of showing his power that way; but he never got an ugly reply from Adam and, though he cursed him to hell twenty times a day, he was fond of him in his savage fashion and ended by putting him in his will to keep Meadow Lane cottage for his life."

"He was a masterpiece with sheep, old Adam was," said Inspector Chard. "I'd say that's why Withers kept him."

"Partly, Thomas; but I hold to it there was something more than that about Merry when he stood up against Nick," explained the head man. "You can only call it the Christianity oozing out of him, like juice out of a ripe plum. Just the essence of the old chap, and it beat Withers in the end."

"The devil's always said to shy at holy water," suggested Toozey, "and Adam's righteous way made him fearless against the master's bluster and threats and was one too many for Nicholas."

"That's about it," admitted Christopher. "I've seen Nick stare at him and scratch his head and frown and look properly puzzled. And it took a tidy lot to puzzle him, too."

"Pity he didn't take to heart Merry's way," thought Chard. "It might have saved the late Withers from a lot of hatred."

"Kind-hearted Merry is by nature," declared the head man of Pigslake, "and always apt to find excuse for failings and hopes for betterment. He never preached, but just uttered his opinions and nothing could shake them. Friendly even to his own body when the rheumatism gripped hold upon him. You'd hear Nick, when he got gout, damn his soul and blast his foot and cuss the universe; but when Adam fell hopelessly lamed, with never a hope to recover any more, he said to me, 'Your body's a bit of a nuisance, Christopher, after the works give out beyond repairing, but you must be patient and remember it has served you faithful for three parts of a century.' Patience was his strong suit and it properly baffled an impatient man like the old master."

William Toozey served more liquor and admired the sick shepherd's philosophy.

"When you've got to the pitch that you can look at everything from the outside, including your own withered carcase, and feel patient still, then I'd say you was tolerable wise, though you might be so ignorant as Adam Merry in general affairs. Withers was a million times cleverer than him, but not so wise in reality. Because he was bone-selfish without a beat of his heart to spare for a neighbour, or a thought for his Maker."

"That's why a lot guessed he might have been hurried to judgment by somebody with a grievance," explained Inspector Chard, "but the Law found otherwise. What did Adam say on that, Banks?"

"You find excuses for the dead easier than for the living," replied Christopher. "He was sorry, because he always held Nick would mellow and mend his ways come he grew old. He made every allowance for his dreadful pangs when the gout took him; but he never grumbled himself, though his rheumatism was a lot worse for him than the gout to the master. 'We old men have to give up our play soon or late,' Merry said to me; 'but I'm cruel sorry to give up my work, because the sheep kept me busy and healthy and was better than any other toil.' Work weren't never no physic to him."

"A great gift to be born like that without having to fight to be good," decided the publican. "With most of those aged blids, the only thing that interests their minds is their bodies and how they can keep the machine on its wheels a bit longer; but Adam rose above that."

"He can eat and he can smoke and, he's often sorry he can't read; but his grand-daughter reads to him, because his eyes have got to be hooded of late and his sight fails him."

"Is the doctor going up?" inquired Chard.

"He's gone. That's why I'm here—Sunday and all. I'm to wait till he gets back and he'll drop in, and if there's anything I can take for Adam, he'll give it to me at the surgery."

Timothy Faircloud had joined the company for the singing to-night and Banks addressed him.

"Haven't seen you of late, Tim," he said. "Got to congratulate you along of the news. You've found the one to suit you early in life, boy."

"We suit each other fine, Mr. Banks, thank you," said Faircloud. "Have one with me and wish me luck."

Christopher agreed to another 'unsweetened' and asked a question.

"Everybody agreeable to your tokening I hope?"

So far as I know. I wasn't asking for opinions. I was telling my intentions when I told people."

"Quite the man I'm sure," grinned Christopher. "But don't you be too grand with us everyday folk. You never know when your elders may come in useful, tiresome though you find 'em. The fortunes of your generation be apt to hang a good deal on the last, my lad."

"If you've got the right brains in your head and the power to use 'em, you make your own fortune," said Timothy.

"Well, here's good luck and may you make a big fortune one day and be a good, faithful husband to Katey when the time comes," answered Banks. Then he drank and continued.

"By the same token there's another bright lad on the war-path, though whether he'll fare so well as you looks to be doubtful. Rupert Canniford have brought our Nora a fine present, so it don't want a very keen nose to smell something in the wind."

"He won't be the only one to try for Nora Withers now," foretold Mr. Toozey. "There's a few held off for fear of her father, but they'll pluck up courage since he's gone."

"Rupert's all right," declared Timothy, "but if he's after Nora, he must think she's come by money. Money's all he cares about."

"No politics, Faircloud," warned Toozey.

"A very promising wife for any man is our Nora," declared the head man. "At Pigslake you can see how the survivor of a miserable marriage may take heart and shine out when their partner's wiped off the map for good and all. So it is with the missis. Also with her boy and girl. Nora's blossoming out like a pot plant."

He laughed.

"What did she say to me a week ago? She said: 'We're like cows, Christopher—like cows that have looked over the hedge into a lovely field for years and years, then suddenly find they can go in.' That's what she said."

Some laughed and Timothy smiled to himself rather than at the story of Nora. He left the bar a moment later and Ned Piper, who had been sitting half asleep by the fire, commented unfavourably upon him.

"You pat him on the back, Banks," he said, "but why? It's a damn silly thing in my opinion for people to let him go on with the baker's daughter. So vain as a peacock and reckons he's grown up, whereas everybody knows, or did ought to, the creature's wanting and never will grow up. A most light-minded thing and his mother's light-minded by nature no doubt. But you can't understand Sam Wish suffering such foolery."

"Why not ?" asked Inspector Chard. "He's got rid of his eldest to a young man who'll have plenty of money, and he bargains for time to pass so Timothy can show what he's good for. A most reasonable plan I'd say and no harm done till the future declares itself. He's timid and shy and not got very good manners, but all agree he's sane enough and you didn't ought to say he isn't, Ned, because that's unlawful."

"I'll say it none the less," replied the sexton, "and I lay my life a day will come when you find I'm right, Thomas."

" 'Tis idle to blame a man for being himself, anyway," summed up Toozey. "Who else can he be, Ned ?"

Dr. Edmund Naylor entered at this moment, looked round for Christopher and marked him.

"You're going to lose your old chap, Banks," he said. "Merry's got too little to fight it with. Outside chopping wood last Friday in the east wind—lungs. His grand-daughter is frightened and the parish nurse can't come. I went to the farm and Mrs. Withers is going to look after him herself to-night. But I'm only too sure. He's very old—how old he doesn't know himself."

He turned to the bar.

"Give me a whisky, William. Then come back with me, Christopher, and I'll make up some physic to relieve him. Mrs. Withers will do the rest."

When they were gone Chard commented on the ancient shepherd's career.

"He was related in a manner of speaking to my wife," he said, "and a wondrous kindly soul."

"There won't be no more blessed dust in the burying-ground than his," declared the landlord, "although no doubt there's lots of blessed dust there, that was called blessed when the parties went home, but forgot these years and years now. A man lives so long as they that cared for him lives, but no longer."

"Followed his master pretty quick," commented sexton. "Merry will go in north side of the tower I expect, or else under our windows. My Alice couldn't be feared of his ghost. A harmless old phantom he'd be."

"Most contented creature I ever met with," thought the inspector.

"And you may say he was happy along of his nature," agreed Toozey, "because contentment is as near to happiness as any tender-hearted man can expect to reach."

They debated the meaning of happiness and William was reminded of something that he had heard.

"We was on that question, along with whether Socialism would bring it, a few nights ago in my bar," he told them, "and doctor, who'd thought upon it, said how you couldn't turn out happiness for all like a batch of bread. He said it to Sam Wish, who was in here. Doctor reckoned what we mean by happiness is an uncertain item and depends on education and the point of view, and training of the mind and the powers of imagination. To the right down poor' happiness means security and enough to eat. They don't want no more than that to make them as happy as kings. To them that never knew what it was to be insecure or hungry from the cradle to the grave, their happiness takes a different shape and they pitch their requirements a lot higher. Only if we was all brought up in the same way and had the same ideas and liked the same things would the happiness of all us men and women be the same. And not even then, said Dr. Naylor, because no two people look at life out of the same pair of eyes. Their hearts and heads and what they shun and what they seek decide where their happiness awaits 'em. He went further and vowed that nobody on God's earth could be perfectly and lastingly happy, except a selfish, own-self dog here and there, because in a world like this one, the woe of the world all around us ought to make everybody short of happy if not actually miserable."

"Us can rule out happiness till we get in the next world then," said Piper, "and tolerable doubtful there. Yet you'll meet a happy man now and again and you wonder what he's got up his sleeve making him so cheerful. When a chap stands a round of drinks, sometimes you may know the reason, but other times you don't, and you try to find out why. Not that I waste much wits wondering about men. There's little I know about 'em, except that great and small are all ate by the same fashion of worms come they die."

"You know a lot more about them than that," declared Toozey. "Adam now. You can say touching Adam that he treated the world a lot better than it treated him. Sheep were kinder to him than men. No luck with his wife and a hard master. Such things might have turned him sour as a crab; but such was his nature that they never did. Name your drinks, gentlemen, them that want another. We're near on time."

VII

HAD Dr. Naylor listened to the inn-keeper's epitaph on the dying labourer, he must have declared material for satisfaction, for he stoutly supported the good sense of his patients in Priory and maintained the superior intelligence of average countrymen as opposed to their urban opposites. Indeed he held that men of the soil developed a measure of mother-wit superior to that of town folk and delighted to quote the conclusions of a famous observer, when he heard his well-loved rustics laughed at.

"Now listen to Adam Smith, the great philosopher and economist," he would say, then give his hearers a passage that he had long since gotten by heart.

"Thus he writes. 'How much the lower ranks of people in the country are really superior to those of the town is well known to every man whom either business or curiosity has led to converse much with both.' There you are, with first-rate authority behind it, and that is as true to-day as when the great Scotsman wrote the words !"

Dr. Naylor could also furnish good reasons for his conviction and explain how the mechanized labour of work-shop and factory tended to make their operators dull-witted, while agriculture and the care of living beasts quickened rural minds.

Now he was called to close the eyes of his aged friend, for Adam Merry succumbed and Priory knew him no more. Gloom followed the death of the ancient man for, on his harmless journey through life, he had made many well wishers.   A larger measure of mourning attended his funeral than that of his master.   Myra Withers and her son and daughter followed Adam's coffin with his few relations; while Jenny Canniford also came and Susan Canniford, her son Harry's wife.

It was Susan who approached Myra when the rite had ended and the little company scattered to their homes.

"May I have a tell with you, Myra?" she asked.   "I was coming up over so soon as I could get a minute, but here's a chance if you can give ear as you go along."

"Of course, Susan.   How can we serve you, my dear?" answered Mrs. Withers.   "You must come up one day, with Harry and a child or two, when you have the time."

"Thank you, I'm sure—gladly we'd come.   For the minute 'tis poor dear old Mr. Merry's cottage, Myra.   It would be a god-send for us in many ways with its four chambers, because we've only got three, and talking it over with Harry last night, he pointed out that when our George comes to work at Pigslake, so soon as he's old and strong enough to serve Jonathan, then I'd be nigh to look after him and save you trouble and so on.   And Harry could go to his work from there so well as from the village.   And, of course, it would be a lift up for him living on the farm.   We was telling about it together half the night and so I ordained to venture to ask."

Myra shook her head.

"Sorry you thought on that," she said, "because it couldn't be, Susan. Meadow Lane Cottage was built before we were born, and has always been given over to the Pigslake shepherd for years and years.   It lies nigh the ewe leases handy for the lambing season.   And Jonathan is going to better our sheep—wool going up and all.   When Adam dropped out, though never a better shepherd than he was, Jack Miller took up the work and Adam learned him everything he knew.   So now, instead of living at the farm, Jack and his wife will go to Meadow Lane.   Afore Christmas they'll get in."

Susan sighed.

"You'll forgive me for asking, won't you?"

"Nought to forgive.   But that's how it is.   And tell Harry we've got a tolerable big job for him before long.   There's none makes up a bank, or clears a water-table better than what he does, and Jonathan wants him here for a month in early spring.

"Thank you, Myra.   That'll cheer him up.   I always feel Harry's a bit undervalued."

"Why should he be?" asked Mrs. Withers.   "Some men have got to do the hedges and ditches, and a lot don't do it half so clever as him.   His work's well known to stand."

Then she changed the subject and admired Susan's children, who had accompanied her to the funeral.

"Have you ever heard your brother-in-law talk of taking a wife, Susan?" asked Myra presently.

"Rupert?   Lor, no!   He comes to see us off and on, if we can do a job to serve him, and he says that if anything could put a man off marrying, it's us. But he may marry yet—not for love, but for a lodge at the Manor. He wants one of them lodges, only he won't have it without a wife to minister to him."

"He gets on all right with Harry, don't he?"

"Everybody gets on all right with Harry. Harry's same as dear old Adam was—the salt of the earth. But Rupert's never done a hand's turn for us—too selfish he is; and when once he lent Harry a pound, us being pushed beyond bearing for the minute, he demanded a shilling interest on the money and never let up for a week till he'd got the pound back. A cruel, mean piece of goods if you ask me, and the wonder is that such a man can be my husband's own brother."

"Nicely spoken, however," suggested Myra.

"Oh yes—to his betters. They think a lot of him at the Manor—so he says. A very good game-keeper no doubt."

"You don't like him too well?"

"I despise him," declared Susan, "and the woman that married Rupert, supposing she came to it, would terrible soon be a forlorn creature when the gilt was off her gingerbread."

They parted at Susan's door, and, passing Peter Honeywood's nursery, Peter himself appeared at work within speaking distance. He was pulling fat, white turnips with a lad to help him.

"Morning, Myra," he said. "Black as a crow I see. I heard the funeral bell. Your old shepherd they told me at 'Pen-in-Hand' last night."

"Yes, Peter. We've just buried Adam Merry."

"Was Jenny there?"

"Yes, she came."

Peter mopped his brow with a yellow cotton handkerchief.

"I see her passing the time very cheerful outside the saddler's along with Pook as I passed t'other side of the road a day or two since. Too interested she was to notice me; but I see her. A most agreeable man Paul Pook can be when he's minded."

"An old friend of our family he is," answered Myra. "We're very fond of him."

"Ah. You might tell Jenny I ordain to come in for a cup of tea Sunday," he said. "And I'll bring her a nice cauliflower and some carrots."

"I'll tell her if I hap to see her," promised Mrs. Withers.

"That being, of course, if she's not otherwise engaged."

"I'll warn her to let you know. She's a popular woman, Jenny is, and gets an invite herself now and then. But she isn't coming to us Sunday."

"Ah!" repeated Mr. Honeywood again. "Enough said."

Mrs. Withers knew nothing of her sister's secrets and felt slightly puzzled to guess what emotions lay behind Peter's exclamation.

"I must be getting home," she told him. "Beautiful turnips you're drawing."

He looked after her as she walked away and evidence of disquiet marked his face. Then he reflected curiously on Myra herself.

"Not a shred of weeds for Nicholas," he thought, "yet she can don her black for that out-worn labouring man!"

Meantime, the plotters were gratified that Peter had seen them together and, when he passed the saddler's shop, both pretended not to notice him and spoke with animation. Now her sister learned from Myra that Mr. Honeywood proposed to drink tea with her on the following Sunday and at first this had tended to alarm her; but, feeling that his intention might provoke the climax she desired, Jenny informed Paul, who expressed a determination to come also.

"I'll drop in first," he said, "and Peter will find me by the fire in your big, easy chair when he comes along with his green stuff. And here's two shillings to get an outstanding tea. I'll clear out after we've finished and leave him in open country."

With resolution Mrs. Canniford concentrated on their food; but the saddler found her extremely nervous when he arrived, and Peter's subsequent demonstration, as he entered in rich attire with a basket of vegetables, did not allay her qualms, for he made no attempt to conceal his astonishment.

"Lord save us! You, Paul!" he exclaimed. "What a world! I always thought two was company and three a crowd, but we live and learn."

"So we do," agreed Mr. Pook. "Live and learn's a very good word. Me and Jenny are old friends and I was pleased to accept her invite. Have you asked anybody else to tea, my dear?"

"No, no, Paul," she answered. "Only you two. Draw up now, please. The kettle's boiling."

Paul picked it up off the fire and showed himself much at ease, while Peter fell somewhat silent for him. He regarded the other man suspiciously, from the corner of his eye, as a toad might inspect a doubtful insect, but presently resumed his company manners and strove to display a like familiarity with the hostess. They talked upon local topics and praised the tea; but in secret Peter was summoning his forces for attack and presently he led the conversation to marriage and addressed Paul.

"'Tis well known, after your sad experiences, that you was never for a second," he said, "and I could understand that, my friend. None felt more put about for you than what I did when that fatal affair overtook your dear wife long ago. A proper tragedy; but I was very pleased when your Ivy came to look after you and take her mother's place in your home. In fact, I often wondered why the girl ever left it. Is she good at figures and up to doing your books and saving you trouble? I hope so."

"She's very good at figures, Peter; but no child can take the place of her mother. And if I ever felt to want to fill it, I'd be called to look elsewhere," replied Pook.

Jenny plunged in.

"And very wise you'd be, Paul. There's none like a wife for a man getting on—as I've often told Peter for that matter. And—and—which of you is going to eat the last muffin before it turns cold?"

"You take it yourself," suggested Honeywood and Pook supported him.

"Let's see you eat it, Jenny," he said. "I doubt you eat enough, for all

Peter's gifts. There's thought to be no cauliflowers like them from his market garden."

"Since you both agree, I'll eat it then," agreed Jenny. "I wouldn't say either of you good men have done yourself very well. But if you've finished, I beg you'll light your pipes. I like the smell of tobacco about the house."

Paul resumed presently where Peter had left off.

"Some say I ought to see my way to another partner no doubt," he told them. "For years and years I felt it would be a bit of a slur on my daughter's mother; but that feeling has pretty well faded now. Ivy shows me things that I'd long forgot, and Jenny's often said how I might be wise to look round for some personable widow that would understand me and feel herself drawn if I set about her properly. But there's advantages to the bachelor state, so I've heard bachelors say."

"Out of their ignorance," murmured Jenny.

"There was a man in the bar of the 'Pen-in-Hand' a bit ago," continued Pook. "A stranger with a sharp tongue—and when talk ran on the married state, he made a very bitter remark indeed. He swore no husband was happy till he was dead and no wife till she'd got her divorce. A nasty view and I withstood him."

"One that drew a blank, or perhaps a bachelor man, like you, Peter," suggested Jenny. "I've heard the late Nicholas Withers say dreadful things like that."

"There may be an ugly truth hid in 'em all the same—present company excepted, of course," replied Peter.

"As a bachelor you can't be expected to know much on that subject," declared Paul. "You wait till you've got the good fortune to find a proper valiant wife, Honeywood. Then you'll tell very different, believe me."

"I've waited and I've watched," answered the market gardener. "I'm the waiting, watchful sort, and I wouldn't say but a bachelor, with my large experience of human nature, haven't got his views of the married state in pretty good order. Everything shows two sides, and it's a nice question whether the failures wouldn't outbalance the successes if we could get the figures."

"That you never will, because there's millions of self-respecting, married people keep the truth to themselves," said Paul. "They don't bleat their happiness, nor yet their private misfortunes, and none but themselves know the inner truth."

Mrs. Canniford considered the matter biologically.

"Some of the most horrible failures can't be hid, as in my sister's case," she said. "The right way is to take the rough with the smooth, same as me and my John did; but in Myra's married life there weren't no smooth and her wrongs properly shrieked to heaven, try as she might to hide 'em. That was an example of a hideous downfall I grant you; but most times, with sensible men and women, the truth of marriage is hid up. There's some things about the male no female could possibly like, and honest men would grant so much as that; but, then again, for all us women know, there's that to us which don't meet with no applause from most of you. You're fussier than what we are. I was often surprised to find my husband so fussy as an old maid over little things I took no count of. But love, when it comes, did ought to cover a multitude of drawbacks. Nothing is perfection, and if the disappointing side of a man outweighs his advantages in a woman's eyes, then you may lay your life she don't love him properly and didn't ought to take him, even if he gives her the chance to do so. Real love soars above ugly details—very likely don't even see 'em.''

Jenny panted after this long speech while Peter grunted and Paul, preparing to depart, supported her.

"Only an empty mind looks for perfection in us mortal beings," he said. "And if the question of love had to decide marriage, then there would be far fewer unions than what there are. If it was the law of the land you must fall in love before you marry—Good God !"

"There's lots of very respectable reasons why folk, getting on and past romantics, should wed if they be wishful to," said Jenny. "Wouldn't you agree to that, Peter ?"

"Life's life and you open a wide subject," answered the bachelor. "But I'd certainly say a marriage of the middle-aged ones, if the man felt satisfied in his mind, didn't call so much for love as bargaining. You've got to sum up on both sides as to whether you're getting good value and act according."

"And a sensible woman would expect to hear what bargain the man might be pleased to offer," concluded Paul. "Now good night, my dear, and thank you for a pretty tea. Good night, Peter. I must tell Ivy to come round and bargain with you—not for marriage, but for some of your fine carrots."

With this light touch, which Jenny much admired, the saddler took his leave and, as soon as he was gone, Honeywood occupied the armchair by the fire and loaded his pipe a second time. She waited for him to speak, but Peter appeared pensive and unusually thoughtful. He sat with his pipe unlighted, his eyes upon the fire.

"A nice man and a true friend, Paul is," said Mrs. Canniford in impartial tones. "You'll always hear a bit of sense from him when he's in the mood to give it."

"A very good saddler I believe."

"A fine workman; but more than that. He's seen a lot of misfortune and it have deepened his mind I'd say."

"Funny how you find people will always praise a man because he's had misfortunes ! As if they were praiseworthy in themselves, yet, so like as not, his own fault."

Jenny struck a match and held it to his pipe.

"I'd say you wasn't quite so cheerful as your wont this evening. What's wrong ? If I can mend it, tell me."

"If you must know," he answered, "to ask an outsider to tea on the self-same evening when I let you hear I was coming, looked a bit thoughtless."

"You wouldn't call Pook an outsider surely ?" she asked. "He was a great friend to my first husband. My first husband, and most like my last for that matter."

But Peter felt in no mood to avail himself of this opening.

"Touching Pook, not a few whispered at the 'Pen-in-Hand' that when your sister got free, that man might be found a bit oftener at Pigslake. What do you think of that, Jenny?"

She laughed.

"You old women in Toozey's bar! What'll you hatch up next? Paul may take another, and she'll be lucky if he do; but could anybody ever imagine that Myra will take another after her fearful career with the first? No, my dear man. Never again in her case to my certain knowledge; but I wouldn't say, knowing him so well as I do, but what Mr. Pook may take another soon or late. There's a rare good husband for a nice woman in Paul, and I've told him so. 'From a woman's point of opinion, you're a fine man running to waste,' I told him."

"Going pretty far that was. I wouldn't give your men friends advice quite so free if I was you, Jenny."

"You never catched me giving you any I'm sure," she said, and Peter returned to Paul.

"Pook ain't a little ray of sunshine in his house I'd reckon. Rather a drear pattern of mind he's got and you'll seldom hear him laugh, joke as you may."

"He'll laugh sometimes, but not much one for a joke. A restful man."

"Restful or not restful, next time I come to tea, if I do come, I'll ask you not to spring no party on me, because I enter this house for very different reasons than a party," he told her, and Jenny felt herself not only disappointed, but annoyed.

"My!" she answered. "You've always given me to understand that you liked other folk and loved a revel. But I won't ask nobody else to meet you if, as you say, you find yourself in a frame of mind to come again."

He ignored this unusually severe speech.

"Between ourselves, Paul hasn't got the money behind him I have," he said. "Along of all the machines used nowadays, and gathering in number, he don't get the work he did."

"I'm sorry to hear it," she answered. "I don't know anything about money, never having had none and not likely to; but I know what it is not to have any, and I'd be terrible sorry if any valued friend of mine was pinched."

"Some wonder he can afford to gallop about after foxes every week. But that's his own business of course. Anyway, horses are doomed in another generation and saddlers like to be doomed along with them," he assured her. "A gloomy prospect for Paul Pook, I'd say."

"Perhaps that's what makes him a thought more serious minded than what you are, my dear," suggested Jenny. "I was going to evensong to-night, but if you'd like to sit on, I'll sit on with you."

"No, I wouldn't say I'll sit on to-night. I've got the indigestion I fancy."

"Oh dear, Peter! Whoever heard of you took that way? Can I do anything for it?"

"You can do this," he said. "You can come and drink your tea with me—not Sunday, but Wednesday next. And there won't be nobody else there either."

"Of course, I'll come," she promised with hope renewed. Then she helped him into his coat and saw him off.

"I'll have one of your lovely cauliflowers for my dinner to-morrow and think of the giver," she cried after him.

Elation and doubt mingled in Mrs. Canniford's mind when he was gone. She did not attend evensong, but washed up, prepared some supper for Rupert and then sat by the fire and measured the results of Paul's experiment.

"We was both very clever," she thought, "and egged one another on. We woke jealousy, no doubt of that, because Honeywood didn't enjoy his tea, and found a lot of unkind things to say about Paul after he was gone. Glaring jealousy that was all right; but we'd hit him a thought too hard for his mind to quiet down all in a minute. He wanted to be alone to think. He wasn't liking me any too well for the minute, and he was hating Paul."

She decided that their attack had succeeded and felt little doubt the following Wednesday would bring her triumph.

"Then," reflected Jenny, "Peter will see his danger, being a clever man enough, dear fellow, for his own interests; and, even if he don't fear Pook, he'll see I'm one to have men friends besides him and might leave him in the lurch yet. Then fear would gather over him like a cloud, and he'd feel he was cutting his own throat to mince about any longer."

She pictured Peter's coming proposal and considered what she should wear.

"To give an invite on a week-day is proof positive he's got the wind up at last," thought Jenny; "but we must be plaguey careful that he never lives to hear how me and Paul hatched a cabal against him. Otherwise his Irish blood would come to the surface and he'd never forgive either of us no more."

This interesting train of thought was broken, for her son, Harry, thrust his head into the door of the house-place, and with him he brought two of Jenny's grandchildren.

"I waited unbeknownst, Mother, till I see Mr. Pook go on his way and Mr. Honeywood follow after," said the man. "I bided longer still lest there might be any more company. Then, finding you alone, I thought as you wouldn't mind if I fetched in and brought Percy and Emmeline to give Susan a bit of a rest."

His parent sighed and rose to greet them.

"That's all right, Harry," she said. "Come in, my loveys."

Two pair of round, inquiring eyes set in plain little faces were raised to her.

"And might you have somefin to eat, Ganny?" asked Emmeline.

"Some nice rock cakes as ever was," she answered. "You sit on the hearthrug and let father have the big chair, and I'll see what I can do for the pair of you."

Gratified by his reception, for he had doubted whether he might be welcome to-night, Harry sat down, removed his hat and sniffed the air.

"I smell Honeywood," he said. "Peter smokes a rich brand of tobacco, beyond the reach of most of us."

Then he lighted his own pipe, while Percy and Emmeline, fortified with refreshment, squatted happily before the fire.

Harry expected to hear particulars of his mother's entertainment, but he would not ask and Jenny offered no enlightenment. She inquired after his work and wondered whether the Cannifords might be invited to Pigslake for Christmas dinner.

"I wouldn't say 'twas beyond belief," declared Jenny. "Myra will like for me to be there, but, against that, she knows you and Susan and the children all come to me on the festival day, so she may not ask me. On the other hand she may ask the lot of us."

"Rupert goes there of a Sunday," said Harry; "but he's the sort that asks himself—very different from me, because I've never invited myself anywhere in my life, and never will."

"The only way to receive is to ask most times," said Jenny, "but not for the like of you, because to get 'no' for an answer always plunges you in despair. Rupert don't mind so much. He's harder stuff than you."

"He called me a blasted fool last time I saw him," answered Harry. "And why? Because Susan had gone behind my back and asked Aunt Myra if she'd let us have Merry's cottage now he's dead. Susan knew that I'd never ask and she reckoned it would be such a surprise for me—just one of her silly, kind thoughts. She's full of 'em, but thinking kind thoughts don't get you anywhere. The shepherd always has that house, so Aunt Myra explained. Rupert's no brother to me, be it as it will, and no uncle to my family."

"He's got his own axe to grind, Harry. He's a pushful, clever man and much valued in the game preserves at the Manor."

"You get a lot to try your faith," he said. "You mark doubtful chaps flourishing like the green bay tree, and think, in justice, you'll live to see 'em get their deserts and Providence down on 'em; but, no; nothing happens. They wallow in plenty all their lives and die in comfort at the end, though well the looker-on knows they didn't deserve none of it."

"Don't you let things like that make you sour," advised Jenny. "You're in good work and well thought upon and respected. That's all you can hope for."

"Nobody respects me. There's something about my trade that makes people think any fool could do it. Whereas the truth is it's a very tricky, difficult trade calling for cruel hard work and a lot of understanding. Only other men doing the same as me can judge of what I do, and so like as not they'd tell you I do it wrong—just for envy. I'd say envy was the curse of human nature."

"Well, if there's them about that envy you, that's a sign some are worse off than what you are," suggested Jenny. "You've got blessings that only God could have gived you, Harry: a good wife and nice children—not to name a faithful mother."

Harry nodded without zest and changed the subject.

"I met young Faircloud a day or two since," he said. "I'm working on Manor hedges, where the cattle have broke 'em down, and coming back I fell in with him returning from the forest. I gave him 'good evening,' for I was never one to visit the sins of the parents upon the children, and he answered 'good evening' to me. But you could see at a glance he thought better of himself than he did of me. That's where the shoe pinches—that every soul I'd welcome with a glad heart thinks better of himself than he do of me—

even a boy like Timothy Faircloud. I'm so used to it now that, if anybody was to treat me as an equal, I'd have a fit most like. Up in the air, Timothy was, but belittled himself to go in step for half a mile."

"He's young and in love with a nice girl."

"Not that he's particular happy for all that. We had speech and I found he was like me in a manner of speaking, though in my case my troubles are real and in his case only fancied."

"What's troubling him then?"

"He feels himself to be under-valued. He worries to think folk don't see what a wonder he is. 'If the people knew what was in me, Canniford,' he said, 'they would be more than a bit surprised.' And I said: 'Well, and what is in you that you're so proud of, Faircloud? If you don't let your good works shine out, how the mischief can anybody know the wonders you reckon are hid in you?'"

"And what did he say to that?"

"He said they'd shine out some day at the appointed time, and I said, if they was so grand as he thought, no doubt he'd get the credit for 'em. 'Not that you need to expect credit where credit is due,' I told him. 'I've done lations of creditable work in my life and shall do much more no doubt, but no man gives me any praise over and above what my own conscience do.'"

"I dare say you did him good, Harry."

"Oh no. I never done anybody good, because none ever listens to me. Him and me are just common objects of the country side. There's a lot like him—queer and on the brink of being shut up—and a lot like me—faithful and leaving the world tidier than I find it, but of no account."

"He may surprise us all yet. With the likes of him you never can tell. The wits ain't wanting. Even his mother has got a pretty good brain and may be better than we think her."

"He's got enough brains to go out of his mind no doubt," admitted Harry. "He asked me if I'd seen the Hunter's Moon back along, and I said I hadn't, and he said 'twas a majestic sight this year and he wouldn't have missed it for money. For money, mark you! And if the boy's moonstruck, God help him."

"The young will be saying and thinking queer things. 'Tis just a last struggle for romantics before they grow up and get to work and face reality," said Jenny. "He's in love, remember. You open air men that work much alone, like you and Rupert and many others, get in the way of brooding and feeding on your own thoughts. But it passes off. Neither your brother nor yet you was much given to it. You never know what Rupert is thinking about at any time for that matter."

"But you can guess. Money's his god!"

"You was always open with your mother, Harry. I wouldn't say you'd ever had a secret from me. A good son for a widow you've always been and will get your rewards and acknowledgments if not here, then hereafter. But don't let yourself go broody. You was one to whistle to your work so sweet as a blackbird in your tender youth; but I never hear you whistle now."

"A long time since I had anything to whistle about," he answered. "Well, you've done me good, Mother, as you always do. And we must hope for better times and a bit of justice. And hope for better times for you, too. Next best thing, if Providence ain't got no use for you yourself, is to see it lending a hand to them you care about."

"Perhaps you will. I'll go so far as to say my affairs look to be coming to a climax," confided Jenny. "But not a word, my dear."

"They climaxes are pretty cold comfort in my experience. Now we'll get along, Mother."

Cheered by this survey of his misfortunes, Harry departed, holding the hands of Percy and Emmeline on either side of him. The little girl hugged to her bosom a bunch of Mr. Honeywood's carrots, while Percy conveyed a massive cauliflower.

Mrs. Canniford kissed and blessed them all before they vanished into the night. Her son's melancholy reflections had not disturbed her in the least, for she was long practised in these recitals of woe. She returned to her own thoughts, completed preparations for Rupert's supper and wondered whether he had spent his leisure hours at Pigslake, or elsewhere.

At nine o'clock he returned and, for once in his life, spoke without reserve both of the past and future. To make conversation, which was always difficult at home, his mother alluded to the recent big shoot at the Manor and, to her surprise, Rupert responded.

"A great success it was. Record pheasants and all good shots."

"Mr. Townley got all the tips as usual, no doubt?"

"Most of 'em. Head keeper always does. I came by a quid myself. Waited on the guns at luncheon. A beautiful day—three beautiful days in fact. The heir was down and that lawyer man. He's a great friend of her ladyship's nephew and they was talking tolerable free together over their meal. One could have picked up a spot of gossip if one had listened; but of course I didn't do that."

"Knew your manners too well I should hope, Rupert."

The game-keeper laughed. "Lawyer drank a bottle of sparkling wine, and then some; but he shot just as straight after as before. A rare shotsman for an elderly chap. I loaded for him and he gave me ten bob, so I made thirty shillings all told. There's another big shoot round Christmas."

"You was ordaining to take a brace of birds to your Aunt Myra, so she told me. Did you manage to get 'em?"

"No. I changed my mind as to that. Pheasants fly everywhere after a big shoot. There will be plenty over Pigslake and Jonathan can get his own pheasants if he wants to."

"How are they all?" asked Jenny. "Nora had a cold last time I was there."

"She's all right. I spent the afternoon along with Christopher Banks, because I gathered that Aunt Myra wasn't particular wishful to see me to-day."

"Never, Rupert!"

"So it struck my mind anyhow. And when Nora offered for a walk, I said I was going to see Christopher Banks, because I wanted his opinion for a friend. I went along to Banks, and then I went elsewhere. I didn't go back to the farm."

Jenny stared. She had been building some secret castles in the air on the subject of Rupert and Nora, but now they threatened to fall untimely.

"I thought you was a bit more than interested in that quarter," she said. "I can't believe you got such a chill welcome as you fancy. Your aunt's well disposed to you, I'd say."

"You know without words if you're on the right side of folk," he answered. "Anyway I do. There was other people there I grant. They had come from a long ways off. So I may be wrong."

"They'll feel pleased enough to see you next time you look in on 'em. Can't be nothing wrong if Nora offered for a walk."

"The visitors was deadly dull and she wanted to be rid of 'em; but I shan't go up for a month of Sundays now. Been there a thought too often perhaps. I've got my pride. Another thing—strictly between you and me, Mother. I grant I was a good bit drawn by Nora for a time and she was coming to like me tolerable well. You always know."

"Why not? You can make yourself so pleasant as any young man, when it suits you."

"I had a bit of a knock, however," he confessed. "I was so set upon winning her that I didn't trouble much about the details, but then the queer thing fell out and, while I found she was going to fall for me, or so it looked, then I began to feel also that I wasn't so keen about her as I thought I was."

"My! What ever has she done? I've always thought Nora was the pick of the basket round here. And now her father's gone, she's that happy and brave and cheerful—a proper good sweetheart for any man."

"She holds her head high and has a right to. Just a thought too fond of making fun of me, but only her high spirits. But there's more than that. I was talking with a man not so long ago at the shoot. One of our beaters and he'd married his cousin, as came out in conversation. And he said—not knowing about me and Nora of course—that it was a fatal mistake and never came to good. He'd got a idiot daughter and a know-nought fool of a son and said he'd warned a lot against it."

"But Doctor Naylor's been heard to tell there's nothing but old wives' tales against, if the man and woman are all right," argued his mother.

"What's an opinion like that to a personal experience? It's a pretty awful thought that I might some day be faced with a lunatic family and the expenses of keeping 'em all in an asylum. You've got to give weight to such a frightful chance as that."

Mrs. Canniford found nothing to say, but she knew Rupert's methods and perceived that he had changed his mind about her niece. She much doubted his story, for it was well within his power to invent a beater with an idiot daughter and doubtful son. Rupert possessed great gifts to bolster his decisions with the practical but quite imaginary experiences of other people. All that mattered was that a hoped-for romance had evidently been nipped in the bud, and Jenny much regretted it. She guessed that her sister would be able to furnish some tangible reasons; but as yet they had not discussed such a possibility, for Jenny was careful to conceal the fact that she knew anything of Rupert's purpose.

VIII

"SOMETIMES," said Susan Canniford, Harry's wife, "my husband puts you in mind of a bullock. I've often thought, to see him squatting by the fire of an evening when he's got nothing to smoke, that you can almost see him chewing the cud. A most melancholy sight and I'll even rob the children of their sweets to get the dear man a pinch of tobacco, which you might say is the only pleasure he'd own to."

Jenny supported this sorry picture with sighs and Harry's privations were sympathetically mourned by Myra Withers and Nora, for Mrs. Canniford's prophecy came true and she with her family all spent Christmas Day at the farm. It was not an apt moment to unfold the hedger and ditcher's tribulations for everybody had eaten a handsome Christmas dinner at Pigslake. Myra, her joy in widowed life persisting, asked them all; and now the men were gone out on the farm, the women and Susan's children drawn up round the fire in the house-place roasting chestnuts.

Nora left her family presently and helped the maidens to prepare tea. It had been a grey day and dusk already prepared to come down, while a sinking sun shot the west with fleeting fire through the clouds. Rupert was of the company and at present out of doors, but, when her daughter had left them, Myra spoke openly about him to his mother, while Susan looked after her children.

"What's come to Rupert these days?" she asked. Something's got on his mind seemingly. I like him tolerable well as you know and I've been a bit interested to see he was after Nora. I don't say I'd have been wishful to lose Nora in that quarter, Jenny, but my objection—the only one that mattered—was them being first cousins. Against that I hear from the doctor that, given good health both sides, there's no danger at all. But the point is this, that he's been very attentive in his spare time and, though Nora only laughed at him at first, she's got to feel tolerable friendly as she knows him better. Jonathan begins to like him well enough too, and Chris. Banks says he's very high thought of at the Manor and will be head keeper in a year or two when Jacob Townley drops out. So I began to feel it might happen. He's a clean, smart man and we can let the past bury the past, which is most times a sensible thing to do. But of late there's a change come over Rupert and I'm wishful to know what's in his mind if you can throw any light on it. If he was only playing about with Nora, then I don't want to see him up here any more."

Jenny, little expecting anything of this kind and knowing only too well that Rupert had changed his mind, found her digestion suddenly impaired.

"I'm sure nothing would have pleased me better than to see Rupert blessed with such a rare good wife as your Nora," she said. "He'll be a lucky man that wins her; but what's in my son's mind I couldn't tell you, Myra. He's not one to open his heart to his mother, like Harry do, and never was. I'd go so far as to say he's considering marriage, but it looks to me as if it was to get a Manor lodge, rather than because he loved any girl in particular.

He can't have the lodge unless he's got a wife, and he might think perhaps that Nora's too grand to live in one of they lodges."

"Has he mentioned her to you at any time?"

"I can't recall him doing so, but I do mind he said perhaps cousins ought not to marry. He'd heard of a case where the family was a great disappointment," replied Jenny.

"I'm thinking of my girl, not your son," declared Myra bluntly. "I know what a loveless marriage is—none better—and if Rupert talked that rot, then he don't love Nora, so all's said. He ain't the sort to let a thing like that stop him if he'd been in love; but I begin to doubt if your boy could love anybody much except himself. However, no harm done. Nora will find all she wants some day."

"And Jonathan, too," agreed Jenny. "When he's got time, I hope he'll meet the right one to please you as well as himself, Myra."

Preparations for tea proceeded, but when Jonathan Withers and his cousin Harry returned, Rupert did not accompany them.

"He's gone to his work," said Harry. "He said that poachers don't respect Christmas Day and there's been traces of 'em in the North wood. A stern calling I grant you, but good money to it and the respect of your neighbours, though why for a game-keeper gets higher admiration than a hedge-tacker I've often felt to wonder."

Rupert had been in cheerful form and brightened the gathering. Now tea completed the party and presently the Cannifords all streamed away with many expressions of gratitude. Percy and Emmeline held their father's hands; George, the future farmer's boy, walked beside his grandmother and talked of the things he had seen in the farmyard; Susan carried her youngest in her arms. They praised the entertainment and were happy; even Harry smoking tobacco in a new pipe, declared that it was a blessing to have spent Christmas Day in the atmosphere of other people's affluence.

When they were gone and Jonathan elsewhere with his head man, Myra spoke to her daughter.

"You can wash Rupert out," she said. "I had a word with his mother. He's up to something; but it ain't you, Nora."

"That's that then," agreed the younger. "I've been tolerable sure this longful time he'd changed his mind. I'm sorry in a way. I liked his appearance and his manner of speech and a good few things about him and I—well I supposed I was growing to care for the man—just tottering on the brink, Mother; but I hadn't fallen in I'd say, and if he's decided he don't love me, then I know where I am."

"That's the way to take him, and any other young fool who doesn't know his own mind," answered the elder. "I don't run him down. I was beginning to think well of him myself; but your Aunt Jenny made it very clear to me he's off you. She don't know why and nobody's sorrier than her, but so it is, and in a case like that you've only to mind you're a Withers and have got your pride and your young life to live and plenty of time to think about a likelier man than him."

Nora nodded.

"I'm happy enough along with you," she said. "You don't want a man in your life to make you happy."

"A long sight more likely to be happy without one," answered Myra.

Elsewhere Mrs. Faircloud and her son had eaten their Christmas dinner with the baker and his wife, and when the lovers departed afterwards, Samuel and Milly discussed Timothy with his mother.

"The cleverness is there, Nelly," said Mrs. Wish. "My husband is amply satisfied with that. Your boy says remarkable things, which, I grant you, don't seem to mean anything in particular, but they couldn't be said by anybody who wasn't smart enough in his way. Only what that way is, Samuel can't exactly see, and more don't I."

"There's a lot he keeps to himself, Nelly," said Mr. Wish. "And Kate says there's a lot he keeps even from her. He's a great one for mysteries, but what a boy of his age has got to be mysterious about, perhaps you know, for be blessed if I do."

"He's a dreamer," explained Nelly. "He lives a sort of dream life of his own, Samuel. I wouldn't say there was any mysteries really; but he makes 'em up and likes to fancy they're real. He always did even in his childhood."

"He talks to himself," said Milly. "Have you ever marked that, my dear?"

"I've overheard him talking to himself," admitted Tim's mother, "but not about himself. He's took to reading a lot and he'll say things to himself he's read out of his books. Just a harmless habit."

"He's got very fine manners," declared Samuel. "What you may call style, Nelly. He eats very nice and at table he looks after the women in a very gentlemanly way. But you can't understand for your life why a man, so finical in his general behaviour, should feel content with woodman's work. Now that is a real mystery."

"And when Samuel asked him how it was, Timothy said trees were his familiar spirits, or some such stuff, and Katey told him he didn't ought to have any familiar spirit but her, and he smiled that superior smile and said she was the dryad to his oak-tree whatever that meant."

"Stuff he gets out of his books, Milly, and I wouldn't say but what he'll see, before long, that he can't live in the woods like a rabbit all his life," answered Mrs. Faircloud. "In fact, I reckon he begins to feel that himself now and again. Tell Katey to keep on at him about it. Meantime, he's learning a lot out of the parcel of books Doctor Naylor gave him."

"He's so hungry for admiration as ever," proceeded Samuel. "It's meat and drink to him to be praised, so why don't he launch out into something praiseworthy, my dear woman?"

"Sometimes," continued Milly, "Tim looks up under his eyebrows as if he was wondering about you, and Katey says he's the same even with her."

"And sometimes," summed up Samuel, "you most feel as if he was trying to pull your leg—a thing I wouldn't stand for a moment."

"I should hope not," said Nelly; "but he wouldn't do that, Sam. I've never known him exactly impertinent to anybody. It's only his way of sizing us up and wondering if he can confide in us. He's timid really, and often timid people, being at heart uncomfortable themselves, make other folk uncomfortable along with them. Just a misfortune of manner, not a real fault."

And while they debated his oddities, Timothy with Katey walked on the hills because he wanted to see the sunset.

"It's a very grand sight when the sky's tolerable clear," he said. "And the sun goes down over the forest now—at his shortest journey. It don't promise well to-night, but sometimes, at the last minute, he'll break through and say 'good-night' to the world before he dips and is gone. The sun's friendly if he knows you're friendly. He's got no brains, but he understands that us living creatures are grander than him, though so small, and he likes to feel we think well of him. They made a god of him in Egypt, Katey, and I expect that bucked him up a lot."

"Well, I make a god of you, don't I ? And very wicked it is of me," said Katey; "but you like for me to praise you better than for me to love you, I believe."

"Praise and love are all right," he answered, "yet the most tremendous thing—what I'd like best of all—is fear. I'd welcome to be feared, because then you know you've got power. You can praise a clever chap and you can love a kindly chap. The world's full of that sort; but the powerful chap—he's the one. I hated Nicholas Withers, but he was powerful—one of the proper, dauntless sort who get what they want and don't give a damn who goes under so long as they come out top. I envied his power to make me fear him. He used his power to be a beast and then—have you ever thought of that ?— then there came one more powerful still and snuffed him out. And so that tyrant man, who tramped over Priory rough-shod and terrified everybody, was only a bag of sodden bones and none went in fear of him any more."

"You can't say that. You can say God Almighty reckoned he'd lived long enough and killed him," argued Katey. "That's what was agreed upon : that he died by an accident, Tim. And an accident's the will of God every time. That's why there's such a cruel lot."

"I never agreed," he assured her. "I always held to it, and still do, that a powerfuller than Nicholas scorned the law and broke the law and killed the man. That's power—and more than power, because him that did that escaped free and nobody ever dreamed who he might have been. A very deep matter that was, with a strong brain behind it."

"Well, talk about something a bit cheerfuller for Christmas Day," she said. "There's your old sun blinking sleepy-eyed and hasting to get to bed."

"He's lazier than we are at this time of year," explained Timothy, "but he makes up for it in June, when he's up and working long before we're up and working."

Through a froth of grey cloud ran sudden red over the naked high tops of the forest. The vapours gleamed to gold and a rift of jade-green sky broke through their brief radiance; the sun signalled his farewell, sank from half circle to one bead of fire and then was gone.

"We think he sleeps, but that's our foolery," declared Timothy. "He never sleeps, else it would be the end of the world. He's always at work and now he's gone to waken up the ends of the earth. His setting for us is his rising for Australia and such like places."

"Did you enjoy father's famous mince-pies?" asked Katey. "You ate two."

"Lovely. He's a master baker. That's his power."

"You'll be a master something some day."

"I am a master something," he said.

"What would you reckon you was a master of, darling? You're my master we all know, but that don't count."

Timothy laughed.

"It's a very queer situation I'm got to, Katey. The people don't know I'm a master and I can't tell 'em."

"Can't you show 'em?"

He shook his head.

"My mastery lies in not showing 'em. If they knew, I wouldn't be a master no more."

"Can't you show me then?" she suggested. "I wouldn't tell nobody else."

"I've wondered that very thing—whether I could tell you; and then I've shut down because you might squeak."

"Talk sense and come home," said Katey. "You're a very puzzling piece of goods, Tim, and if I find you so, knowing you as I do, well may other people."

"When we're married perhaps I'll tell you where my mastery belongs. Perhaps I'll even give common people another chance to find it out if I get the proper chance myself to show it. And don't you say I'm your master, my lovely. Nobody's your master but yourself. If people love each other same as you and me, there's no talk of mastery between 'em. They're halves of a whole and if one half was to master the other half, or even try to, they wouldn't be lovers no more."

"That's sense," agreed the girl, "and I'll remember it."

"And another thing," he said. "I couldn't love you better than I do now; but if you was to know all about me, you would love me better than you do yet."

"I never, never heard you talking such a lot of muddle-headed nonsense as what you are to-night," vowed Katey. "For the Lord's sake put your arm round me and come home to tea, else they'll think we're lost, like the Babes in the Wood."

He obeyed and she spoke of everyday matters.

"Do you see much of the Canniford men?" she asked.

"Yes, I oft see 'em. Rupert's all right; Harry's the go-by-the-ground sort—just one of the powerless everyday kind."

"A bit ago I thought from what Nora Withers told me, that Rupert was after her. And I could see she was a lot interested and making up to like him. I wonder. A bit of a come-down for her I'd say, unless she really loves him."

But the subject did not interest Timothy.

"There's play-acting at Honiton to-morrow," he said. "I'm going.

Would your father let you come if I was to see you home after? I didn't name it to him—too doubtful."

"Not doubtful at all. They don't hold with that sort of thing and I don't feel to care about it, Tim. You can tell me how you fared after."

"I don't reckon I'll like it myself," he said, "but it's a chance to see play-actors, which I never have done. I play-act to myself sometimes when I'm working and say speeches out of Shakespeare. And then I feel myself like the man who made the speech."

"You go then, and get some other chap to walk home with you after. It's a tidy long way to Honiton."

"I enjoy to be alone in the night-time. So does Rupert Canniford."

"In his business you've got to be a bit of a night-bird; but not in yours."

"He has owl's eyes, Rupert has. A great gift for him. But I can see by night very well myself."

"Why should you want to? You're a day creature, same as me," said Katey. "I ain't feared of the dark, but I wish the lamps would come to Priory all the same. There's talk of 'em."

They went back to the baker's and found tea awaiting them. Then the little party broke up and Timothy returned home with his mother. He spoke of Rupert and told Mrs. Fairclold what he had heard.

"Would you say it was a good thing for him to marry Nora Withers?" he asked.

"Couldn't tell you, Tim. I don't know much about either of 'em. Mr. Withers liked his daughter very well, but he hadn't no use for the Canni-fords."

"Another thing has been said, Mother: that Honeywood, the market-gardener, wants to marry Mrs. Canniford but hangs fire a bit. I heard it at the 'Pen-in-Hand'."

"Between ourselves, Tim, I gave Jenny Canniford a tip on that subject—quite private," murmured his mother. "Yes, I stopped her, and told her she might be wise to see Mercy Grepe if in her opinion Peter Honeywood wanted a push."

Nelly laughed at a recollection.

"She was a good bit startled when I talked to her; but I think she must have understood that I hadn't anything to gain. Whether she ever went to Mercy I couldn't tell you, but nothing don't seem to have come of it if she did."

"There's a spot of power in 'Mother Forty Cats'," declared Timothy. "I'm quick to see power in anybody, but where does a frail, old atomy like Mercy Grepe come by her power? You hear the people grant she's got something they have not. What is it? It hasn't made her anywhere noticeable."

"She's above wanting to be noticeable," said Nelly. "That's her fineness, that she don't care two pence for the things most folk care about. Money and goods mean nothing to her, but she's always ready and willing to help anybody. That's her power. She only asks to live so long as she can be useful and she's got a lot of wisdom hid from most, but always at their service. And a woman, with a point of view like that and gifts same as Mercy has got, is so uncommon rare that any fool can see it and respect her and give her her best."

"There's witches in Shakespeare. Powerful witches, too, that work their tricks on common folk and drive 'em to do murders. There's what you may call good murders done in Shakespeare and what you may call bad murders, Mother."

But Nelly was not interested in murder.

"Come to think of it, Mrs. Wish told me something about Jenny Canniford that sounded as if she'd taken my advice and seen Miss Grepe after all," she said. "They're whispering now how the widow looks to have got two strings to her bow and is often seen having a tell with Paul Pook. And if Honeywood was in proper earnest about her, you'd think that ought to quicken him up, for fear he lost her."

"Pook's a damn sight finer man than that little, round-about chap," Timothy told her. "Pook rides to hounds and is well thought upon by the quality. And Mr. Withers thought well upon him, too, else he wouldn't have left him his splendid horse. Mr. Withers wouldn't have looked twice at Peter Honeywood."

"There wasn't many he troubled to look at twice; but I don't know a thing about it. Perhaps we shall hear the gardener's mustered up courage to ask Jenny; or perhaps we shall hear she's given him the slip and took the saddler."

"Maybe Mercy Grepe knows," suggested Timothy. "Not that it matters a lot what a parcel of old fossils may decide to do."

"Jenny's no fossil," answered his mother, "and the men are both well to do and would lift her out of her poor circumstances."

In truth Jenny herself could have thrown no light for any confidante, because her own experiences and the course of her experiment had but entangled her in further complications, some of exceedingly disturbing nature. She had kept her promise to Peter and drunk tea with him on a week-day at his comfortable dwelling beside his land; but yet again she had found her hopes of a climax postponed. He was still labouring under considerable annoyance, spoke a great many edged words, obviously aimed at Paul Pook, and adopted a minatory attitude to herself. He had even hinted at a disappointment in the difficult business of reading human nature.

"Even our nearest and faithfullest and best understood friends will sometimes flash out with a side of their characters we didn't know was there and cause us a proper pang," he had said, and then proceeded, by implication, to let Jenny know she was responsible for his discomfort. The meal he had furnished was indifferent and compared ill with those she had prepared for him, while the entertainment as a whole proved bleak and unsatisfactory. She felt secretly indignant, did not even trouble to regret his alleged disappointment and revealed no warmth whatever.

"A woman," so Mr. Honeywood had said, "if she finds herself drawn to any outstanding man, did ought to put him on a pedestal all alone, and there shouldn't be no other man but him on or near that pedestal in my opinion."

And Jenny had answered somewhat tartly.

"Pedestals be meant for statues of dead men, not for living ones, and I wouldn't say at this moment, Peter, as I've got any particular, outstanding man asking for no pedestal."

Since then, however, things had resumed their even tenor; the market gardener continued to visit her as usual and behaved as usual, sometimes indicating that the vital word was upon his tongue, at other times revealing general doubts as to the married state and once going so far as to say that, if you found yourself devoted to a female, the truest kindness might be preservation of a platonic affection and consequent continued respect. When he had seen her with Mr. Pook, or heard reports of such a meeting, Peter was austere and remote; at other times, if no disquieting rumours had reached his ear, he resumed the old friendly and cordial relations; but now had come and passed another Christmas and Jenny's heart fainted. Indeed a far more distracting experience than Honeywood's diversity of moods began to confront her, for the contrast between the saddler and her adorer threatened to create increasing inroads upon Mrs. Canniford's peace. Paul she well knew was only pretending and, indeed, had confessed in private that he began to weary of the business; but even in his present, simulated role, her better and closer acquaintance with Mr. Pook had deeply impressed Jenny. She found in him a quality of calm and restraint that Peter lacked, and more than that: there were occasional indications that Paul felt a measure of genuine good will to herself that made her very thoughtful. Defying Honeywood, she had asked his pretended rival to come to tea yet again; and he had come and uttered a warning.

"Dammy!" said Paul, "we're going it, ain't we, my dear? We must watch out we don't over-do this nonsense, else our play-acting might end in earnest."

"Not on my side it won't," Jenny answered; and that had vexed the saddler somewhat, for, as she had long discovered, a man's a man. But knowing her ally for ever committed to widowhood, she felt no fear, or wish to unsettle his resolves.

Yet Jenny unconsciously continued to contrast Peter with Paul, a depressing mental occupation. Rupert, who had perceived the drift of affairs but was ignorant of the secret behind them, openly made a comparison much in favour of the sportsman.

"If Pook's after you, Mother," he once said in his brutal fashion, "you'll do very clever to give Tubby a miss. Pook's worth a hundred of him and don't dance about all dolled up with his trinkets like a barbary ape. He's a man, and good value I'd say for an old bird like you."

"There's things you didn't ought to dare to open your mouth about, Rupert, and that's one of 'em," she answered. "You don't talk much to me best of times, and the less the better if you trample in like that where angels would fear to tread. It's well known that Paul Pook don't take another wife and if old friends can't continue so to be without aspersions thrown on 'em, more shame to the people."

IX

THE supporters of the 'Pen-in-Hand' were used to give an annual concert early in every new year and always strove to furnish some novelties when the occasion returned. But the choir of glee-singers had ever been a backbone to

32

these entertainments and they were now rehearsing industriously under their conductor, Mr. Joseph Bowring, an old and energetic musician, who for forty years had played the organ at Priory Wesleyan Chapel. Timothy had joined the singers and was welcome, while on hearing his adult voice, the master of the proceedings invited the young man to sing a solo. To Katey's delight and at her urgent prompting he agreed and was busy learning a Shakespearean lyric, to be sung to an ancient melody. In season and out Timothy practised his solo, singing it at home to his mother, in the forest to the trees and woodmen, and under the tuition of the old organist. As the time approached, he became a little nervous and hated himself for being so. His Christmas outing on Boxing Day at Honiton had interested him no little; but the business of the theatre awoke no answering thrill. He felt that he would have enjoyed the play—a Sheridan comedy—better if he had read it to himself in the quiet of his home.

He sang well enough at the concert and received a friendly greeting; but another local man—a day labourer with no great voice and abundance of humour—received a much greater ovation and, for encore, gave the audience a popular music-hall ditty which awakened enthusiasm. The incident spoiled Timothy's pleasure and opened his eyes. He was satisfied with his reception until the other man sang; then he perceived the difference. He sulked to his mother when they went home together and asked her why the people liked the feeble fun of the comedian more than his own effort; but Nelly told him not to be foolish.

"What d'you think?" she said. "Laughter was welcome, because little offered for laughter in the glee singers and piano playing, and the vicar's reading. And there was nothing to laugh at in your song, except when Miss Wilson didn't get off sharp enough in the second verse. That amused them, though it didn't ought. But when a crowd of all sorts comes together for a bit of amusement, they want to laugh. Everybody wants to laugh sometimes—hungers to let themselves go and have a good shout. So, when Arthur Tanner, with his funny face and funny song, gave 'em a chance to bawl a bit, they jumped at it."

Timothy regarded this explanation moodily and at a later time found Katey of his mother's opinion.

"You was high-class, Tim, and I heard a man near me and mother in the audience say how you'd got a very sympathetic voice if it was trained," she told him. "But low-class folk like us ain't educated up to being high-class, and you know how thankful you always feel to anybody who can make you laugh. I wish you was more of a laugher yourself sometimes, though perhaps you don't think laughing is very high-class in itself."

"Them that laugh a lot mostly laugh at nothing," he said. "I've noticed that. I can laugh as well as the next one when there's anything worth laughing at. And that's jolly seldom."

"There's different sorts of fun, of course," she agreed. "What amuses people most in the world is to hear tell about other people in a cruel mess. Everybody roars at that, especially if they're comfortable themselves. And the funniest thing of all is to hear somebody laugh at himself in a mess. Then

D

your heart goes out to him.   You yell with laughter, but all the time you wish you could lend him a hand."

"I'm more what they call a strong, silent man myself," he said, "but if I'd heard that chap say my voice wanted training, I'd have told him it was trained."

"Would you say that, Tim?"

"Trained all I want it to be.   If I ordained to make my living by it, that's different; but I don't.   To live by singing at concerts before a lot of everyday people would drive me silly."

"Yet you face up to people better than you did.   To get up and sing before a lot of folk that have paid sixpence each to hear you is a pretty brave thing and I was pleased to see you do it," Katey assured him.   "And far ways the most beautiful object in the hall I thought you."

She had wondered whether the stage play at Honiton would attract him, but felt rather relieved to find it had not; for other girls often told her that, with a face like his, her lover might want to be an actor some day. He explained, however, that it was not so.

"You've got to pretend you're somebody else all the time," he said.   "In one play you've got to pretend you're wicked and in another you've got to pretend you're a saint.   I don't want to pretend I'm anything but myself. I like reading about the heroes and villians and heroines and what they're up against; but my own life is a lot more interesting to me than anything I read about other peoples' lives."

"I couldn't feel like that," confessed Katey.   "Your life and father's and mother's lives, and the children's lives—they all look to be a lot more interesting to me than my own."

At the 'Pen-in-Hand,' when the concert was over, many of the choristers assembled to consider their achievements, and Arthur Tanner received full measure of applause.

"You was top hole, Arthur," said Mr. Toozey.   "You brightened up the show, which dragged a bit to tell truth.   I'd say if you'd come of an acting family instead of a navvy family, you might have figured very well on the stage."

"I've seen a lot of merry men in the circus of old that wasn't half so merry nor yet so funny as what you can be, Arthur," declared Ned Piper, the sexton. "It takes something a long shot out of the common to make my wife laugh, but she did to-night.   Never seen her in a better temper."

"Laughter's prone to put you in a good temper," said Toozey.   "That's what we find so soothing to it, Ned.   It may leave you aching in queer places, but it makes you happy for the minute and feeling kinder to the world at large."

Dr. Naylor was in the bar and praised the concert.

"A very good show and much to your credit, Joseph," he declared. "You got the best out of the material and showed how good the material was. Congratulate you, Joe."

Old Mr. Bowring rose from his seat by the fire and bowed.

"Thank you, Doctor.   Yes, the boys did remarkably well—a good concert—one of the best I remember."

"What did you think of young Faircloud, Mr. Bowring?" asked Toozey.

"He was all right, but can't forget himself when he's singing, William," answered the musician. "A good tenor voice with that nice quality that always wins a welcome. Many better voices than his just lack that unconscious something which wakens sympathy. A subtle thing. You can't teach it, of course, and it doesn't belong to the singer's character, but just something in his vocal chords. I've heard great voices that hadn't got it— grand voices powerful enough to sing against brass—and I've heard other voices that weren't so wonderful, but didn't lack that precious something that appeals. Timothy's got it, and when his voice broke, it came out in his proper voice."

"He had something in his boy's voice, too," said Toozey.

"He had," agreed Naylor. "Just that unearthly treble you hear now and again that touches your heartstrings as no grown-up voice, however beautiful, can touch 'em. Sang like an angel and looked like one now and then."

"But it's just an accident and not part of the young man himself in Faircloud's case," declared Bowring.

"Tim's what they call an egotist," he continued, "and I wouldn't say there was much outside himself really interests him."

"Not an artist?" asked the doctor.

"A bit of an artist, but a difficult fellow. Takes rather a mournful view of life—prickly. He sang very well in the glees—better than in his solo," answered the old musician.

Then Naylor spoke.

"When you come to bed-rock," he argued, "there's not much outside our selves really challenges any of us. Our interests may be large or small, but we are the centre of 'em. 'Egotist' is the right word for Timothy as you say, Bowring. And the mischief with his sort is that egotism often leads to pessimism—taking a black view of things in general, especially if your own affairs don't prosper too well."

"You can't prophesy much about a boy of that age," suggested Bowring, "but he's got an active mind."

"He's unstable, like most lads and you can't predict when he'll steady down, but I hope he will," summed up Naylor. "To be wrapped up in yourself is bad, and pessimism is bad, because it leads nowhere and is unfruitful for yourself and everybody else."

"This here egotism ain't unfruitful in itself, Doctor," suggested the landlord. "There's some only live to feather their own nests and do it very clever."

Harry Canniford's melancholy voice supported Mr. Toozey. He had been to the concert with his wife and Jonathan and Nora Withers, and turned into the bar afterwards.

"That's right. Look at my brother, Rupert. What you may call an own-self man if ever there was one—always out for Number One and making a success of it. And for my part I say and will maintain for us that put others before ourselves, life is terrible after you're grown up. I was happy enough when I was a boy—not since."

"Well, don't cry about it," snapped Ned Piper. "What's the matter with your life ?.. A good, patient partner and plenty of children and plenty of work. What more do you want, Harry ?"

"We say 'Yea' to life, or 'No' to life," Naylor told them. "You can divide people into two classes. We're built to say 'Yea' or 'No' and carry on according; but to say 'No' is to refuse to pull your weight. Never you say 'No,' Harry, for all good sense prompts us to say 'Yes.' The motives may be good or bad, but England stands where she stands by saying 'Yes' and getting on with it. There are nations that say 'No' and go down. Set your heart on something, Harry. Useless to whimper."

"You wonder why you was born now and again, all the same, Doctor," protested the hedger and ditcher.

"We all do that, my dear chap. Men have been wondering why they was born ever since they had wits to wonder with."

"Any fool will find a reason for something his heart's set upon no doubt," agreed the old organist. "If you've had a good time off and on and followed your bent, then you can allow at the end that your life was worth living. Music made my life worth living. Fox-hunting and saddler's work made Pook's life worth living; doctoring and curing people made the doctor's life worth living; selling good beer to his neighbours made William's life worth living. So you could go round. In a word useful work makes your life worth living."

"Some say work's the snag that don't make life worth living," asserted Toozey; "and some get a sudden experience that will change all their opinions in a single night, like the Light that shone on Saint Paul, and make all their opinions go down the wind at a breath. Human nature's full of surprises like that. You can't count for stability in young or old when they get hit on a raw spot. Take Nathan Goodenough, Colonel Tomlinson's head gardener at 'The Elms.' Most curious thing ever I heard—how a kind act will lead to perdition."

"What's Goodenough done ?" asked Ned Piper, and Toozey filled some empty glasses, then told them.

"Changed his point of view: that's what he's done, Ned. And why? Along of a rich gift, which in all reason ought have made him thank the giver, but did the opposite and turned him against the giver. You'd say that's a riddle beyond solving, so 'twas. And I'll tell you the gift first, and then what it done in the queer mind of Goodenough. To begin with Mrs. Woodrow, the laundress, and a better woman never walked, had a most unfortunate accident with the colonel's new winter pants. They was extra thick and fine, such as the colonel favours in winter. Well, Mrs. Woodrow came to fearful grief with the things and shrunk 'em out of all knowledge and belief. She ruined 'em in a word and owned up bravely to her error and Colonel Tomlinson forgave her—like the good Christian he is. And then he minded Nathan in his kindly fashion and reckoned his under pants, though lost to him, might very well serve his gardener a turn, him being a six foot man himself, but Nat little more than five. So Goodenough gets the garment and no doubt he expressed his gratitude properly enough at the time."

"What's contrary to human nature in that ?" asked Piper. "Who'd have done different, Bill ?"

"Wait," continued Toozey. "The surprising thing followed. Come a proper cold morning, his wife put out the pants and Goodenough got in 'em and was amazed to fell the richness and the warmth and comfort of such high-class stuff. Of course they were beyond anything in his experience and he marvelled to find how good he felt in 'em and how they helped him to stand to work. All went very well seemingly till Mrs. Goodenough took 'em away from him to wash and then, back in a pair of his own unders, the Devil tempted Nathan in a manner of speaking, and he asked himself why the hell there should be such a mort of difference between what he was used to wear and what the colonel was used to wear. 'All men are equal in the sight of God,' he said, 'so why should my pants be so thin as a winter hedge and the colonel's pants overflowing with fatness and heat ?' His wife couldn't tell him the answer to that and now the man's gratitude have turned into envy and he says it was an eye-opener to show how shameful the poor are treated ! And so, from being a peaceful man, Nathan's leapt up into a fiery Bolshie ! Which all shows you how evil may come out of good and the fantastic ways that people behave."

"Them pants acted on him like a poison," commented Piper. "An eye-opener, as you say, and an eye-opener for Colonel Tomlinson, too. He won't much like that if it gets to his ears."

"He don't," said Harry Canniford. "It have got to his ears and he don't like it. My wife knows Goodenough's wife and she's afraid of her life the colonel will take action; then Nathan will get another eye-opener yet and maybe find his job gone."

"Human nature's full of things like that," declared the old organist. "Human nature's a devil's cauldron one day and you despair of it; then the next day, it's bursting with promise and making a good contribution to progress. You'll get a bloody war full of horrors to-day, and to-morrow Handel writes his 'Messiah'."

"Just according whether we let Reason rule over us, or turn our backs on Reason," suggested the doctor. "When Reason gets a free hand, which is mighty seldom, then you'll see progress, Bowring; but when we quarrel, with less instinct than the beasts, and fly at each other's throats, then we go backwards again. If you look at the things we are most thankful for, you'll see that use of our reason was responsible for most of them."

"Yet I've heard parson preach how our reason's a snare and isn't always to be trusted," said Mr. Toozey.

Upon this thorny problem fell the hour of closing time, while elsewhere during that self-same January night, there might have been observed another dawning example of human nature's bewildering ways. Given a knowledge of cause, doubtless most mysteries cease to be anything but natural effect: the inevitable result of activities that created them; and even without such explanation, we are often quite content to welcome the fascination of mystery in itself and may resent the cause responsible for it, should that appear. Rupert Canniford, during the course of this evening, created foundations for such a mystery; but from the hour when his perplexing performance challenged his neighbours, to the day that linked cause with effect, and all understood, a lengthy period extended.

The game-keeper, though at leisure on the evening of the concert, did not attend it. Music had never struck a chord to enlighten his spirit and was little likely to do so; neither did he wait outside the concert hall to see his mother home after the entertainment. Yet he was outside when the audience emerged and thinned away, and his eye skilled to see in the darkness, found no difficulty in recognising a solitary female figure. It was Ivy Pook, who came to the concert and now prepared to return home. Had she been accompanied, Rupert might have abstained from approaching; but now he did so, waited till she was free from the little crowd, then quickly joined her, much to the girl's surprise. They knew each other and had met not seldom at the Manor during past days when chance brought Rupert to the servants' hall; but no friendship existed between them. Indeed the man was apt to jest at Ivy's expense behind her back; while she remembered how he suffered imprisonment and always declared that only the Christian charity of her old mistress had saved him from destruction. He never was among the males who wakened any ray of interest in Paul Pook's daughter and she had even been heard to doubt whether his reformation, though so far steadfast, would prove enduring.

And now he overtook her two hundred yards from her home and greeted her in friendly fashion.

"Good evening, Miss Pook," he said. "You'll wonder who 'tis in the dark, but I can see in the dark myself and I felt sure 'twas you. We haven't met this longful time now; but we often talk of you at the Manor. I'm Rupert Canniford."

"I mind your voice, now," answered Ivy. "I haven't been up over just lately, though I find myself welcomed when I do go."

"I should think you would. I always felt you was the leader after Alfred Bodkin—the butler. He's going by the way—retiring. But not until Lady Garland passes out."

"I knew 'twas in his mind to do so," she said. "When her ladyship dies the new master will come into command and Mr. Bodkin don't care about him and never did."

"Why not?" asked Rupert. "He's a very good sportsman and very well liked by us out-of-door people."

"The outdoor point of view is different from the indoor point of view," answered Ivy.

"That's a clever thought," declared young Canniford. "And no doubt a true one. You indoor people see more of an employer than what we do. A man may be a good shot and yet not a nice chap to wait upon."

"My father thinks well of him also from the outdoor point of view," continued Ivy. "He's met the gentleman in the hunting-field and says he's an excellent fox-hunter and may come to be Master of the Hounds one day."

"I lay he don't ride so well as Mr. Pook," declared Rupert. "I'm no rider myself, but I know a fine horseman when I see him. I expect your governor's mightly glad to get you home again."

Secretly amazed, yet not ungratified by such unexpected interest, Ivy replied:

"It was my duty. I could have gone to a very great lady if I'd minded to when I left my dear mistress; but I felt it was time I went into private life and looked after Mr. Pook. And I found it was more than time, for he'd got into a good bit of a trough and a lot called for doing. A man slips into untidy ways terrible quick and untidy ways means an untidy mind."

"I couldn't live with an untidy mind myself," he said. "Nought saves time like tidiness I find. We bachelors are mostly tidier than married men in my experience. A man happily married gets such a lot done for him."

Ivy considered this and approved it.

"A proper wife would naturally take pride in seeing her husband's comforts were watched over," she said.

"So she would, and a decent husband would be properly grateful and do his part to reward her. Between father and daughter the case is altered, yet I can say from my own experience, between mother and son, I show my mother I'm grateful in every way I can."

Ivy planted a barb—an art at which she excelled. As yet she felt no personal interest in Rupert.

"That ain't the general opinion about you," she said. "I've heard one or two tell—no matter who—that you're a bit hard on your mother, and close as wax."

Somewhat disconcerted, the other answered.

"I'm sorry to know that. I ain't the sort to boast, but you won't hear my mother say I'm a bad son, Ivy, and I would be properly sorry to think you thought I was. I'm not one to care a lot what other folk think of me. A good game-keeper, which I claim to be, cares nought as to other opinions so long as his master and his conscience are on his side. But now and then you catch yourself hoping this person or that thinks well of you, and I'm always glad to know your father thinks well of me, same as I do of him."

"I never heard him say nothing against you, nor yet for you."

"He wouldn't to you. Why should he? But it's a tolerable good rule to come to man or woman with an open mind and not let the folk decide you whether you're going to like them or not."

"Which I always do," said Ivy, "and shall so continue."

"It's the only honest, fair way. But difficult for people when they spare a thought on me. Because, you see, I did wrong when I was a bit younger. Got under a bad influence and did wrong. And was very properly punished for it."

Acute suspicion wakened in Ivy's breast. This did not sound in the least like what she had always imagined Rupert Canniford to be, and once fixed impressions concerning a fellow-creature have been entertained, it needs massive evidence to shake them. However, the fact that a young man was walking beside her and talking seriously to her went some way to unsettle the listener's judgment.

"You made good after, by all accounts," she said.

"I tried; but nought clings so close to you as being locked up. Once you've been in clink, Miss Pook, that's the thing that sticks in people's memory, and no matter how straight you go after, you'll never shake it off while there's anybody alive to remember it."

Didactic by nature, Ivy improved the shining hour.

"A person's wickedness holds your mind a tidy sight longer than a person's goodness," she admitted, "because back-sliders is such common objects; but you can only go on showing the past have buried the past, Mr. Canniford. Then, if you don't back-slide, the folk'll come to believe it."

"You're pretty wise seemingly," he admitted, "and I hope you're right. If you know yourself going straight and trying your best to make good, then you don't worry so much about what other people think. Inspector Chard knows I'm all right and our head keeper knows I'm all right. So do my relations, and I'd very much like to think your father and you felt to trust me. I'm a lonely man you see, as them in my trade are apt to be."

"I've always felt myself," she said, "that if your conscience is clear and gives you no reminders, then other people don't matter such a lot. You naturally wish to stand well where you belong; but I've always felt, while I knew myself to be doing my duty in every particular, that nobody didn't ought to ask me to do more."

"You certainly did no less in your career at the Manor," he replied. "But my duty, as it looks to me, often don't seem to be quite the same as it looks to other people. Have you ever marked that ?"

"Yes I have—very often indeed," she answered. "Even in my own father's case, since I came home to minister to him, time and again him and me don't see eye to eye as regards my duty to him. But none-the-less I do it."

"I'll bet you do."

"Yes, I do. There's such a thing as entertaining angels unawares, Mr. Canniford, and though I wouldn't set up for being an angel or any such creation as that, yet I do what I may. I wouldn't say I entertain my father, and a lot he does—silly habits and such—don't entertain me; but I do my duty and trust him to see where I'm right and he's mistook in fullness of time."

"He will, Ivy—if I may call you Ivy," prophesied Rupert. "Such a fine man as Mr. Pook knows good sense when he sees it. It takes time for us men to realise what a good woman can do for us. Now I must get home and hear what mother thought of the concert. Did you like it ?"

"Yes—a very good concert, Mr. Canniford."

"Call me Rupert next time we chance to meet," he begged. "Good night and good luck."

The game-keeper vanished into the darkness and Ivy returned home, mildly excited at an event so unusual. Instinct opposed suspicion in her mind. Affable conversation with a young male had stimulated her desire for a partner; while the fact that she had long shared a general distrust of Rupert among her friends tended to check any lenient leanings in his particular direction.

She prepared supper on returning home and when Paul appeared at half past ten o'clock, Ivy had already eaten hers, but remained to look after him. It was indeed a feature of her attention that she always accompanied his meals—a source of private irritation to her father, who had long been accustomed to eat them alone and hated modification of his table manners.

She told him of her recent experience.

"Fell in with Rupert Canniford coming back from the concert," she said.

"Music not much in his line I expect. Didn't know you knew the man," answered Paul.

"Oh yes. The outdoor people came and went at the Manor. We was well acquainted enough to pass the time of day."

"A very good game-keeper and clever in wood-craft, Rupert is. Otherwise I don't know. Hard outside and downy inside they say."

"I keep an empty mind myself about people," said Ivy. "By their works you shall know them. He was in a serious mood and seemed pleased to talk. He opened up a bit about himself and reckoned his misfortune in the past is still remembered against him. He seemed to think nothing was harder to forget about a man than that he'd once been reached by the arm of the Law."

"I shouldn't have thought that was likely to weigh with him," answered the saddler.

"He wants the good opinion of some of us," continued Ivy, "but don't fret about that of the folk in general. He's pleased to think you believe in him for one; and I told him, if his conscience was satisfied he was doing his duty, that's all that matters. He said he was a lonely man by the nature of his trade."

Mr. Pook made no comment on these remarks, but asked about the concert. He did not, however, forget his daughter's experience and a day or two later, when Mrs. Canniford, still faintly pursuing her deception, came into his shop, he mentioned it to her.

Jenny was depressed and had dropped in to chronicle the fact.

"He took his tea with me again last night," she said, "but he didn't bring no vegetables and there was nothing doing. He said he'd seen you on your horse going fox-hunting and wondered how you could spare such a lot of time away from your work. Always has a dig at you like that. Then he got friendly as usual and praised me and himself and thought it was wondrous how we saw alike and so on. But, as I say, nothing doing, and all we have done by the looks of it is to make him hate you."

"That don't matter," he assured her. "I'm all right, but, so far as Honeywood's concerned, I doubt we can do any more. Our friendship suited me very well, Jenny, and I enjoyed it for itself; but it isn't advancing the good cause, if he's not getting forwarder."

"It's done just the opposite," she confessed, "because, without any effort on your part, Paul, and just in the natural course of our pretence, you've thrown a light on Peter and showed me more about the man than my affection for him brought to my notice. The last thing you'd have wanted to do, or me expected; but there it is—just where you happen to be strong, Honeywood's prone to be weak. And I believe he knows it and that's made him nasty where you're concerned. You do get jealous of people if you know they're wiping your eye in a tender quarter, and seeing you riding a horse—a thing he couldn't do for his life—and knowing you're a finer man and better preserved than what he is at the waist-line and so on—it all mounts up into a grievance."

"That's quite all right; but what's the use if it don't spur the fool? What does he want?"

"I'd say he wants me at his own good time, whenever that may hap to be; but the ugly fact is, Paul, that little by little, I begin to feel I don't want him so much as I did. I want him, of course, and peace with honour, as they say; but not to the same pressing extent as what I did want him."

"In that case I've done more harm than good," he said. "A pity; but not my fault, Jenny."

"More you might say my misfortune than your fault. Yet maybe a blessing in disguise. You've shown up, by accident so to say, the weak spots in Peter's character, and now, if he ever rises to it and offers, I may be able to show them to him and help him mend 'em."

"The weak spot is so weak that it's enough to make you lose heart about him," declared Paul. "I don't pretend to understand the man and I'd dearly like to talk straight to him and, if nothing comes of it and he's finally down and out and got his dismissal from you, then I will talk straight to him and show him the born fool he was. In the meantime we can go on as we're going a bit longer I suppose. Though I don't like it too well."

"I've confessed to Myra," Jenny told him. "'Twas against the grain to keep any secrets from her and I never was one for secrets in any case. She's not particular helpful, be it as it may, because she don't know why the mischief I want another husband for. She grants I was fortunate in Canniford, but can't see much in Honeywood except his money. She agreed it was uncommon kind of you to lend a hand. Only she pointed out that, as the world knows you never ordain to take another, there wasn't any reason to think Peter would feel you made any difference."

· "There's something in that. Perhaps he don't," agreed Paul. "In which case our trouble's wasted."

"He wouldn't be so venomous against you if we hadn't touched him up," she said and Pook changed the subject.

"What's this I hear from Ivy?" he asked. "Sounds to me that Rupert's been telling her a parcel of lies. And he's not one to put himself about unless there's something to gain by doing so."

"Why should he put himself about to tell lies to your girl?" asked Jenny. "He hasn't named her name to me."

"All I've heard about him was from Myra last time I was at Pigslake. She said that Rupert looked to be after Nora."

"That's off," explained Jenny. "I think he was for a bit; but he changed his mind in that quarter. He's personable, Rupert is, and though the folk say it's only the men run after good looks, I can tell you a handsome man often wins a girl's heart, just because he's got a nice face and long legs."

"I was only wondering to hear Ivy take such a broad-minded view of him and why he'd stopped to speak to her," explained Paul. "Perhaps he'll tell you when he hears she spoke favourable of him. But there's nothing to Ivy worth his attention or any other man's attention. I wish there was."

Mrs. Canniford well knew that Ivy belonged to a type that awoke little save ribaldry from her son; but she questioned him on the following day and found him serious, though apparently uninterested.

"Ran up against her after the 'Pen-in-Hand' concert," he said. "Couldn't but speak a word, because we knew one another in a fashion when she was at the Manor. I'm rather sorry for girls like that. Plenty of common sense and good workers, but nothing more."

"She's always been wishful to find a husband and haven't thrown over hope yet I gather," answered Jenny.

"She's going to be disappointed I expect. Still a good, useful woman, as women go, and may satisfy somebody yet."

"To want to be married and find you can't is a very painful situation," declared Jenny. "It's a situation few men have got to face, because almost any man can pick up a female, if he's got the power to offer her a decent home. But Ivy with her poor looks and creeking voice, like them corncrakes, has only her fine feelings for duty and her faithful nature to offer a man. But men, especially young men, want more than that."

"I'd say they mostly do. Perhaps somebody will fetch along presently who's deaf and blind, and try for her. I see her good points all right."

"She'd wear very well," admitted Jenny, "but few would like to feel they was going to live their lives along with that sort of pattern. And she'd last for ever. She's the sort that's never young and never old. They go on, like a 'grandfather' clock, years and years."

"Good staying powers, no doubt."

"Yes, they have. Something few men have got. If Ivy was to marry by any outside chance, she'd long outlive her husband I expect—unless the man's patience got exhausted and he was to forget himself and do her a fatal injury."

Rupert stared.

"Well, I never! Fancy you harbouring such a thought as that!" he exclaimed. "I'm ashamed of you."

"I ain't harbouring nothing, my dear. I never was a harbourer. I'm only saying what might overtake poor Ivy if she married the wrong sort of man; and as, with her longings in that direction, she'd jump at any sort of man, you see there might come a day——"

"Does Paul Pook set much store by her?" asked Rupert.

"He used to when she was at the Manor and only came and went. But not so much now she's come home for good and made him her duty. A grown-up daughter over him gives Pook all the misery of changing his bachelor ways and none of the compensations a wife have got to offer."

"Well you ought to know," admitted her son. "Perhaps that's why your market-gardener hangs fire such a lot. Belike 'Tubby' weighs his comforts and freedom against his poor, old, patient lady friend."

Mrs. Canniford flushed.

"Love you as I do, Rupert," she said, "I've never heard a man so coarse in his speech as you can sink to be now and again."

X

WITH Spring a new pattern was woven into the texture of some lives in Priory, developing designs that challenged others. According to custom, change and movement were created by the activities of the young, while middle-aged carried the chief burden of life and assured its progress and advancement, and the old abode in their cubby-holes, only to awaken fleeting comment when they left them for the grave. Not that those of mature years and experience confronted no excitements and challenges; but they were trained by life to keep their affairs to themselves, or among themselves; and it was the young who gave evidence of most lively intention and cared not what comments their elders might be pleased to offer.

Timothy Faircloud for example revealed to his mother that a concentration of his faculties and a dawn of abiding interest began to awaken for him. The change was gradual but began to furnish evidence of a new outlook and orientation. It could not alter his disposition or quality; it never for a moment shook his steadfast affection for his sweetheart; but it dominated his days and filled his leisure. It qualified his devotion to out-door labour and largely unsettled his vague and ineffectual opinions. He became an industrious and inveterate reader, developed a thirst for literature and welcomed new books. Such illumination could not be concealed. Indeed Timothy made no effort to conceal it. He was proud of it and loved to give evidence of his new learning and widening horizons. Here opened a new channel for the attention of other people, a fresh opportunity to win the personal attention he desired above all else. But something still persisted beyond these evidences of growth—a sense of past achievement hidden in his mind that supported and comforted him by its knowledge, yet troubled him for the reason that it could never be imparted to another, or reward claimed in shape of applause. This his mother dimly appreciated and his sweetheart more certainly knew. Katey felt that these comforting memories still supported him, yet some inhibition prevailed to prevent particulars being spoken; but what they were and why any outstanding achievement on his part should be hidden from her, she could never guess. Not seldom his approaches to these concealed performances had much mystified her, for it was impossible to connect them with any action in the young man's competence; yet gloomy and tragic considerations often occupied his rambling utterance. He would speak of sinister events, remote indeed from himself, yet justifying the evil doers, and explain that crime might be fruitful of good, given a high motive to commit it. He declared Shakespeare's support of this contention and told Katey that, if you knew where to look in books, you would find that right and wrong were but interchangeable words signifying the point of view and having no relation to reality. He often muddled himself in his endeavours to define the subject of his thoughts, and he never failed to confuse the simple material of Katey's innocent and mother-taught mind; but she loved him not the less for his fruitless reflections and was always glad when he abandoned them and returned to the pleasanter topic of themselves. Much he revealed that she was able to carry happily enough to her parents; for it had now become established that Timothy was resolved to abandon the life of a woodman. This he announced and gleaned satisfaction from the general applause that greeted his intentions; but as yet his purpose for the future was hidden; and whether he knew it himself remained a matter of doubt. Mrs. Faircloud could throw no light upon the subject neither could his betrothed; but Nelly inclined to believe that her son as yet had no definite ideas.

"Something will come to him out of his eternal books some day," she told Mrs. Wish, "and then we'll know. What it may be I couldn't tell you, but if it points to him going away from Priory, then I shall go along with him."

"So long as there's money to it and a respectable calling, all will be well," agreed Katey's mother. "But it will soon be getting time for him to think upon our girl's future home and his powers to support her in it. They can't start without them."

"So I tell him," agreed Nelly. "and he's well alive to it."

But while Timothy's dynamic promise interested his own alone, the rumoured enterprise of another native son was of a sort to challenge a larger audience and raise more active doubts. For at this season there winged a whisper hinting at activities, so amazingly improbable, that it was long before any, familiar with the character and reputation of Rupert Canniford, felt disposed to credit them. They stole as rumours will, through holes and corners, by way of key-holes and entrances unguessed into the conversation of gossips and intelligencers, first to be laughed at, then to be listened to, presently to take substance and solidify until finally attaining their place among accepted and authentic facts. In such a case few presume to question the implicated parties themselves and, when the story gathered weight and busy people were prepared to prove and quote good evidence that Rupert was keeping company, Priory waited in patience until he himself, or the object of his devotion, should proclaim their conclusions.

A side-light will serve to introduce the game-keeper's incomprehensible romance, for there came a stage of development when the lady felt need for inspiration and suppprt. Then met two women who had never met before; but while one knew all about the elder, the other was only aware of her visitor's existence and ignorant of all else. Ivy Pook, however, shared her father's estimate of Mercy Grepe, for Paul greatly esteemed her, and though his daughter might claim a measure of culture, as the result of many years' service with a kindly and intelligent mistress, she was not devoid of superstition. Thus when problems of immense significance confronted Ivy and there rose a challenge much desired though little expected, while tolerably clear in her own mind, she had reached a point when it occurred to her the. impartial opinion of a notoriously wise person might be worth seeking. To ask for advice is by implication to admit doubt, if not actual ignorance, before better knowledge and she knew of none other to whom such an admission was going to be made. Her father's sagacity she held in poor esteem and, in any case, a woman would be more likely to understand than a man. Good sense suggested some outsider, who might counsel and then be dropped, and two possibilities occurred to her. These were the vicar's wife, whom Ivy knew and much respected, or Mercy Grepe; and she decided that it would be more satisfactory to approach the white witch. 'To ask for advice isn't to take it,' thought Ivy, 'and if the lady advised something and I turned it down, then she'd think ill of me and mightn't forgive me; but if 'Mother Forty Cats' was to advise contrary to my feelings, she wouldn't care whether I took her advice or not, so long as I paid for it.' She made no appointment and told nobody of her intention, but called at Mercy's little house on a Spring evening. She knocked and was invited to come in.

"I'm taking tea, but can give heed to you if in my power to serve you. Who might you be, my dear ?" asked Mercy.

"You know my father, though you don't know me," Miss Grepe," explained Ivy. "I'm Mr. Pook's daughter, I have left Lady Garland and am home and looking after him now."

"You're Ivy then ? Of course. And never a better man than your good father to my knowledge. Sit you down. But if you feel to want a bit of sense over and above what you've got yourself, why didn't you seek him ?"

"You know by instinct whether a man s got the sense you want, or a woman's more like to have it," explained the visitor. "And in the matter I've come about I can't think a man's any use. In any case I'm most like to make up my own mind after all's said."

"When it comes to the point, most people do," agreed the old woman.

"I'm a very independent girl, Miss Grepe," continued Ivy, "and well educated and got what you might say w quality and character. But you're known for large experience and good-willing and I'd wish for you to say how my affair strikes your attention. But you must regard me as a customer, because time's money and I'll pay you half-a-crown if you've got the time to listen for an hour or so."

Mercy gave the remains of her meal to a cat, tidied her table and bade the visitor proceed.

"That will do very well," she said, "so tell me how it is."

"I'll traverse over the grounds then," promised Ivy, "and you stop me if I'm not making myself clear, Miss Grepe. When her dear ladyship failed and took to her bed and lost her mind, or pretty near all of it, I wasn't wanted at the Manor any more; so I returned to look after my father. But though you may, so to speak, devote your intentions to a parent if you've got proper daughterly feelings, that don't stop you getting on with your own life and it don't change your ideas in general. Well, in any case, I found myself to be the marrying type of woman, well adapted to be a wife and mother, if God so willed. You leave such things in Higher Hands and don't dwell upon 'em, but carry on just hoping ladylike that your fate will some day bring you acquaint with a nice man, and you'll fill his eye and answer to his standards and find he answers to yours. But the right man don't come in sight just because you feel you'd welcome him if he did, and between ourselves, I never had an affair and no man, right or otherwise, ever showed any signs of interest in me. Of course a young, religious woman of my class wouldn't allow her mind to dwell on this man or that in particular, because it's their part to make the advances and our part to size them up and consider their natures, and wait to see if any tender feeling for 'em may happen to awake in us. So that's how I stood when I left service. I never felt to be on the shelf, as they say, but just in my prime of womanhood and in the open market, and ready and willing to consider a husband and a home if they were offered and equal to what a woman like me might demand. Given such a man, I knew he'd get good value and could trust myself to be a very sufficient wife to him, being well educated and faithful to the death. And I may say nothing that has happened since makes me doubtful on those points."

"And what has happened since?" asked Mercy, as she stroked a snow-white cat, now exalted to the place of honour on her lap and promising to become a mother."

"Well, quite unexpected and unforeseen," continued Ivy, "a man has loomed up into my life with strong expectations of stopping there and being the big noise in future. It wasn't so much I felt any great surprise at that, because I'm not the sort that warns the male to keep his distance—not the neuter kind of women, only created to be useful to other women and without no prospects of their own. Far from it in fact—a woman with strong maternal instincts and plenty of room in her heart for a godly and masculine fashion of partner. No, Miss Grepe, I didn't feel no astonishment to find I'd won attention and if it had been somebody different—a thought older and with a more solid standing behind him—I should have relied upon my own feelings and not consulted a third party in a sacred matter like love. But the astonishment was in the man that had come forward—you might say the last man in Priory, or anywhere else, that had ever harboured in my thoughts. I knew him and I knew his story and there was nothing there to awaken any lasting affection in my mind. Quite the contrary you might almost say, though I've always been one to judge people by my own know-ledge of them and not through hearsay, nor yet rumour."

"Very nice," declared the listener. "The proper way, Ivy. And what was his story?"

"A bit clouded. There were facts in his story not over-much to his credit, but against that in fairness you had to remember that nobody is faultless, and that the young man had lived down his past and conquered his tempta-tions and was now well thought upon by his employers. Justice is my second nature, Miss Grepe, so I was in duty bound to take that to account."

"You'll be aiming at Rupert Canniford," said Mercy.

"Yes—him. Or it might be righter to say he is aiming at me. That's the astonishment—not an unpleasant astonishment when I got to know him better, because there's a lot in Rupert open to my understanding and hidden from other people. We've grown little by little on to terms of friendship, and so soon as the man unfolded his feelings and let me look into 'em and get a grasp of his inner nature, I found he'd been a good bit misunderstood by the parish in general, and ran his life on higher principles than he was given credit."

"Fancy that!" said Mercy.

"Yes. And then my astonishment waned out. Because, though at first I was a lot surprised to think such a man had figured me up and found what he wanted was there, I little imagined that he could be what I wanted; but, after hearing his opinions and his ideas of the sort of wife he some day hoped for, then I saw what had drawn him, because I was exactly the type of woman he dreamed about, but never expected to find."

"You've kept this business to yourselves so far?"

"So far. But we're reaching to a time when I've got to give Rupert something in the nature of an answer. I've contrived to let him have a good many of my spare hours and it's leaked out, one place and another, that he's concentrating a good bit on me."

"What does your father think of him, Ivy?"

"Father's quite in ignorance of what's arisen, or what Rupert's wishful to happen; but he thinks well of Rupert in general, though considers him to be a bit downy. Father wouldn't come into the picture in any case, except it would mean that he lost me and went back to his bachelor ways."

"Well," said Mercy. "Now you've told me what the game-keeper thinks of you; and next you can tell me honest what you think of him."

"I think if ever a man was going to be the richer for a woman like me, Rupert's the man. I see a great field of usefulness along with him, and where you see a field of usefulness opening out before you, then the question of your duty faces you of course. I want a husband and ain't afraid to say so to a wise and secret woman like you, Miss Grepe; and though if I was to wait my time somebody else might come along to suit me better than Rupert, I doubt it. The fact that a personable, clean man like him has come along, cheered me in itself, because where a man like that leads the way, others may follow; but for the minute I had to pay his advances respectful attention of course, and the more I've got to understand him, the more I doubt if he's not worthy in himself. Mind you, he's not deep nor yet downy as father fancies—not where he finds himself understood. He's quite open with me. He admits frankly now is his appointed time for a wife, because of the Manor lodge he badly wants to inhabit next autumn; but he makes it clear that he'd never have married just for convenience, if a woman he couldn't love for herself had not come along. I think he feels in a sort of fashion I was like the Bible lamb catched in the thicket, and just appeared at the right moment by God's will."

Mercy gave a subdued laugh.

"You don't want to be catched in no thicket with Rupert Canniford knife in hand," she said. "Then your instincts made you say 'Yes' to him and return the affection you talk about? If that's so, what's the other instincts that made you feel you'd like another opinion?"

Ivy considered this question.

"I could hardly put a name to 'em in so many words. There's your whole future life in the balance when you decide upon taking a husband. I've got a strong opinion that I might be wise to enter into marriage with Rupert; but once I say 'yes' to the man there's no going back on my word. I'm like that: my word is my bond."

"You want another opinion to help you take him with a good conscience," suggested Mercy; but the younger opposed this suggestion with some warmth. She flushed and answered sharply.

"My conscience has nothing at all to do with it. If my conscience had got anything to say, it would have said it. I don't go to a fellow-creature on any subject where my conscience have spoke."

The racy narrative of Rupert's enterprise had long since reached Miss Grepe's ear. Authentic and trustworthy witnesses reported the spectacle of him, accompanied by Ivy, on the confines of the forest and elsewhere. She had, as a matter of fact, not seldom met him by appointment in such secluded spots as his official duties demanded; and like not a few others Mercy had wondered what the game-keeper might have in view and whence came his inspiration.

"I don't hold this to be a matter of prayer—not yet," concluded Ivy. "God helps those who help themselves—so we're given to understand— and I reckoned that if I could get an outside opinion from a clever old woman like you, that might be helpful, or, of course, otherwise."

"I can't say I know the young man himself," replied Mercy, "and most like you don't know all there is to know about him yourself. Not that anybody ever knows all there is to know about any of us, from the cradle to the grave. But there's one knows a great deal more about Rupert than anybody else and have had a close experience of him all his life. Known him longer than anybody else could, and that's his mother."

"I haven't got any use for Mrs. Canniford—none whatever," declared Ivy. "What she may know, or thinks she knows, about her son, I couldn't tell you; but she let me see very clear what she thinks of me. That was a long time back when first I came to my father, and she was most contemptuous and said cruel and monstrous things to my face. And I'd never pay no heed to her opinions on any subject whatever."

"Don't sound overmuch like Jenny to be cruel and monstrous to a younger woman," commented Mercy. "I've found her to be kind-hearted and well-intending. She loves Rupert and was always a very good mother to him. You could trust her to say nothing that wasn't worth your attention."

"If it happens, then I'll go before her and not sooner," declared Ivy. "It would be a triumph for me in a manner of speaking to face that woman tokened to a man, and her own son at that, because she told me, blunt and brutal, in my own father's house, that I mustn't count on marrying anybody. But I don't want none of her opinions on Rupert, and I wouldn't trust a word she was to say whether she praised him or blamed him."

"Poor speed for a mother-in-law if ever it comes to that," murmured Mercy; then she lifted the white cat off her lap and mended the fire.

"Smell of Spring in the air these days," she said. "There's something in Spring air more gracious than any other time. It goes through your lungs, then it gets into your heart and then it rises to the head. Few understand that, but I discovered it for myself many years ago; same with plants: Spring sap gives each herb its proper nature and all should be gathered in May month to get the best of 'em. Well, Ivy, now you see I couldn't go so far as to reach a final opinion on what's best and cleverest for you to do, my dear, because I ain't versed deep enough in your characters. You have given me a pinch of

yours and I see the sort you are—independent as you told me. You might
neighbour very well with some fashion of husband and there's many a middle-
aged man might see eye to eye with your plan of living and find your ways
fit in very nice. But not so many young men would. Because Rupert says
he would and perhaps even honestly thinks he would, there's no certainty he
might not live to find himself mistook. I can only make a picture of him in
my mind from the facts known about him—not just the opinions floating
around him. They're as like to be false as true—more like to be. But the
facts are in his favour. He shines in his walk in life; he's made good; he's
proved worth his money and will rise so high as a first class game-keeper can
rise. You'll know the manner of his calling and how it keeps him from you
by night and so on and you'll surely hear him well spoken about by his employers. There's one fact some might say was against him, but, there again,
he may have explained the ins and outs of that in a manner to satisfy you. No
doubt he's well equal to doing so."

"If you mean when he was sentenced to prison——" began Ivy; but the
elder shook her head.

"I don't. No decent man or woman is ever going to bring that against
him—especially after the fine manner he atoned for it. You can wipe that off
the score, and him none the worse—perhaps all the better. Sometimes when
a man comes to his turning point, he'll find it sharp enough to give an ugly
wound; but it's for him to set about to make it heal and leave no scar, and
I'd say Rupert did that. But there was talk he'd took up with his cousin.
Mind you I don't want to know a thing about the details and it may not even
be true or worth a second thought. Still you ought to feel clear on a happening like that."

"I'm glad you mentioned it," declared Ivy. "I'm very glad you did hear
that lying story, because it serves to show how things get misrepresented.
The truth about that is just contrary to what you heard. In all innocence,
liking the Withers people very well, Rupert took to going to Pigslake after his
Uncle Nicholas was dead. And a very warm welcome he had; but little
guessing what was in Nora's mind, he took a cousinly interest in her and once
went so far as to buy her a necklace. Nothing in that at all and, if she'd
spared a thought to Rupert's opinions, Myra Withers would have seen that a
light-minded girl like Nora couldn't suit him, nor yet attract him in any serious
fashion. But all the same, drawn no doubt by his fine appearance and
friendly ways, the girl fell in love with Rupert, much to his confusion and he
made good his retreat so fast as he was able. And that shows how quick
people are to read wrong motives and talk scandals where none ought to be."

Mercy brought the conference to an end.

"Well, my dear, upon the main question, I don't feel it would be exactly
proper or fair to give any advice whatever," she said. "There's your heart
and head both ought to come to the task when you give a fellow man or
woman advice and, in my experience, if they say the same thing to you, then
you can utter it and hope you have been of service; but if they say different
things, then you need to bethink you and weigh 'em against each other. And
that's where I stand this minute. There's much doubtful that no living
creature can prophesy with sureness and one such thing is how any marriage

however full of promise, is going to pan out, but your heart always says to you, 'Give 'em a chance; don't come down on what they are feeling like a frost to nip true love and the chance of a triumph.' And your head may agree to that and say the betting is all for a happy marriage and Providence can be trusted not to smash up their little dreams and hopes. But in this case while my heart sees you're in love with young Canniford and want to marry him, my head tells me it's a case where there didn't ought to be any hurry. My head says, 'Keep company for a bit longer; let him practise patience and show you if he's got the strength of character you think, while you show him a few more of your qualities and opinions."

Ivy rose and fetched out her purse.

"The answer to that is that I ain't growing any younger and Rupert wants the Manor lodge," she said. "But all the same I'm very much obliged to you for your opinion. He's pressing for an answer and now I'll tell him he can count upon it by a fixed date; and before I see him again I'll fix the date; and that ought to satisfy him."

She produced half-a-crown which Mercy did not hesitate to accept.

"Meantime don't cherish no unkind thoughts against Rupert's mother," she urged. "You'll be quite mistaken to do that. She's got her difficulties like all of us."

"I don't want any advice on that subject."

'Mother Forty Cats' saw Ivy to her garden gate and looked up at the sky.

"New moon in the old moon's arms, I see," she said. "And if you chance to want my opinions again, Ivy, you can get 'em without paying any more next time."

Elsewhere others canvassed the exciting fact that Paul Pook's daughter looked to be engaged to Jenny Canniford's son, yet so many suggested reasons to oppose any such fantastic theory, that doubt prevailed.

"In murder cases," said Inspector Chard, "you look first and foremost for motive, where most like the clue is apt to lie, and in marriage cases as often as not, a bit of routine inquiry will surely find the motive and satisfy you. It may be a good motive, or else a bad one."

It was at the 'Pen-in-Hand' that Thomas Chard expressed this view and the landlord praised him for doing so.

"The case in a nutshell, Tom," said Toozey, "and that's precisely why this interests the people out of the common. Some men never want the reasons for anything and accept the facts without wasting time to find what lies behind 'em; but when it came out that Rupert Canniford was keeping company with Ivy Pook the minute after he'd thrown over Nora Withers, then us educated and intelligent men asked each other why he did it."

"And the minute you can't find a shadow of reason for a thing, then the wonder grows," declared Chard. "Any policeman will tell you that. Nought quickens the public mind like a mystery and that's why we think such a lot of them bright lads at Scotland Yard when they solve one."

The old organist happened to be amongst his hearers. Local gossip did not interest Mr. Bowring very often, but Chard's assertion did so.

"And what is the mystery, Inspector ?" he inquired.

"The mystery, sir, arises from a thing happening which don't bear no explanation on its face," explained Chard. "Mary Ann—that's Mrs. Chard —she put it like this. Here's a chap—namely Rupert Canniford—well known to be close and after the main chance, which in his case is money; and this man has set about to find a wife, for his own reasons. Well and good—no mystery so far. But when you think upon the young woman he appears to be courting, then the puzzlement arises. If Ivy Pook—the maiden he's after—was one of they comely creatures rich in promise to the male eye, then you might say what more natural? You might even imagine that love was the reason of Rupert's efforts and that he had found himself overcome by a beautiful object and set out to win her."

"There's no object that would be more beautiful than money in young Canniford's opinion, Thomas," said Toozey from behind the bar.

"I'm coming to that, William," answered the Inspector. "That's true, and in the case of Ivy, though she's a good girl and worthy of her father, the looks to awaken any high affection in Rupert ain't there, to say it kindly. With Ivy there wouldn't be no love at first sight to carry a man off his feet, and in any case the game-keeper wouldn't let the loveliest that ever was stand between him and his liking for cash. But none the less, he wants her and seems tolerable safe to get her, so the next question is, what rewards may Rupert be looking for?"

"He may have higher principles than you imagine," suggested Joseph Bowring. "Why not be charitable and give the lad credit for good sense and good judgment, Inspector? He may have found in Paul Pook's daughter qualities that outweigh good looks and promise to make a valuable wife."

"He may," admitted Chard, "but that's a good bit out of the picture of Rupert, Mr. Bowring. No word against him in general. He's a very fine built young man and a very good game-keeper and worthy of credit for living down his past; but let me flow on. The question is why he wants to marry Ivy and the answer has yet to be found. Now we're on delicate ground and stop me if I go too far, William. But motive takes us to Ivy's financial prospects as the only possible reason why Canniford's on her trail, like a weasel after a rabbit, and where do we find ourselves then?"

"No politics, Thomas," warned Toozey.

"I know, William, but looking at the inquiry from the view of a police-man, there ain't no politics. On the trail of a mystery everything sinks into its proper place for the police and they can't suffer any considerations to come between them and their appointed task. So it must be granted that, apart from her own savings, which can't amount to big money, Ivy has nothing to tempt Rupert, or prompt him to this rash act. We'll allow for argument's sake she has her father behind her; but Pook's a man in his prime and good for another five-and-twenty years very likely, if he don't come to no harm in the hunting field. Which Rupert very well knows and he certainly isn't banking on Paul's money—much or little."

"Another thing, though delicate ground as you say," agreed Toozey, "and dangerously near the limit of talk I favour, Thomas, but the fact remains that Paul might take another wife himself. I don't think so for a moment, because he's expressed himself very definite on that subject to me on more than one occasion; but you never know and I've heard his name breathed in connection with somebody. Such things must be thought upon and nobody would be like to take 'em up quicker than Rupert."

"There you are then—all clear and orderly," answered Chard, "and where are we now ? Face to face with the mystery, and I for one, policeman though I hap to be, can't see no light."

"Have you learned Paul Pook's opinion on the subject?" asked Bowring.

"We haven't named it before him and I haven't heard that he's mentioned it," answered Toozey. "By a side-wind I don't know whether he would worry a lot."

"Better be charitable and large-minded, then," directed the old musician. "If the only way to get to the root of the matter is to credit young Canniford with good sense and perception, why not do so, Chard? Then you not only have a motive for his intentions, but a good motive. And with a good motive available, why worry yourselves because you can't find a bad one ?"

"There speaks the Christian," agreed Toozey, "but you don't know Rupert, Mr. Bowring."

"And we've got to look at the case from Ivy's point of view also," continued Chard. "That's another angle of the mystery. Here's an indoor servant, or such she was, on the one hand, and an outdoor man on the other. Very seldom you'll find an indoor woman fall in love with an outdoor man."

"True love wouldn't trouble over a little thing like that," declared the landlord. "I'd be disposed to think that Ivy, well knowing herself not for every market and yet very ready and willing to wed, which she hasn't concealed, when she found herself in reach of the promised haven, didn't hang fire for a moment. Women like her, longing for a husband, would very soon find herself in love with anybody who showed the least inclination to want her. She'd be easy meat. No mystery there, Thomas."

The inspector prosed on.

"There's a minor point that throws light in a manner of speaking I grant you. Rupert's set on a Manor lodge and he can't get it as a single man. That's a reason for marriage viewing the question, by and large; but again no reason for choosing Ivy. There's plenty of more personable ones than her would take the man."

"Time alone can show the inner meaning," concluded Toozey, "and meanwhile we'll try to take Mr. Bowring's good tip and hope Rupert's moving on a higher plane than what we're disposed to fear. And why ? Because there don't seem to be no other plane he can be moving on."

Half a dozen men had been listening to the trio and now the subject was dropped and conversation became general, as Rupert himself joined the throng with his brother, Harry. The elder's hand was bound up and he was full of an accident that had overtaken him at his work.

"My own, trustable bill-hook turned against me, souls, and very near took off my guide finger. You'd almost say the forces of Nature plot to overthrow an innocent man some days. And I may lose my finger yet."

They condoled with him while those free drinks, often poured to comfort the unfortunate, flowed for Harry and hopes were uttered that his finger might be spared.

"If 'tis took, my life's work ends," he said. "'Tis the reigning member without which all's lost."

XI

AFTER due consideration, Ivy Pook decided that the wise woman was for once in error. Indeed she regarded Mercy Grepe henceforth as a mistaken and inefficient prophetess, who had won her shadowy fame upon no basis of reality. Indeed, looking back afterwards, the saddler's daughter puzzled to know what whim could have driven her to consult any other arbiter than her own sound judgment in a matter so vital. She and Rupert were now on exceedingly close terms and, with considerable patience and industry, he had won her trust and even a measure of affection. His own purpose in this calculated bid for a partner he kept to himself. It was not laudable, yet, as time passed, an impulse quite praiseworthy had developed respectable emotions which could not have been expected to spring from their secret source. Human nature abounds in these paradoxes, for figs will sometimes spring from thistles, and refreshing fruit appear on boughs that offered no promise whatever. Rupert's enterprise arose from a disreputable determination to profit from knowledge acquired by accident; yet, having launched upon a piece of cold-blooded calculation without one single worthy motive to condone it, now better knowledge of Ivy awakened the consciousness that her bleak attitude to life and her practical outlook, so different in all else from the kindly trust she displayed for him, might wear well and provide all that he was ever likely to desire. While love did not enter into the prospect, he began to find himself under less and less compulsion to pretend it and was relieved to find that Ivy herself neither demanded nor displayed any trace of romance. She was not by nature emotional and the fact that a good-looking and masculine type of man would be ready and willing to marry her proved amply sufficient for Ivy. They soon abandoned any make-believe and met upon the same ground of a possible union convenient and desirable for them both. In order to enjoy the amenities of a very comfortable lodge on the Manor estate, she knew that Rupert needed a wife, and confident that her own physical appeal was adequate and her good intelligence an added asset, the young woman felt herself an excellent bargain for Rupert; while that he should have found all he needed in her was highly gratifying. It showed that her own self-confidence had never been misplaced and patience was now duly rewarded. She welcomed the idea of living within the precincts of Tudor Manor, where so many years of her live had been profitably spent, while to be the wife of the future head game-keeper promised a certain measure of distinction in the little commonwealth. It is probable that even had she earned the reason for Rupert's initial approach, she might have forgiven him and still decided to wed. Prosaic were the lines of the courting, yet clear-cut and definite; but she had always felt a desire for some second, unbiased opinion on Rupert's character and to learn how he struck an indifferent but orderly mind; and it was this impulse that had taken her to Mercy Grepe. He was apparently frank enough himself and anticipated her own somewhat uneasy and minatory attitude to the little matter of Nora Withers, for knowing that Ivy must learn of his operations at Pigslake, Rupert had spoken first and explained his doubtful performance in a manner to satisfy her.

Now Ivy accepted the game-keeper and no direct hint of what awaited him reached her father's ear until the deed was done. Though he had been chaffed about the rumours already upon the air, Paul was never one to indulge in wishful thinking at any time and attached little importance to the jests afoot on the subject. He knew Rupert and felt as positive as need be that nothing more grotesque than the idea of Ivy captivating such a man could be imagined. He suffered his own minor tribulations at this season and had already directed Mrs. Canniford to visit him less often. Their plot having failed, Paul desired that it should now be forgotten between them; yet when she agreed and approached him no more, a sense of loss haunted the saddler for a time. This indeed he confessed when next they met by accident.

"Lord! how quick a habit over-gets you!" he told Jenny. "Blessed if I'm not quite pleased to see you, Jenny!"

"And always will be I hope," she said. "You done the cleverest in your power, and I miss you above a bit for that matter. There was one bright side to our failure, because I've got to hear a lot of your good sense and felt proud in a way to be seen with you round about. But that's over now and I'll ask you to let me have our paper back, because you might die, my dear, which God forbid, but if you were taken, that paper would fall into other hands."

"You shall have it," he promised. "I'll look it up. How's Peter behaving?"

"Much as usual. I'd say if anything he's getting nearer to it. I see it hover on his lips off and on; but I don't care so much as what I did."

"You're still in the mind to take him, however?"

"I couldn't very easy have the face to turn down the man now after all that's passed."

Jenny suddenly laughed, and Paul stared with considerable surprise in his wistful eyes, which made her laugh the more.

"No wonder you gaze at me to hear me laugh, my dear man—a woman with no great call for amusement best of times. But I think now and again that if he rose to the words at last and asked me to marry him, what the mischief he'd do supposing I said I wouldn't! And when I picture such a scene as that I can't but laugh."

They stood in the open street at the time and Mrs. Canniford giggled helplessly for a moment, then wiped her eyes with the corner of her apron, while Paul regarded her solemnly and shook his head.

"You mustn't let any such wilfulness overget you," he said, "though I'll confess, if such a thing was to happen to Honeywood, he'd mighty well deserve it."

"His Irish blood would boil to the surface," sniggered Jenny. "Poor man—what a shock! I doubt he'd ever forgive me. But I'll put such thoughts out of my mind. You're quite right, Paul."

"Remember your age," he warned, "though you never looked it."

"Better I was to bide single perhaps," she said. "It comes over me tolerable often now that it ain't ordained for me to take another."

He asked a question before they parted.

"Has Rupert dropped anything in your ear about marrying?"

"Not him," she answered. "After his affair with Nora—to call it an affair—I'd say he'll lie tolerable low in that direction for a time. Not that he'd ask my advice."

Mr. Pook nodded and they parted; but it so happened that he obtained direct information on the subject not long afterwards.

At the inn only one general sentiment prevailed when Rupert's engagement was definitely announced by himself. Wonder found the company little disposed to make immediate comment; but the customary free drinks greeted his news and not until after he was gone did argument intrude. Mr. Toozey's supporters rarely displayed a cynical outlook upon the vagaries of their neighbours and might usually be found to take tolerant views. To-night, the startling fact accepted, their chief concern was still how to explain it, and Peter Honeywood opened an investigation by paying Inspector Chard the compliment of asking his opinion.

"As a policeman used to seeking out motives, what would you say was back of that, Thomas?" he asked.

"When you say 'motive', you're up against it instanter," once again replied the inspector. "When two people come so closely together as to favour marriage, you'll generally find their reason lies well within common knowledge; and even if it don't, nobody's much troubled and nobody needs to think that anything devious, or disorderly lies behind. But knowing these particular parties you feel curious."

"Why?" asked Samuel Wish, the baker. "Why do you all seem to reckon it so wonderful?"

"Along of the parties, Sam," repeated Chard. "Here's a young man who's made good and is well thought upon, and a woman passing plain with nothing to her to challenge Canniford and, between ourselves, a bit of a thorn in her father's flesh; so wonder arises."

"I'd say this," argued Samuel Wish. "He wants a wife and has found a woman, who in his own opinion would make him a good one. He's hard-hearted, close—granted—but that kind suits some women better than the large-hearted, open-handed, easy sort. She may like his point of view and feel he's the man she could picture her husband to be."

"She'll give him no chance for jealousy anyway," said Honeywood.

"And he won't give her none," prophesied Toozey. "She's a few years older than Rupert, but that wouldn't trouble him. You can't judge from what we know of Rupert how he's strike Ivy Pook, nor yet, from what we know of her, what there was that took him."

"Reasons no doubt there were, but no call to think 'em bad reasons," said the baker. "They haven't committed no crime."

"No crime, Samuel, and I'd be the last to look for it; yet they still have committed a wonder," repeated Chard. "I may have gone deeper into it, by my training in the law, than what you have, and I'd say the wonder lies along with Rupert, not Ivy. There's nothing wonderful she should have jumped at Canniford; the wonder is that he should have given her the chance."

"That's what I say," agreed Peter Honeywood. "You don't jump at rice pudding when there's cherry-tart on the table, and plenty of girls round about are quite so virtuous and high-minded as the saddler's girl and a lot likelier to live with. You can't deny that, Samuel?"

"There may be but I wouldn't condemn Rupert on that account," answered Mr. Wish. "I'd say it was her character that marked her out in his eyes as the one most likely to make him a fitting partner."

Ned Piper, from his seat by the fire, introduced a less charitable probability.

"Bunkum, Samuel!" he said. "What led the man to pick her up at all? Does a chap like Canniford go out of his way to run after a woman like her, because he thinks her likely to make him a tidy good wife? He knows the general opinion of Ivy and knows what she looks like and have heard her guinea-hen voice. And that's enough for any man of Rupert's generation. Do us run about to find what's hid in a crab-apple? We damn well know."

"I don't want to throw any reflection on Rupert," continued Chard. "All the same it continues to be a wonder and we must next ask ourselves if his motives aren't high, what the mischief are they?"

"No need at all to ask yourself such unchristian questions," answered Wish.

"It's stretching Christianity to believe in his motives all the same," said Honeywood. "No aspersions; but we shouldn't have all felt so powerful sure there was a mystery if there weren't."

"That's your bad nature, Honeywood," replied Mr. Wish sternly, "and when you talk of stretching Christianity, you're no Christian yourself. You people want to find a bad motive, because it would be more exciting than a good one, and I don't think the better of you, William, for letting 'em do it. Good night all."

The baker went to work and Toozey admitted his impeachment.

"I stand corrected," he said. "I've broken my iron rule over this job, so no more of it."

"Let Chard go on," suggested Honeywood. "We'll need to stop in a minute because, so like as not, Pook will come in for a drink himself. And we ought to touch him for a round, because this will be a bit of luck he little counted on."

"No politics, Toozey—just deduction," explained the inspector. "We're all friends and all wish the parties well and hope the marriage is going to be a winner, but, win or lose, we can go on asking ourselves what questions remain to be asked."

"There's only one question worth asking, Thomas, and that's in a nutshell," declared the sexton bringing his glass to be refilled. "Why the devil did Rupert Canniford fix his affections on a frost-bitten virgin same as Ivy? And you can go on deducting till Doom afore you'll answer that."

"You must remember there's nothing behind Ivy, Chard," warned Honeywood. "At best she don't carry any great promise of cash because, between ourselves, Pook ain't a very snug man."

"And another thing," added Ned Piper. "There's nothing to forbid Paul from marrying again and some say, for all his resolves never to do it, he looks as if he might change his mind."

Peter's eyes glinted; he frowned and breathed hard suddenly but said nothing; while Chard spoke again.

"If that's true, then we can't deduce any future money value to Ivy that would waken interest for Rupert."

"So we're left pretty much where we began," summed up Toozey. "We're left before a puzzler beyond our power to dissolve, so no more politics in any case."

Elsewhere two people explained the attachment in their own fashion. On a day when Katey Wish brought Timothy his dinner, they approached the engagement from quite a different angle and the young man only wondered, from his personal knowledge of love, how it might operate in the heart of another. He sat and ate under a wide belt of larch, all emerald green again on a day of silver mist in Spring.

"I wonder," he said, "if Canniford and Ivy felt a pinch of the fine things I and you felt when you took me and told me you loved me. Would it be possible for a tolerable old woman like her to feel a quarter what you did when you knew I loved you?"

But Katey was not Nora's first friend for nothing and hated the gamekeeper heartily.

"You can't dare to bring a blessed thing like our love to mind when you think of Rupert Canniford," she asserted. "I only hope she will marry him; then he'll get a bit of what he deserves I expect; but she may have the sense to see through him yet before it's too late. Nora told me all the ins and outs about him of course and she says her everlasting sorrow was not in losing Rupert. That was a matter of thankfulness as I've often told her. But her sorrow was in being chucked by him before she had time to do the chucking herself. And why he changed his mind, just after he'd begun to make Nora feel he was good enough, nobody will ever know. To go after Ivy straight from a girl like Nora was the foulest insult of all, as any woman but Ivy Pook would have seen; but no doubt he lied about that and calmed her down."

"He wasn't much one for the girls," declared Timothy, "and I've heard him say tolerable scornful things about all of them. Contemptuous he was, and foul at that, so I don't suppose he's likely to love Ivy for herself."

"I'm dead sure he isn't," said Kate. "Some men can't truly love a girl; they only love hunting 'em. Being a game-keeper no doubt he's got a love of hunting in him. And some women love them hunting men for that matter. But all hunting's cruel, so father says, and Rupert's a cruel beast anyway."

Timothy considered this.

"You can't judge a man on his trade. He's a killer of vermin. He gets his living that way, same as a butcher slaughters the people's meat. He's not got the heroic nature to rise up and kill a man, or anything like that. That's what you understand by a 'killer.' But he's mean and too small-minded to run any risks."

"He won't kill Ivy," foretold Kate. "He'll find, if they ever get married, that he's caught a tolerable tough piece, quite so clever as he is himself. She may give him the surprise of his life when she finds out what he is, and puts a pinch of poison in his tea some fine evening. Then he'd go after all the hawks and weasels he's killed himself."

Timothy grinned at this suggestion.

"Would you say it was no certainty yet, even though they're tokened before the parish?" he asked.

"There's never no certainty with a shifty man like him," she answered. "He's hunted Ivy, same as he might hunt any other creature, and no doubt she felt mad with joy to find a man was hunting her; but anything in trousers could have caught her if he was fool enough to want to."

"My," said Timothy. "You do properly hate 'em, don't you? But I dare say a right down ugly woman, passed over for years and years, would like to find herself being hunted after all. I grant that."

"Ugliness is nothing," vowed Katey. "You see lots of ugly girls married and happy and successful. But Ivy Pook's got a cheerless nature and don't feel too kind to anybody. There's nice ugliness a man can neighbour with very well content and it's only outside, but Ivy's—there, I'm wasting our time yelping against the woman. Drop it and tell me what you're doing in the woods.'

In another quarter Mercy Grepe had heard the match proclaimed; but it was not until an evening when Rupert's mother visited her that she learned particulars.

"If you'd push a few of they cats out-of-doors I've got something to tell about," began Mrs. Canniford, after she had been admitted, and the wise woman without comment banished numerous familiars from her dwelling-room.

"You look pale," she said. "When I see you coming, I hoped it was good news, my dear."

"I've got very near past the time when news is ever good," sighed the widow, "but news I certainly do bring, though no doubt you've heard it."

"Your boy and Paul Pook's girl—yes, I've heard."

"Heard it before I did myself I shouldn't wonder. How many may have picked it up before it came to my ears, the Lord knows; and when I did, it came like a thunder-clap."

"Rupert didn't give no hint what he was up to?"

"Not a whisper. I doubt if he'd have told me when he did—two nights ago—if chance hadn't drove it out of him."

"Sit down and tell me," suggested Mercy, "and don't worry. I'll make a pot of tea."

"It went like this," began Jenny. "Rupert, after he'd took his supper, didn't go out as usual; but he was off duty till next day and he sat on and smoked his pipe, using my box of matches to light, as he always does when he's home. He'll even save down to a match. I wasn't much in a mood for him that night along of a lot on my mind besides him, so I asked him if he was pushing off to the inn, or going to stop. 'Because if so,' I said, 'you can help me wash up.' 'I'll help you if you want me,' he said. 'I'm through with talking now. Nought so tiring.' 'You never talk to tire yourself—not to me,' I answered him. 'There's times when you need to talk,' he replied, 'and there's times when you can be expected to relate the result of your talking. I've had a tell or two with Ivy Pook, Paul's daughter, lately. She don't like you I find.' Well, I ask you, Mercy, if that weren't about enough to bring a drop of lemon to any woman's tongue? And I'd heard the same shameful fact in another quarter, too, for Pook himself told me that, for reasons unknown, his blasted Ivy didn't like me !"

"Keep calm, my dear," begged the old woman. "Tea's brewing."

"Mind you, up till now I hadn't the ghost of an idea as to what Rupert was doing, so I answered pretty sharp about Ivy and said he must be tolerable short of women friends if he had to fall back on her. 'She's a spiteful, back-biting bitch,' I said, 'and I'll warn you, Rupert, you're out of your mind to have any truck with the creature.' For once," continued Jenny, "my son was astonished; but he wasn't so much surprised as what I was a minute later."

Mercy pressed a cup of black tea into the visitor's hand and added a little milk.

"So that's how you came to hear, my dear ?" she asked.

"He gave me one of his rare laughs; then he said, 'I'm sorry you take that view, Mother, because Ivy will be your daughter-in-law inside two months. I'm going to marry her.' I fell back in my chair and felt the blood rush out of my heart and thought to faint. I was out of hand, but I drawed in a deep breath of air and he went on talking, but showed no concern for me."

"I can see it, Jenny; I can see it all," declared the elder.

"He upheld himself of course. He made out his case. 'There's a lot more to Ivy that meets the eye,' he said in his cold voice, talking as if she was a specimen insect in a museum. 'Her face would frighten a hedge-pig no doubt,' he went on, 'but I ain't one to marry for decorations. She's a woman and she can cook and she knows the value of money and she respects my opinions on that subject. I don't find her a bad sort by any means and share her general views of most people. She's got sense and she's no gadder and would rather work than play, same as me.' I'd collected myself by that time; but knew it was wasting strength to argue about her. 'There's her famous temper and her croakin' voice,' I murmured to the man. 'Nobody won't hear no more about her famous temper,' he said, 'not after she's married me. I'll cast out her temper, and her voice won't trouble me neither. I'm a peace lover and her voice will darned soon be stilled when I don't want to hear it.' That was a glimpse of Rupert at his deadliest you might say."

Mercy nodded.

"And if it had been anybody but Ivy, I'd have felt sorry for the woman," continued Rupert's mother. "He didn't say much more however. 'You must see her and find you were wrong about her, and she must see you and find she was wrong about you.' They were his last words on the subject, and then he spared a thought for me."

"And what did he think on your account ?" inquired Mercy.

"He said. 'You'll be alone when I settle at the lodge; but you've got two old gun-dogs running after you and now you'd do well to decide which you're going to take. And when you go to one of 'em, you'll be all right and free of anxiety.'"

"Two old gun-dogs?" asked Mercy.

"'There's only one after me, Rupert'," I answered, "and he's a market-gardener, not a gun-dog, and I much wish you wasn't so coarse."

"'Then what about Paul Pook?' he asked. 'It's common knowledge Paul's in the running, or seems to think he may be. And if the coast's clear and one of 'em has fallen out, why don't the other speak?' And then in his merciless way, he said one more thing. 'If you ask me, Paul's worth a million of 'Tubby' as a man, but against that I reckon 'Tubby' have got most money, and money's what you've wanted all your life, like most other people, so you'd best to net him and be done with it'."

"With a man like Rupert," said Mercy, "you always know where you are. They people who don't talk a lot often have the art to say much in little."

"I never heard him talk so much before," admitted Jenny. "And when he'd said that, he got up and went out of the house and left me in a proper miz-maze to think I'd ever borne such a man."

Mercy smiled. She had been amused to learn that Ivy declined her advice, but was not surprised and now hoped in her philosophic fashion that the young woman would prove to be right and herself mistaken. But it was her rule never to divulge to another the name of any client and she did not tell Jenny of her future daughter-in-law's doubts.

"Well, you know where you stand now, my dear, and, in such cases, if we can't help, no cause to hinder. Maybe they see alike in the things that matter to them and will pull together very well."

"You must give and take in marriage," replied Jenny, "and Rupert was never a giver in any sense. As for her, I'll summon religion to my aid when she comes before me and more than that I can't do."

"And yourself now?" asked Mercy.

"I stand where I was and my trouble's wasted and your advice didn't work, good as it was," replied the widow. "Me and Paul have tried our best and gone tolerable far at that; but now he ordains that we must drop play-acting, and who shall blame him? We done all we could and I'd go so far as to say I enjoyed it, because the better you know Pook, the better you like him and he's felt well disposed to me also. But that's finished and there's a feeling coming over me that Peter knows it. Between ourselves, I catch myself not liking Peter so well as I did. Of course Paul never intended any such thing, but to the seeing eye, he shows up Peter here and there. I tell myself it's treacherous to think the thought, but there it is. An inner voice whispers that Paul's got a finer character at bottom, though he don't amuse me near as much as Peter do. He ain't got quite such a light touch as Peter when he's in the mood. But that's how I stand, and security further off than ever."

"Security's the bed-rock we'd all anchor to if we knew how," agreed Mercy. "How would it be, I wonder—as a last shot at Honeywood—a dying effort, so to say—if you was to tell him in the course of conversation that you have decided to bide single for the rest of your life? It would be neck or nothing in a manner of speaking and you might lose him on it; but if he really thinks you're ready to take him and wants you still, as no doubt he does do, then it might loose his tongue at last."

"I could," agreed Jenny, "and I could do more. If that spurred him to propose marriage, I could turn him down after all and what a fool he'd look if I did! But I've got to a pitch now I'd rather like to turn the tables on him. I'll think upon it, Mercy."

"Don't do nothing venturesome that you might be sorry for afterwards," begged the old woman. "He'd be all right once he was wed, and if he came round after you'd refused him and said he'd built his future on having you for his wife and so on, well and good, then you could admit the case was altered and, if he wanted you, that was different."

"I'll turn it over," promised Jenny again, "and let you know what arises; and bless you I'm sure for your comfort, cold though it is. I haven't seen Paul yet, but no doubt he'll be a lot more light-hearted over this match than what I am."

Mrs. Canniford was right. When next they met the saddler walked as jauntily as a young man and she had never seen an expression of such serenity upon his face before.

"Well, my dear woman," he said, "I hope you're as pleased over this good news as myself."

"Rupert and your Ivy?" asked Jenny, without enthusiasm. "I guessed you'd take a hopeful view."

"Why not?" he inquired. "Best news I've heard this longful time. Surprising I grant, but top hole in my opinion. I've always stood up for Rupert and, though I never pictured a fairy story like this, I can assure you nothing will please me better."

"From your point of view it do, no doubt, Paul."

"Don't it from yours? What's wrong with it?" he asked. "There's no doubt seemingly. Ivy didn't beg leave from me and I lay Rupert didn't invite no opinions from you. Just told you, same as she told me. And I hope to God you didn't try to put him off her, because I'd never forgive you if you did."

"It would take more than me to put Rupert off anything he wanted," said the game-keeper's mother. "He's very well pleased with his bargain seemingly and spoke tolerable good sense about it. But you never know what's hid in Rupert and you'll need to keep him up to the mark very likely. If you take my advice, you'll give Ivy a pinch of cash when they wed. That's more certain than anything to make him faithful."

"I'd thought the self-same thing," he said, "and I've let Rupert know it. In fact I've gone so far as to name a hundred and fifty pounds if they're man and wife before hay-harvest."

"Then it will happen, I expect."

He mentioned another subject.

"All looks to be shaping pretty much as I could wish now, Jenny; but I haven't put my hands on that paper you signed—not yet. I could have sworn I'd stowed it along with other documents in the right hand drawer of my business desk; but so far I don tfind it. However, it's sure to turn up."

And in the bosom of his family Harry Canniford considered his brother's step with suspicions deeper than anybody else.

"Would you say it was going to come to good for 'em?" asked Susan, and Harry shook his head.

"Knowing Rupert same as I do," he said, "I'd feel it was most like coming to good for him; but little like to do so for her. He wants the lodge and the only way to get it was a wife, so he got one. That was easy. There's lots of meek women that like his over-bearing, brutal sort and would have took him, well knowing he spelled safety if no more; but I can't fathom out why he picked Ivy. He lives for the main chance and nought else, so you may feel sure that he knows something she's told him hidden from the world at large; but whether she told him the truth, or invented some hopeful story to snare him, I couldn't say. A clever lie about money would be just the bait to catch Rupert."

"Ivy Pook wouldn't be smart enough to invent nothing to snare Rupert," said Susan. "More like the other way round and he's snared her for his own deep reasons. I wouldn't be her for a lot."

Harry agreed that this was probably the case.

"If no true love went to their tokening, then they're heading for a fearful failure," he decided. "Love's beyond Rupert's powers I'd say and she couldn't awaken it in any case, so his motive must be bad and we did ought to see him cast down presently. He was never any brother to me, nor yet brother-in-law to you. Other folks' poverty always turned Rupert's heart to stone."

"More and more of the people seem to have no hearts left in 'em as they get older," said Susan. "I wish us hadn't made Rupert stand godfather to our eldest. We ought to have known it was a vain honour to pay the man."

"I've often been sorry myself," he said. "I only done it to please mother, He'll never be no shadow of use to George."

XII

PAUL's daughter had now reached a stage of complete confidence in her future husband. His frosty love-making quite satisfied her and she respected his downright and definite way of regarding the problems she brought to him. It might have been said that both were far more interested in the Manor lodge, which they would soon inhabit, than in each other, for Ivy was full of ideas upon the subject and Rupert announced his plans also and proposed to see that they were carried out. They did not clash, for the decorations, new wallpaper and household conveniences he left to her to arrange as she pleased. He was more interested in improving the little garden and arranging adequate quarters for his dog and ferrets. Those in authority were willing enough to serve him in these matters, but Rupert displayed lavish ideas when not called to pay for their fulfilment, and the land agent deemed it his duty to check certain suggestions on his part while complying with Ivy's wishes.

Industriously they proceeded to prepare for their united life and, since no sign of rift occurred and they were much together, the folk accepted this nine days' wonder and found new interests. It was remarked that Ivy had made Rupert come to church to hear the first calling of the banns, and numerous eyes were fixed upon them when the announcement had been made, but neither evinced any emotion where they sat side by side with Rupert's mother.

Jenny's affairs had distracted the lovers, for a remarkable discovery on Ivy's part called for her sweetheart's attention. She brought it to him, as she now brought everything, and left it for Rupert to take any action he might think necessary. She and her future mother-in-law had come together and were now on terms of somewhat frosty friendship. Neither pretended to any enthusiasm for the other, but each conducted herself with decorum, and in view of the fact that her father evinced such pleasure at Ivy's coming departure, Mrs. Canniford accepted the situation and already planned her future to meet it. She would have liked to go and live with her sister at Pigslake, where all was peace and Myra's tonic support might have been counted upon; but no such suggestion came from Myra, who felt so well content with the conditions of widowhood, that she displayed little response to Jenny's desires for the security represented by another husband.

It was then that Ivy had informed Rupert of her remarkable discovery and opened his eyes to a mystery. They were walking out together and Rupert carried his gun for he was on his way to work.

"It's like this," said Ivy. "Father's apt to be untidy and, going in his room when he was out, I saw a proper litter on his desk. Needless to say I didn't go near his papers, but marking one on the ground under where his feet went, I stooped down and picked it up. I was just setting it along with the rest when I chanced to see your mother's name to the bottom of the communication, though a glance showed me that my father had wrote it and, as everything to do with your mother did ought to go before you, I felt it my duty to cast my eye over it."

She produced the document and handed it to Rupert.

"I won't pass no opinion and leave you to do what you think proper, my dear. Or, if you tell me to, I'll hand it back to my father without a word."

It was dusk and Rupert lighted a match to read his mother's undertaking.

"It looks like something a thought devious to me," suggested Ivy. "But I wouldn't like to think our parents were indulging in anything underhand, and more would you, I'm sure, Rupert."

He read the secret undertaking and whistled. Then he laughed.

"Downy old dodgers, ain't they?" he asked.

"Best to give it back if you feel 'tis no affair of ours," answered Ivy. "How d'you read it?"

"No," he answered. "I'll keep this for a bit. It wants thinking over. When you get a spot of news, your first thought—at least my first thought—always is if I can reap any advantage out of it. That's what they call the instinct of self-preservation and every living thing has got it. Any gamekeeper will tell you that. On the face of it this don't look as if it was any business of mine; but I'm not so sure."

"How d'you read it?" asked Ivy again.

"It means your father was agreeable to help my mother catch 'Tubby'—that's Peter Honeywood; but Mr. Pook, not wanting to get into a mess himself, or be misunderstood, made my mother put the plot on paper for his own safety and satisfaction. Then they went to it and he began being uncommon attentive to mother, to make Honeywood jealous and spur him on. So far they've failed and I'm rather glad they have; but I fell into the general mistake and thought your father had changed his mind about keeping single for evermore and had turned his thoughts on mother."

"Now you see the truth then," she said, "and I'm glad you do, Rupert. I wouldn't expect there was going to be a lot to father when he passes over, but every penny ought to be mine in God's good time, and I'd much object to the thought of him marrying again."

Rupert considered this.

"A very proper feeling," he said. "And I'm with you. But I'll turn it over. Honeywood's got good money, so they say. But you can't make a man marry, though you may stop him from marrying if you have the power. I'll think how best to get something to serve us out of this. Don't you name it to anybody meanwhile."

Thus the discovery was left in Rupert's hands and when they parted and he went to his work, he occupied the nocturnal hours with reflections equally dark. Upon the whole he felt something desirable lurked in his mother's promise to his future father-in-law, though in what way benefit might accrue to himself was not apparent. Their enterprise had ended unfruitfully for the plotters; but Rupert's instincts already suggested that profit might be extracted from Paul Pook for the return of this understanding. He confessed to himself, however, that a man cannot reasonably blackmail his future wife's father, nor in any case, as reason assured him, was the discovery likely to command a stiff price. Moreover, his own mother being as deeply involved added another difficulty to direct action. Then Rupert surveyed the matter from quite a different point of view and began to see light. A new and brilliant angle of approach suggested itself to his ingenious mind, whereby any future hope for Ivy was not lost and his parent's unfortunate circumstances also mended. Rupert knew that in all human affairs nothing could be counted upon with absolute certainty save the inevitable circumstance of death; but a method by which Mrs. Canniford's agreement might yet be used with likelihood of success finally presented itself and he completed his vigil in quiet elation. He decided that the parties to this undertaking were of far less importance than the victim against whom their endeavours were designed. His purpose grew with astonishing speed and he saw its speedy approach to flower and fruit. As he pursued its speedy development he marked that one aspect and consequence was little likely to please Ivy; but this fact did not deter him from proceeding without consulting her. Everything was cut and dried in the young man's mind before he went home and while the ultimate issue still remained a matter of doubt, one swift and definite sequel appeared assured.

'That'll be the end of Tubby once for all,' he told himself, 'and a good riddance. Him off the map, the decks are cleared; and that's going to be where I come in. With some women I'd be kept out and told to mind my

E

own business; but I know mother like a book and it ought to be easy enough, though all turns on her of course.' He considered Jenny's reaction on discovering that the market-gardener was finally and irrevocably lost and decided that she would weather the shock. 'It may not be such a deuce of a facer in any case,' he reflected, 'and if the luck's with me, she might even feel thankful come presently. There must be a side to marriage with Peter Honeywood that was dreadful for her to think upon sometimes.'

There remained the exact nature of his coming stroke and here craft would be needed. Rupert inclined towards an anonymous approach, since he had no wish that Ivy or himself should be implicated in the attack now to be launched against Peter. And this he determined from no fear for himself, but because his apparent innocence would much strengthen his hand when future phases of the incident called for action.

'If he knew I was at the bottom of it, Paul Pook would get nasty with me,' thought Rupert, 'and if he thought Ivy had done the trick, he'd hate her worse than he does. But if some unknown outsider gives the show away, then we're all right and no call for me to put no pressure on my future father-in-law.' Finally he spared a thought for Ivy herself.

'With her sense of duty it will be best not to put any pressure on her,' decided Rupert. 'Her sense of duty might well spoil all and be tiresome, so she shan't know a thing about it.' He was impressed by the exceeding simplicity of his conclusion. It seemed that the mountain of his reasoning and secret debate had produced no more than a mouse, yet he was well satisfied that nothing better could have appeared. 'Half the battle in a case same as this,' he told himself, 'is to do something that can't be brought home to you and know nought about it afterwards'; and upon this principle Rupert proceeded. When next they met on the following day he told Ivy a lie, which appeared so probable that she believed it without difficulty.

"A bothersome thing happed after I left you last night," he began, "I dipped in my pocket for a cartridge to load my gun, because I always load when I go in the preserves, and all unbeknownst to myself I must have dropped that nonsense mother signed for your dad. Stupid of me, and when I found it weren't there, I had a look where I must have dropped it. 'Twas gone, however, fallen in some hollow most like. It don't matter a lot all the same, because, thinking it over, I can't see what good it would have served to let 'em know we'd found 'em out. Nobody likes to be found out and laughed at after. There's a lot of touchy fools would forgive murder before laughter. Such a caper's better forgot, and I dare say Mr. Pook has forgot it ere now and mother too."

"So long as no enemy don't find it," she said.

"Little likely in the Manor woods. And they couldn't make top nor tail of it if they did. The thing's dead now in any case. And we can't mention it without telling 'em you found it under your father's desk and read it. And that might strike him as a funny thing for you to do."

"I'd thought of that myself," confessed Ivy.

"I quite agree it was your duty to read it and bring it to me," declared Rupert, "and admire you for doing so, but he might feel different. The middle-aged don't like to look silly in the eyes of their children, though they mostly do."

"If you hadn't lost it, I'd have slipped it back under his desk and let him find it," said Ivy. "He may remember and worry to think it's gone."

"If he do, he'll soon forget it," promised Rupert. "He'll have your marriage on his hands now. He's asked me about that and I've told him it can't be too quiet. 'Keep your money in your pocket,' I said. 'We'd hate a lot of silly expense and don't want nothing in the nature of a flare up.' And he allowed he was very glad to hear it. He's given you a nice bit of money as it is and far better what he's got should be saved than spent."

She admitted this and turned to the scene of their honeymoon—a problem that interested her more than Rupert. Indeed they tended to differ, for Ivy much desired to revisit London and show him some of the sights, whereas he had never seen London and never wanted to do so. In olden days, when Lady Garland repaired to town in spring, Ivy had accompanied her to the family mansion, and her desire was to see the metropolis once more; but young Canniford anticipated no pleasure from any such experience.

Mature thought satisfied Rupert that his present inspiration was sound and, a few days later, he posted his mother's undertaking, without any comment whatsoever, to Peter Honeywood. For once some prevision for another person than himself moved him, for while he guessed that the immediate results of this action must be painful, he looked ahead and perceived the possibility of a sequel surely destined to atone. Thus it came about that in an unguarded moment, when Jenny stood at her cottage door chatting about nothing in particular to a neighbour, there burst suddenly upon her, as she afterwards declared, one of the most unexpected and distressful experiences in her life. She had spent some time at Pigslake of late endeavouring to make Myra take a charitable view of Rupert's coming marriage; but Mrs. Withers would not forgive Rupert and declined to feel any interest in him.

"No good talking," she said to Jenny, "and no use pretending. He's up to some low-down game and hatched some cunning plot, and for my part and my children's part, we never want to see him again. You're all right and Paul Pook's all right. A better man never walked; but his Ivy and your Rupert are a beastly pair in my opinion and you'll both be well rid of 'em when they go and live to the Manor lodge—if they ever do. But so like as not he'll give her the slip at the last moment."

Somewhat hurt by these stern words, Mrs. Canniford had decided to abandon the farm for a while and allow Myra to make the next approach. Now her personal affairs were thrust harshly upon her. Mr. Honeywood's last appearance had been at tea, when he had praised her hand with a plum cake, but made no demand for it on his own account; yet now, at an unusually early hour, he suddenly appeared and bore down upon Jenny. It was only an hour after breakfast and Peter's very gait as he approached indicated that exceptional reasons had brought him. Nor did it take long for the widow to perceive that his reasons were unpleasant. He was clad in his working clothes; not a jewel made glad his person; he wore a black bowler hat and upon his red face there sat the nearest thing to a scowl she had ever seen there. The neighbour hastily withdrew at his approach and a moment later he stood on one side of Jenny's wicket-gate while she greeted him from the other. His jaws were working and for a moment he was dumb.

"He properly glared at me, but couldn't find no words to open with," said Mrs. Canniford, when she related the incident afterwards; "but I saw that he was angered to the roots, so I spoke first."

This indeed she had done.

"Why, my dear man !" exclaimed Jenny, "what evil have overtook you ?"

Then Peter spoke in a strange and formidable voice.

"'Tis what's overtook you, I reckon," he replied. "Step in your house, please. I've heard something."

"And not too good news by the sound of you," she answered. "Come in by all means. Always welcome as you well know."

He followed her without more words and when they were in her kitchen and the man had taken a seat and put off his hat, she spoke again.

"Early hours. Will you have a nice cup of fresh milk and light your pipe," suggested Jenny; but he declined.

"No, I don't take no milk, nor yet light no pipe under this roof no more," he said. Then he drew out a handkerchief and mopped his head, while his jaws still worked. For some reason the widow did not find herself as stricken as she expected. That he had come to quarrel was evident and, imagining no possible reason why he should, her temperature also rose a little and she resented it.

"If you're in trouble," she told him, "I'm sorry; but why your trouble should make you run across Priory to be rude to me, I'd like to know."

"You're going to know here and now," he answered, "and more than that: Old Pook's going to know too."

"Is he ? I shouldn't call him old whether or no."

"Be damned to his age and be damned to him. Now you can listen and I don't want back answers neither. I've respected you for a good few years now, as well you know, Jenny Canniford."

"Why not ?" she asked.

"No reason till half an hour agone when among my business letters was an envelope conveying to me this document, showing under your own hand how you and Pook plotted against me for a purpose. And when that purpose was reached, the document was to be destroyed. Instead of waiting with patience and womanly pride for me to speak at the accepted hour, if so I willed, you went behind my back and wove a dirty trap to thrust yourself upon me and jump down my throat for greed to get me to the altar, and all the time prancing before the parish and pretending to be a high-principled, self-respecting woman well worthy of a man like me."

Jenny felt the blood rush to her face, then retreat again; but she kept her wits and made no reply whatever. He had ceased and awaited her answer, while her silence put him out of his stride.

"A very monstrous thing and well you may turn red upon it," he continued, "and well may I thank God I was let into a sight of your hookem-snivey nature. You've done evil, and you've failed, and I'm saved instead of lost, which I should have been if I'd offered for you."

Then Jenny spoke.

"I ain't going into no details," she said. "And I wouldn't stop here any longer if I was you. Best to push off. But I'll ask for that document, because it's my property and I'd dearly like to know how the mischief it reached your hand."

Peter declined her request.

"Not till I've shown this to Pook you don't have it," he replied, rising and returning the agreement to his pocket. "We'll hear what he's got to say next and I may go further and hear what other folk have got to say. And now I'll leave you for the last time, Mrs. Canniford."

"You can't go none too soon for me, Mr. Honeywood," she answered, "and you've misread my character, and may God forgive you for it, because I never will. 'Tis you are shown up, not me, and when you find a straighter, cleaner-minded woman than what I am, and one who had more respect for your character than what I had till now, I'd like to see her."

"It's off—all off once for all," he answered, "and no more women for me, straight or otherwise. Be damned to the pack of you !"

Jenny observed that he had lost his fire and walked down the garden path with a bent back.

"Yes," she said, claiming the last word, "it's all off as you say, if ever it was on, and angels wouldn't bring it back again. I never had in my mind for an instant moment to take any other man but you, and if I haven't been patient and long-suffering, waiting till your insulting caution was at an end, then the Lord never made a patient woman. But it's off as you say, and I'll be very well content to bide the relic of a better man than you, who valued me and died blessing my name."

It was the turn of Peter to adopt silence. He shuffled away and, after he was gone, Jenny's fighting spirit failed and she returned, limp and stricken, to her home. Her indignation cooled; her heart sank; tears sprang to her eyes and she let them fall. Then she calmed down, licked her bruises and felt deep yearnings for a sympathetic confidante. The circumstances however forbade any confession save to Mr. Pook himself and for him she began to feel genuine sorrow. He was a sensitive creature and an exposure of this kind could not fail to try him sadly. She had bluffed Peter to the best of her power and was of opinion that she had come fairly well from the ordeal, but what would Paul say ? His case was far more grave than her own, and it looked safe to assume that she must suffer in that quarter also when the saddler discovered the disgrace into which she had brought him. She decided that if Paul was also going to be angry with her, then one fair argument should oppose his annoyance. That the fatal document had ever reached Peter's hand could only be through Mr. Pook's carelessness, and if he declared a grievance, surely she might oppose it with a greater ? He had told her that he could not find their agreement; but it was now hideously apparent that somebody else had done so and sent it anonymously to the subject of the plot. Here arose matter for prolonged reflection and Jenny marvelled why either of them should possess any enemy capable of such an unfriendly action. To imagine secret foes, or put a name to them, lay quite beyond her power.

At this juncture in her melancholy reverse there came distraction. Along the garden path crept two little figures, hand in hand, and two little ugly faces peeped up at their stricken grandmother. They were Emmeline and Percy. To Myra, in strictest secrecy, Jenny had often confided that she won far greater pleasure from her grandchildren than their parents, and perhaps unconsciously aware of this fact, not seldom, when enabled to do so, Emmeline and Percy would escape from home and make for Mrs. Canniford, the elder. When they were missing, Susan, their mother, always knew where to find them, but seldom before the children's purpose had been attained.

It was Emmeline who spoke.

"Granny darlin'," she said, "have 'e got a spot of somefin' for me and Percy to eat ?"

The plea was often whispered and never denied.

"Yes I have then, my lovelies," answered Jenny promptly, and her thought sweetened.

She kissed them and spoke what came to her mind.

"And when you grow up, Emmeline, remember the only happiness worth a mite is to be got by trying to make somebody else happy. If you try to make yourself happy, you're a born fool, because it can't be done."

When their mother presently appeared full of chiding, her offspring were refreshed and equal to supporting the censure.

"Us have had a hugeous dollop of seedy pudding be it as it will," said Emmeline. She was fond of this expression, often hearing it upon her father's lips.

Susan turned to their grandmother and perceived that she had been weeping.

"Don't tell me the children have made you shed tears, else Harry will never forgive them," she said.

"No, no, my dear, not them," said Jenny. "A cold in my head I expect. They'll never make me cry, nor yet make you cry, please God."

When they had gone she considered how swiftly she might approach Paul and feared that Peter had already done so after leaving her. This proved the fact for, on reaching Mr. Pook's shop, she found him working at some new harness and he told her that Honeywood had presented himself with the shocking news.

"I know why you're come," he told her, "because Peter said he had let loose on you first."

He, too, observed that Jenny had been in tears.

"No cause to let this show-up get you down," he continued. "In a misfortunate affair of this kind, the first thing is to keep your nerve and look all round it, Jenny. And what do we find ? The fault was mine ever to make you sign the paper."

"He'll flourish it all round the parish before nightfall," said Jenny, tears returning to her eyes.

"Don't cry," continued Paul, "and you can take this to your comfort : he won't flourish it round the parish for two reasons. Firstly because I've got it in my pocket, and secondly because, up in the air as he certainly is, he'd know he couldn't do that without looking terribly silly himself. He came in here gobbling like a turkey cock and put the document in my hand, and after I'd read it over and seen what it was and heard how he'd come by it, I stuffed it in my pocket and said it was a private agreement I'd happened to lose and felt glad to find again and would destroy. He was a lot disappointed to find me so cool, for nothing chills a man in a rage so quick as finding the enemy not put about. I talked sense to him, and reminded him it was all his own fault for treating an exception of a woman, with a stainless record like you, as if she was a doubtful customer, and I said you were well in your rights to try and bring him up to the point and get on with it.''

"He's got on with it anyway now," said Jenny. "He's dropped me, and I told him I was thankful to God he had done and wouldn't marry him now for anything on earth.''

"So he told me, and I was glad to hear it. We've cleared the air if no more," replied Paul. "He had grown to be a good bit of an incubus in my opinion and didn't know his company where you are concerned, else these things wouldn't have fallen out. So much for that and, very like, you'll live to look back and be thankful he's gone for good. Or he may change his mind presently and come sneaking to your feet like a spaniel so humble as need be. But what's got me for the minute is how the mischief ever this bit of paper reached him of all people. That looks the most serious thing to the whole affair. Now, just when life turns cheerful for me and the coast going to be cleared after Ivy's married, down comes this queer bit of work. Who the mischief done it? And how did they do it? I'd swear on the Book I never dropped your paper out of doors. I couldn't do so, because I'd lost it and didn't know where it had got to. Then we're faced with the cruel, ugly fact that it was found in my house, or among the papers on my desk, where I'd piled them to look for it. But there again, it wasn't among them, because I'd already turned them over.''

Jenny's thoughts drifted upon his daughter; but she was cautious.

"Have you asked Ivy if anybody came into the house and was left in that room while she went to seek you, or anything like that?" she suggested.

"I have not," he answered, "because no such thing could have happened. None goes in that room but me and her. That's why I say it's ugly. If by ill chance she came on the paper, she might have cast her eyes over it. She might even have thought it was her duty to make it known, because her duty to my certain knowledge almost always takes a very unpleasant shape for somebody else. But how could her duty have led her to do an anonymous beastliness like this? I don't like Ivy and she don't like me, but never in my life did I do a thing to make her a secret enemy.''

"It wasn't you, I'm sure," said Jenny. "Never a better, patienter father than what you've been to the girl; but it might have been me I'm fearing. She don't like me at all, though I've tried my bestest to pleasure her since she was going to marry Rupert and enter our family. But long ago I hinted that she wasn't one of the outstanding beauties of the parish, and she never forgot it and may never have forgiven it. And so—though I blush to think such a thing—she may have seen her chance to put a spoke in my wheel with Honeywood.''

Paul considered this view.

"If that's true," he said, "she did you a good turn where she thought she was serving you a bad one. In which case you may say Providence put a spoke in Ivy's wheel, not in yours. But blood's thicker than water and I wouldn't like to believe, whatever her feelings about me or you, that she would give us a stab in the back same as this."

"She couldn't fail to know this was going to be terrible unpleasant for you as well as me," admitted Mrs. Canniford. "And how's she the gainer anyway? You've given her a grand marriage dowry, whatever you think of her, and, if she's got eyes in her face, she must know she's as plain as bread and have catched a husband on some other hunting ground than her appearance."

Paul laughed.

"We'll rule her out," he said. "She don't solve the mystery in my opinion and no lasting harm can come of it in any case, except to the conscience of the anonymous person."

"Them that would do such a godless thing are little likely to have a conscience I'd say," declared the widow, "but if you can take it in such a large spirit, I'll try to do the ssme. And thank Heavens you've got the document, because, without it, anything Peter likes to say will only make the people doubt if he's telling the truth."

"That's right," he agreed, "so you and me can go our ways in peace. Our own ways without fret from outsiders. You're free and may make some marrying man happy yet, and none better pleased than me if you do; and I'm going to get my old couple back to look after me, same as before Ivy came and sacked 'em."

"A very clever thought, Paul, because they well know your ways and understand you must have your comforts."

"My ways are easy to understand, my dear, and all I ask is to be allowed to pursue them. Ivy understood my ways only too fatal well and found it her duty to block every one of 'em she discovered."

"Her ways being not as your ways I'm afraid," sighed Jenny.

"I wonder sometimes whether Rupert have got any ways in particular," mused Paul, "because if he has, she'll discover 'em to a dead certainty."

"He's got his ways all right," she assured him, "and I'd feel sorry for any woman born who thought to change them—duty or no duty. You see me and you are what you may call an easy-going pair, my dear man, and not the fighting sort. We only ask for peace and neither of us would oppose our own children. I'd say I've gone down like a reed in the wind before Rupert these years and years, and you've gone down before Ivy; but now our crosses will be lifted in that quarter, and how the pair of 'em may face matrimony, who can say? We can only hope it will be holy matrimony; but we can't promise it—not on our general knowledge of 'em."

"The sparks will fly no doubt; but I hope there won't be no general conflagration," said Paul. "Neither of 'em is a fool and they must have a tidy bit in common somewhere, else it couldn't have happened. For my part I've always thought well of Rupert in his business. He's hard, but a good keeper's got to be hard, and so long as Ivy don't dare to question his duty, or let her ideas interfere with his comfort, they may carry on as well as most married folk."

Paul lighted a match and consumed the cause of their confusion.

"Keep a good heart," he said, "and remember what you owe yourself.

Be dignified, Jenny, and carry on same as usual, as if nothing had happened."

"I'll try," she promised. "You might go so far as to say my dignity was lost; and if you ever find out who done this, Paul, let me hear who 'twas. Because I'd be wishful to keep clear of them."

"I certainly will," he promised. "There's a snake lurking in the grass somewhere and, if a man, you can trust me to deal with him. Knowledge have a knack of confounding your wisdom sometimes. You can be wise and carry on all right without knowing a devil of a lot, Jenny."

This reflection was beyond Mrs. Canniford and she changed the subject.

"For the likes of me I don't count on wisdom, nor yet happiness," she said. "All I pray to my Maker for these days is to find myself on firm ground. You've done most generous for Ivy and I wish I could do likewise for Rupert, but I haven't got no money to name. I'm sewing him six very fine wool shirts, however, and I get peace so long as I'm at 'em. It's a sad thing that he can't expect nothing in the way of a wedding gift from Pigslake, but so it is."

"I know all about that from Myra," said Paul. "To an old friend like me she can speak as she minds and no harm done. Better draw a veil over the past. Nora's all right and interested in somebody else by all accounts. No hurry for her."

Ivy intruded at this moment.

"Your dinner's cooling, Father," she said, then turned to Jenny.

They kissed when meeting now—as a matter of convention, but without ardour.

"Just telling your dear father how I'm building some fine flannel shirts for Rupert against winter, Ivy, and I hope you'll watch out and not spoil 'em when the time comes. Wool's often a sad sufferer in the wash."

"You don't need to feel no cares on that account, Mrs. Canniford. I know all there is to know about washing wool. Her ladyship was a great one for wool and never let it go out of my hands."

"Is she like by good chance to send you a wedding present, I wonder, when she hears tell about you and Rupert?" asked the elder; but Ivy shook her head.

"She would have for sure; but she's long past giving presents now. I asked one of her nurses—the cleverest of 'em—when I was up there to tell her how Rupert Canniford was going to marry me come June; which she did do. But she said the result was a blank, because Lady Garland had long forgot both Rupert and myself. People don't interest her no more—only her food. I think sometimes, if she was to see me, her memory might flicker up; but of course I couldn't ask for permission to see her."

"I dare say it would only hurt you if you did," said Paul, "and certainly do her no manner of good."

"Hovering on the brink no doubt," suggested Jenny, "and nobody was ever readier for flight upward than what she is. And Rupert blesses her name to this day—the only name I've ever heard him bless for that matter. And when she's gone, he's going to put in to be one of the bearers."

Ivy showed pleasure at this thought.

"A most proper idea for Rupert," she declared, "and I'll keep him up to it when the sad day comes. Sad for us I mean, not for her ladyship, because every day more on her death-bed, is a day less for her in her heavenly mansion."

"You was always a clever one at arithmetic, Ivy," said her father.

XIII

THE life-long friendship of Katey Wise and Nora Withers had already experienced a strain when Katey became engaged to the son of the family enemy, and to avoid that complication they agreed that Nora must not know Timothy. She herself declared no aversion but it was understood that Mrs. Withers would not tolerate any communion with Nelly Faircloud's son, so Timothy and Nora did not meet. His sweetheart, however, had painted him in colours so brilliant to her friend that Nora would much have liked to know him and hoped, in future time, to do so. Katey was always welcome herself at Pigslake but, on the occasion of numerous visits, icy silence concerning her betrothed had been maintained. Now arose a trifling complication for the reason that Rupert Canniford, having no particular companion to fill the office, fell in with Timothy among the woodmen at the Manor and invited him to be his best man. Such a suggestion greatly pleased the younger, who considered it a compliment, and indeed Rupert felt friendly enough to Nelly's son, admiring in a fashion his love of the wild and the sort of life the gamekeeper himself best enjoyed to live. But, when she heard the news, Jenny felt in no small concern, for Rupert had long since ceased to be a welcome sight at Pigslake and it looked exceedingly doubtful whether the Withers folk would pay any attention to his approaching wedding or respond to Paul's invitation to attend it. The matter was still in the air and Mr. Pook himself felt uncertain whether Myra might care to join the wedding party; but that Timothy was going to be Rupert's best man, and therefore entitled to attend the marriage feast, promised to banish any hope whatever from the farm. Jenny pleaded with her son, and found him quite indifferent.

"It don't matter a button if they come or if they don't," he said. "There's nothing to be gained out of that lot and I've other things to think upon for the minute in any case—you among the rest."

Why she occupied even a corner of his mind Jenny was at a loss to imagine, but a fortnight before the marriage date she learned.

Mrs. Canniford soon found that Peter had now determined to know her no more. The next time they met in the open street, he marched past her looking straight in front of him and she perceived that Paul's prophecy had failed. The market-gardener was gone, and his disappearance from her life created a void. 'If I hadn't tried so hard to get him, belike I'd never have lost him,' she reflected, 'but things being what they are, I can't find it in my heart to blame him.' She wondered whether Mr. Honeywood experienced like emotions, but guessed not. 'His Irish blood will rage against me for evermore now,' she thought. 'I can only forgive the poor soul and keep out of his way.'

It was about this time that her younger son took a high hand with Jenny and asserted himself in a manner beyond her experience. Like a wolf upon a lamb Rupert descended and though, in the welter of concern thus wakened, she could not fail to feel her welfare appeared for once to be his prime purpose, the violence of his ideas and the stark nakedness of his words when he set them before her, cast Mrs. Canniford into further tribulation. He stayed at home one night after his supper and displayed his usual indifference to her feelings; but he was in a good temper and Jenny felt that he meant well. In truth Rupert prided himself thus far upon the success of his own devious enterprise, for the plot to destroy all hope for his mother in the direction of Peter Honeywood had clearly prospered. Everybody knew of the breach, while none but the sufferers and Rupert himself understood the reason. Ivy was quite ignorant and her future mother-in-law did not interest her in any case. But sharp eyes had marked Peter pass Jenny in the open street without acknowledgment; even Harry Canniford was aware that weeks had passed since her admirer came to Sunday tea with his mother. Nor had he failed to remark her unusual and persistent melancholy.

"She's a good bit under the weather," he told Susan. "She misses Honeywood, and she went so far as to tell me she'll miss Rupert when he goes."

"Us ought to think upon a wedding present for him," said Susan. "He won't get many."

"He ain't the fashion of man to earn many presents," replied Harry, "and Ivy ain't the type to get any at all. I shan't do nothing myself and he's making difficulties to the end, because to choose Faircloud for his best man was to defy Pigslake. Not that other peoples' ill conveniences ever troubled him."

Now, having lighted a pipe, Rupert struck harshly into his mother's affairs.

"Seems like you've given your fancy man the go-by now," he said. "I'm too busy to take note of such things for the minute, but so they tell me at the 'Pen-in-Hand,' and I'm very glad to hear it for that matter. What's happened? You're well out of it anyway. He'd have driven you daft. He's a tyrant under his grinning face, as them that work for him would tell you."

"I don't want to discuss Mr. Honeywood, Rupert," she answered. "It's enough that he hurt my feelings very bad, and I hurt his still worse, so we dismissed each other."

Rupert smiled.

"I'd have given a finger off my hand to hear you," he said, "but you're sure it's final? You ain't waiting for him to crawl back and find you've conquered him after all."

"No," she answered. "I'm not waiting for anything like that, Rupert. I've no wish to conquer Mr. Honeywood any more, nor let him conquer me. I wouldn't take the man now if he was twice what he is, because he forgot himself last time we met. A man with his yearnings for precaution didn't ought to marry anybody. His hair will grow white and he'll be in his eighties before he comes to a conclusion."

"Too late then," agreed Rupert. "Would you say that hob-nobbing with Paul Pook had helped you to see he was a better man all round than Peter—a sort of husband worthy of your famous gifts ?"

"I ain't got no gifts and never claimed none," replied Jenny, "but this I will say: if there were more like Paul and fewer like Peter the world might be a happier place."

"Honeywood at his best never held a candle to Pook—you'd agree to that ?"

His mother hesitated.

"It may seem a mean thing to say, Rupert, but in honesty, knowing the both of them, I'll grant Paul is trustworthy."

"Trustworthy—yes, and like to make a husband to suit you better ?"

"I won't be mean," repeated Jenny, "and if I was to run down Peter Honeywood now he's sunk into my past, people would only say it was sour grapes, because he's had enough of me. There was a lot of him I much admired and he had a cheerful outlook on his prosperous days and a funny story to tell you now and again and a nice basket of green stuff off and on. A lighter touch than Paul, and a lonely woman like me, with two sons that never made a joke in their lives, certainly did find Honeywood a ray of brightness now and again. And a ray of hope also. But if you take the higher view, then I can admit to you in private, Rupert, that for trustable qualities, Mr. Pook's the finer man. He wears better, if you understand me."

"I think a lot of him myself and he thinks a lot of me," answered her son. "He's took to me tremendous since I fell in love with Ivy, and he's told me in so many words that he couldn't have wished for a better man to have her than what I am."

"I know he's very relieved about it," admitted Jenny. "And a nice bit of money he's giving her."

"Well then, how would you like to marry Paul ?" he asked, "because, if you would, you damn well shall marry him."

Jenny gasped.

"If I have many more shocks from you, Rupert," she said faintly, "you'll see me drop down in a heap and die under your eyes. Nobody ever tore the common decency out of life like what you do."

"No need to twitter about that," he said. "Stick to facts and trust me. I'm a darned good son if you only knew it and wishful for you to be all right when I clear out."

His mother pressed her hand to her bosom and strove to steady her breathing.

"You'll puzzle and terrify me to my grave," she said, "and I'll ask you a question for yours. How do you dare to take Paul Pook's name in vain like that, and tell me 'tis in your power to give him to me if I was to want him ? Have Ivy Pook weakened your brain ? Don't you well know her father will never take another having had all he wanted, and more, with his first ?"

"Don't chatter," continued Rupert. "I'm very well intending towards you and why not ? You was a good mother to me according to your limited lights and, for once, I can do you a rare good turn. Nought in it for me neither. Just a happy thought on your account. All I need to know is whether you want Pook, or don't want him. If you can see yourself wed to the man and making a success of it, well and good. If you don't, you've only got to say so. Don't bleat about it—just a plain answer before I clear out."

Jenny, however, would not oblige him. She stared at her son and shook her head.

"The only way with you, Rupert, is to sink to your own low levels seemingly," she said. "I've tried time and again to lift your manners, and I lay my life you don't talk like that to Ivy, else she'd never have took you. And it's a pity you can't pick your words to your mother nicer; but I feel touched to hear you say you're well intending to me, though not knowing any reason why you should not be."

"Get on with it," he said, rising and preparing to leave her. "Between mother and son can't we have plain speaking? Yes or no's easily said."

"I see the point of that and I'm glad you feel there ought to be understanding between mother and son, Rupert," replied Mrs. Canniford. "I've always been only too wishful for understanding with people all my life, because half the pitiful messes on earth happen where there ain't none. And for your ear alone and sacred at that, I should be willing to take my valued friend, Mr. Pook, if the idea got in his mind—not otherwise."

"Right," said Rupert, preparing to depart. "Then it mighty soon shall get in his mind, Mother."

"Wait!" she said. "Hear me, Rupert, and mark what I told you. If the idea got in his mind—them were my words. Not if the idea got in your mind as it looks to have done. You haven't got the touch for a delicate subject and never did have, and for you to dare to tell him this would be fatal to my good name. You asked me a terrible impertinent question and I've returned a true answer, and that's the end of the matter if you've got a spark of proper feeling left in you."

But Rupert was out of the house before she had finished and, in growing disorder of spirit, his mother viewed the future. 'Now they're both gone,' she reflected, 'and I shan't even number Paul among my men friends no more, because once this was to come to his ears, he wouldn't know me, but pass by on the other side, same as Peter do. And well he might!"

Of this disaster she heard no more immediately, yet further cause for tribulation overtook the widow when, a few days later, Rupert announced that he had invited Timothy Faircloud and his sweetheart to tea on the following Sunday.

"He's going to stand best man for me and civility costs nothing and I'll pay you a shilling for the food," promised Rupert. "You'll like Katey: she's a smart little piece and Timothy's all right in his way. You've got to have a best man seemingly, though Lord knows why. And Ivy's looking round for a bridesmaid. She hasn't got many girl friends, thank God. We've agreed the fewer outsiders poking into our lives, the better."

"Never you said a truer word than that," his mother told him, "and I wish you'd practised what you preach, Rupert, and didn't poke into the lives of your betters; but I'm not against Faircloud and Milly Wish's daughter coming to tea, though I feel terrible 'feared your Aunt Myra will think it's treachery in a manner of speaking for me to have any truck with that boy. Your stock don't run too high at Pigslake, be it as it will, and I'm cruel afraid none will join up at the wedding from that quarter."

"To hell with 'em," he said. "Let 'em bide away. Timothy and Kate come to tea Sunday anyhow."

The lovers duly appeared. Changes of view had developed in the lad of late and his future wife confessed herself as uneasily proud of them. He was restless and egotistic as usual, but he had continued to develop an intense zest and eagerness for books, while their influence began to assert itself profoundly. They were in process of purifying his speech as well as tincturing his mind. He delighted to utter startling novelties, and when Katey sometimes protested, he admitted that the new ideas had come from reading, but that he had already thought these things and now could claim support from printed authority. He began to love books for themselves and show an instinct to collect them and care for them.

"He's getting that clever there won't be no bearing him one of these days," so Katey told her mother; "but all to the good, because the more he reads, the less he dreams. He's prouder than ever now he's getting a fine way of talking, and it all points to the end of his woodman's work when he finds something more in keeping with his intellects. He knows he's very near finished at the Manor now."

The parents applauded Timothy's progress and Samuel Wish held it more than time.

"He must put off childish things, like cutting down trees and planting new ones," the baker told Katey. "All very right and got to be done, but what you say is true. He's reaching to his full strength of brain and that will teach him he must turn to indoor work, where the money is."

Timothy had expressed this opinion himself.

"The time has come for me to rise above a day labourer," he told Mr. Wish. "I love the trees, same as I always have and always shall; but I love my wits better and must polish them brighter and brighter for Katey's sake as well as my own fame."

Fame continued a very steadfast beacon in the growing intelligence of Timothy; but as yet, though acutely conscious of it already and quite convinced it was well earned, circumstances kept him dumb. While inclination prompted a yearning that, in one quarter at least, it might be told and praised, he hovered still upon the brink of confession in that quarter. But mistrust of the result held his tongue. Sometimes he felt that a stupendous and triumphant response was assured; at other times the outcome looked more doubtful. So he put it by until further light should shine upon his new horizons, seeking from his reading to find that light. But it was typical of Timothy that he only regarded the secret evidence of his powers from a personal angle and only fitfully considered how the revelation, if ever he made it, might affect Katey.

Now they came together and took tea with Mrs. Canniford and her son. Jenny knew him well enough by sight and admired him exceedingly, but she had not heard his voice before, save in singing, and felt during his visit an uncomfortable sense that the home of Myra's sister was no place for him. She also recollected acutely her sole meeting with Timothy's mother, Nelly's advice on that occasion and the miserable result of taking it. But the youth was on his best behaviour, courteous and attractive. Jenny felt a liking for him wake within her, perceived that he approached manhood, even wondered whether a dawning moustache would mar his face or improve it. His manners delighted her, for she had not seen a male wait upon females since her husband died. Even Peter had never displayed such attention at table; while, contrasted with Timothy, Rupert appeared little better than a bear, both in voice and gesture. Katey, who already knew Mrs. Canniford, displayed naïve pleasure at Timothy's performance and told Jenny, when they talked together, that her betrothed was much gratified and flattered at the distinction put upon him.

"I always wanted to show him to you if you were willing, Mrs. Canniford," she said, "but I never thought he'd stand so high with your son as to be chose for best man."

The entertainment passed off without a cloud and after the lovers had departed together, Timothy declared the whole business very mysterious.

"Because of Pigslake," he said. "We don't live more than half a mile away and the Withers folk pass you by as if they didn't know you were there, yet Mrs. Canniford could let me come to her house and certainly Rupert thinks well of me."

"So do anybody else if they know what you truly are, and your mother too," said Kate.

After they were gone Jenny discussed them with her son.

"He's not a gentleman really, of course," she said, "but he's picked up their ways something wonderful and their book language and everything. Where he got 'em I couldn't tell you."

"Nelly could—or perhaps she couldn't," grinned Rupert. "But he's all right—just the figure-head for a best man. He's all for reading books now he tells me. I often find him with his nose in a little book when he ought to be earning his money in the woods."

"Katey says he's making a collection of 'em. In fact she told me at tea, when he was talking to you, that the boy spends too much money on them. But his mother has took out a library subscription for him, so Katey tells."

"He's reaching a point when he'll quit the Manor," predicted Rupert. "I can see it coming. He ain't built for forestry, more than a hunter's built to pull a farm cart. Books are choking him off manual labour same as they do lots of others."

"So his young woman says," replied Jenny. "She told me her father was at Timothy to go in a town for what they call the higher education, which leads to better money; and then he'll most like find something to do, with promise and security to follow."

"He's torn in half, because he's well content to bide with the trees," explained Rupert, "but you can't have it both ways. I'm the same myself for that matter. I might have done more for myself black-coated, but I'd rather be a poor open-air man than a rich indoor one."

"Your dear father was the same and you get that feeling from him, Rupert," she declared. "He always said household air lowered his spirits, and when he got down, as he often did, poor man, he'd rush out in the open air—even by night sometimes—and sleep under a haystack and return cheerful again."

It was about this time, within a month of his wedding, that Rupert proceeded with operations involving his promise to his mother. They were crude and highly offensive, but that troubled him not at all, nor did the possibility of failure give him any concern.

He approached Mr. Pook on a night when they left the 'Pen in Hand' together and asked for a few words upon an important subject.

"It's going to surprise you above a bit, so I'll come in for half-an-hour and you can hear it sitting down," he said.

"What's in the wind now," asked Paul. "You young shavers live at such a rate and take everything in your stride; but at my time of life, I find your mind's apt to work slower and steadier. When I want speed, I get on my horse, Rupert."

They sat together presently and had the house to themselves, because Ivy was from home visiting some of her mother's relations.

"Light your pipe and listen," began Rupert. "Marriage is like death seemingly. Before you enter into it, you have to take a last look round you and satisfy yourself your affairs are in order and them dependent on you safe and so on. Or so I feel it. In my case there's only mother. Harry's no use as you know and, in future, I shan't have it in my power to help her, because a wife comes first and a son can't never be the same to his mother after he's married. I see that and Ivy agrees with me."

"All very true," agreed Paul, "but not leading anywhere in particular I'd say."

"Yes it do, because I think a deuce of a lot of my mother. She's the finest woman in the parish in my opinion, and I'm not at all disposed to see her out in the cold all her life—a woman made to partner a good man and be the apple of his eye."

"She is that," admitted Paul.

"I held my hand," continued the game keeper, "I held my hand though burning with impatience, for Honeywood to speak, because he made no effort to hide his feelings. But the fat fool hung fire till I was sick of the sight of him. And then I couldn't but see you thought a lot of mother, too, and you don't need for me to tell you, Paul, I'd a million times sooner you had the blessing of mother in your life than 'Tubby'."

"Meaning Honeywood ?"

"Yes, meaning him. Grows more like one of his own vegetable marrows every day to my eye. As a man he ain't in your class and never could be. But all these things was outside my pigeon and not my business for the minute."

Rupert trod warily now and gave no hint of the truth.

"Then what happened ?" he continued, "I find the market-gardener, for some dirty reason known only to himself, has gone off mother, and mother—so I was thankful to hear—though outraged to her bones, didn't feel so put about as you might have fancied she would have. You see, while he was philandering with mother and drinking her tea and flashing his trinkets about and throwing her a carrot or turnip now and then, as if she was a rabbit, you came along and showed a lot of interest in her and opened her eyes to what a man can be. She mighty soon found there was a proper gulf fixed between you and Peter, and the result of that was, when he went off the map, she didn't feel so terrible cast down after all. And that's how it stands at this moment."

Rupert stopped and lighted his pipe, while Paul considered whether to tell him facts, already only too familiar to both of them. He decided, however, that this could not with propriety be done since Jenny's secret must never reach her son.

"That's how it stands," agreed Mr. Pook, "and I wouldn't say that it was any business of yours to bring the matter to my attention, Rupert."

"None, none, except that a son's business did ought always to be his mother's happiness and contentment," replied the younger. "But I'd go so far as to say, with all respect, that it was your business. A man like you stand head and shoulders above us everyday men, and I've always felt a deep respect for you and been jealous to keep your friendship and proud to have won it. That you well know, and when you agreed for me to have Ivy and told me you was well suited, I felt properly bucked up about it to think I'd have such a father-in-law as you. And I felt there wasn't nothing I wouldn't do for you to show my gratitude, and I feel so still."

"That's all right. I don't want no gratitude and shall always be willing to befriend you for Ivy's sake and your own also," promised Paul.

"And thank you for them words, Mr. Pook," answered Rupert, "but we're travelling away from mother. Now, if you'll excuse me, there's first what you think of mother and next what she thinks of you. And I know what you think of mother, else you wouldn't have paid her such fine attention of late. You was always her first friend in the old days as I well remember after father died; but nothing to it then, though she'd often sing your praises; but now there is something to it and that's where my gratitude comes in, because I know what you think of her, and I'm doing all this talking just because I want to tell you what she thinks of you at this present moment."

"I've every reason to believe she thinks of me as well as I think of her, Rupert," said the elder.

"In that case I'm wasting my wind and your time, and I'd like to think that was true," declared young Canniford. "Because, if it was true, then there's nought between you and mother and I'd wish you joy of each other and feel it was the best day of my life if you two joined up."

"Curious talk from you to me," answered Paul. "Very curious talk indeed in my opinion."

"Never a talk more curious I'd say," agreed Rupert. "And nothing more curious than for me to be talking at all, because I'm no talker in general as you know. But I've very near finished now and I can do with a drink when I have. We come next to the fact that my dear mother is fixed in her opinion that you'll never wed again and, when she told me that, I told her how circumstances alter cases and how a wise man like you was never known to let a determination, grown to be years and years old, hamper his movements when the scene had changed like it has changed for you."

"As to that, my mind's open as every man's mind should be," said Paul. "I demand liberty of action from my neighbours same as I grant liberty of action to them, so long as their actions keep inside the law. That's what they call democracy, Rupert. And democracy's another name for freedom."

"So I've always understood, and so long as you hold yourself free to marry again, I'm much hoping you'll marry mother, because I well know what an addition to your home you'd find her," proceeded the widow's son. "I ain't blind. I know very well indeed that Ivy—clever and precious creature though she is—haven't added to your comfort nor yet your liberty. Love her as I do and you do, I can see with half an eye that she wasn't planned on a pattern to make her your right hand. To me she'll be my right hand without a doubt; but not to you. What you want is the seeing eye and a clever touch and the understanding that you've got your own ideas of comfort and convenience, and nothing on God's earth must happen to interfere with them ideas. No daughter can look in her father's heart like an experienced and loving widow from outside, and along with mother you'd find that she'd add to your well-being at every turn and be like a coal fire in an empty grate— properly change the whole scene of action for you."

"My life !" said the saddler. "You never gave me to understand you thought such a lot of Mrs. Canniford, and you never gave her to understand you thought such a lot of either, if you'll pardon my saying so."

But Rupert brushed away this idle comment and took no notice of it.

"Another interesting thing is that she loves both dogs and birds same as you do. You always run a fox-hound puppy for the Hunt and if you under-took a dozen, they'd be safe to win her affection. You wouldn't be content to the full without a dog-lover for a wife and no doubt you've marked that Ivy don't over-much like dogs indoors. I'd say she was cold-hearted about dogs, but I shall learn her better presently."

Rupert ceased for a while, but Paul made no attempt to fill the silence. He rose, however, and fetched out a bottle of unsweetened gin and two glasses. They were sitting in the kitchen and he now brought water from a tap in the scullery that opened from it. Then he helped his visitor and himself and at last spoke.

"There's a good many would feel you were treading on holy ground to-night, and tell you to clear out, Rupert, and show a bit of annoyance over what you've got the face to talk about; but I like to see good motives working in my fellow creatures when it can be done, and though I've never yet marked you particular taken by the thought of helping other people, I'll go so far as to say you've got some idea to help your mother, though you've took a shocking line to do so."

"And you—to help you too. You can't deny the effort includes you," argued Rupert. "I ain't much for friends as you know, but no man who knew you as well as I do and have gained so much out of your good sense and is going to marry your daughter for that matter—no man situate like that would lose a chance to pleasure you if in his power. I've thought a deuce of a lot about this and hoped a deuce of a lot, too, when I saw how the cat looked to be jumping; and now I've screwed up courage to mention it. I didn't mean no shock to your feelings, but I put two and two together and looked at it from the viewpoint of you and mother. And it seemed to me there was a chance to further the only two people in the world I care a button about—after Ivy, of course."

"And how did you come by the queer piece of information that your mother was so amazingly well disposed to me that very like she'd take me if I offered ?" asked Mr. Pook thoughtfully. "In certain directions, Rupert, I may be said to know a lot more about your mother's character than what you do. And there's no shadow of doubt that she was going to take Honeywood if he'd given her the chance. Now things have happened in that quarter outside your knowledge, but not outside mine, and knowing human nature a long sight better than you do, I'd say a time may yet come when Peter's going to see what he's lost and ask her to forgive him and let the past bury the past. And if that fell out—well, there's never a more forgiving woman than Mrs. Canniford."

"You needn't to think twice about that," replied Rupert, "because I'm in a position to tell you Honeywood's wiped out of her path like a bad smell now. I never knew her to bristle with righteous anger same as she did after he dared to forget his manhood and fall out with a woman like her. She was thankful when she found herself to be free, and I bet you were the first to hear it."

"It was a very complicated row between 'em—I'll tell you that much, Rupert, and some might say that the man had a tolerable good case; but I'm with you to the extent that at present your mother don't feel to have any further use for him. If he came back with his tail between his legs, however, with her long experience of him as a follower and her kindly and pitiful nature, she might take him back."

"Never on your life! He's gone for good and all. And though I well know you hadn't no hand in it, her better knowledge of you had already showed up Honeywood a lot to his disadvantage. Long before the final crash between them that was."

"I'd want to know one or two home-truths before I——" began Paul. Then he broke off, since any preliminary inquiries concerned Jenny rather than her son, and asked a question.

"I'll do this much," he said. "I'll give you the credit for favourable intentions, Rupert, and allow you meant well, because I can't see how you meant anything else. No more as to that. But where would you stand if I told you, once and for all, my mind's made up never to marry again, no matter what the temptations might hap to be?"

Rupert sighed and emptied his glass.

"I'm sorry you put that question, Paul," he answered, "for it was the last I expected and rings like a tolling bell to my ear. I've built up a lot of hope on this subject, and looked far ahead for both our families, and I've asked myself time and again if there was a snag in it and so on, yet couldn't for my life see but what it promised untold good fortune for all concerned. Lations of good, not only for you and her, but Ivy and me."

"Has Ivy had a hand in this job?" asked Paul, "and if so what line did she take?"

Rupert sighed again and shook his head.

"I always face up to facts, same as you do," he answered, "and here's another painful subject that I'd hoped would never be brought to your notice. But you go to the root as is your custom and won't be denied truth. About my future wife I'm sorry to say two things, and very painful things they are to me; but it looks as though you'd got every right to hear them, Paul, and you shall hear them. Ivy don't like my mother—first person on God's earth that didn't like her, I'd say. And as to that I'll trust time to show her what my dear mother is. No feeling against Ivy in mother's mind, needless to say. She's all for welcoming my future wife and being a second mother to her as you know. That's the first unfortunate thing, but there's another that's even worse. Now I'm on delicate ground, because between father and daughter no outsider, even the woman's husband, did ought to push in, and this is entirely your affair. I've argued against her till my tongue was tired in my mouth, but she's got a will beyond shaking as you've found for yourself no doubt. And her will is that you shouldn't marry again. She's took that extraordinary line and made it bitter clear to me that, though eager and well pleased to enter into marriage with me, she's dead against you taking a second, or having a companion worthy of you to make you a happier man and the richer for a partner. I couldn't believe my ears when I heard such an opinion; but there it is—stuck in her so hard and fast as her backbone— and argue as I might nought could budge it. Flying in the face of decency you might almost say, and no business of hers in any case. It properly terrified me to hear such a thing and I'll confess to this, because if you hear a sane and affectionate creature, and engaged to be your wife, go off the handle like that without a shadow of reason, you ask yourself ugly questions about it. No girl ever had a better father and your good should be her good. Then why in the name of fortune does she want to bitch up your show with her own show all complete and a devoted man like me waiting for her? It makes you look ahead a bit and feel the earth shake under you."

"I know that feeling with Ivy myself," confessed Paul, "but don't see no reason why you should."

"For my mother's sake, not to name yours. If my mother's to be left in the lurch just for the reason that my future wife don't like her, or else for the reason that Ivy don't want you to go your own way, then, me being as you may say only human, she would begin to look a thought different in my eyes from what she does look at present. If I heard that you were to be left a lone man just because she willed it so, and mother was never to have nothing but a frosty welcome if she ordained to come in my house, then—well, I needn't put it in words, but you can see what I might be tempted to do. It's never too late to bide free, before the chains are fastened."

A look of frank alarm contracted the elder man's features.

"Too late—much too late—for you to talk like that, Rupert," he said, yet without conviction.

"No, it isn't. I can face the consequences. And I'd have right and reason on my side. And that's the answer to your question I'm afraid, Mr. Pook. If you don't feel a woman like mother would better your manner of life and make you a more comfortable and contented man, then I'm much fearing I shall begin to ask myself if you are not right and the single state ain't best after all. I don't handle words very clever I grant you—deeds being more in my line—and if I've said anything that sounded wrong to your ear I'm very sorry for it, but you asked a plain question and I've given you an honest answer, harsh though it may be. What any other people but you and mother think don't matter a button to me, but if you're against me, then I can only say I'm cruel disappointed, and in that case I'll bide a bachelor and watch over mother, and you can keep Ivy to watch over you."

"What they call an ultimatum I believe," mused Paul. "You're an overbearing, insolent chap, but so clever as a ship-load of monkeys seemingly. I'll swear I never had an insight into your true character before to-night, Canniford."

"Don't you let no anger against me cloud your judgment," begged Rupert, "and don't look so grim as a ghost about it. I wouldn't make an enemy of you for a Jew's ransom, Paul, and whatever you may decide, I shall never feel nothing but respect for you and your opinions. We'll leave it at that. There's a fortnight yet, but if you convince yourself it will be better for your young woman to stop with you than come to me, I shall respect you just the same. With your quick-moving mind you won't take long to decide. And meantime not a whisper to either of the females of course."

"Holding a pistol to a man's head," answered the saddler—"that's what you're doing."

"No need for nasty suggestions like that. I'd sooner hold a pistol to my own head than yours. I'm only thinking for us all. To lose Ivy would be a terrible blow for me and for her too; but she's a mark on duty at all times and if you ordain that's got to be my duty, she shall find I can do it."

"Go home," said Paul. "Do get out of my sight, Rupert, and leave me in peace. For the moment I feel that I never want to hear your voice again and the longer I listen, the more I'm wondering what's back of all this. What the devil are you marrying Ivy for? But don't answer. Go and I'll turn over the situation in my own time."

Rupert shook hands cordially and cheerfully.

"Nothing could be better," he said, "and what you ordain I will faithfully abide by."

"I doubt it," replied Pook. "I'd so soon believe a dog fox as I believe you."

XIV

NELLY FAIRCLOUD paid another visit about this season to Dr. Naylor on behalf of her son. For herself she became increasingly conscious that Timothy's mind was widening fast and through the clouds of his increasing knowledge a fixed star began to shine. He continued wayward as of old and his point of view shifted when new lights shone upon his intelligence. Though vain and avid of recognition still, easily cast down by any harsh word or fancied slight, swiftly elated by a word of praise, or any display of interest in his opinions, a distinct and master bent began to declare itself, and upon this subject his mother desired to consult the doctor. He had always been her friend and entertained for her a very genuine regard undimmed by any reflection on Nelly's doubtful past.

"Come in, my dear," he said, when she paid an evening call and found Naylor in his garden. "How's the world treating you? I know how you're treating the world and your good willing to the neighbours."

"I'm all right, Doctor," she assured him. "I'm come to an age to settle down. I can look back placid on the past now and remember good and bad without much fret about either. I was built peaceful by nature and maybe too apt to please folk when I knew that pleasing them would please me too. But that's all over and done with. I ain't restless no more. My restlessness has gone into Timothy and 'tis about him I'd like to tell you. You've been so properly good to him and plastered him up with books, and they've learned him such a lot and woke him up in such a wondrous way that I've got to feel there's big changes coming. So, of course, I thought upon you as I always do where he's concerned."

"Quite right. I'm tremendously interested in the boy," said Edmund Naylor, "and I'm glad—very glad—my advice about reading has helped him to come out of his shell a bit."

"More than that," she explained. "It looks as if books was grown to be his first friends, Doctor. Of old, as a child, he'd pick his own queer friends—not out of humans, but just dead objects."

"Inanimate objects—not necessarily dead, Nelly."

"Trees come first and his soul went out to trees. And there were other things I'd sometimes hear him talking to himself about—any odds and ends he'd picked up into his thoughts. But trees stood before all else, and now you may say books have took the place of trees. Not only what's in the books, but the books themselves. He'll welcome a new book and turn it over, like a child with a new toy, before he reads a page of it and he treasures his books and looks after 'em like a hen watches over her chicks."

"Dear me—that's interesting. But if his mind is bent in that direction then perhaps he's got some deep, inbred instinct for books. They're a passion with some people—like old furniture and china are with others."

"I believe he feels that way by them," declared Nelly, "and if he's to find his proper occupation along with books, I was wondering what he'd come to be. It would mean living in a town most like, wouldn't it, Doctor?"

"Before we go into that," he answered, "let us consider where he stands with regard to Katey Wish and yourself, who are the two people most concerned. Is he all a son should be to you and does he do all he can to add to your comfort and convenience?"

"Yes, I'd say he does. He's a very good, orderly boy. Still wants to be something different from what he is and still talks about wonderful things he's done and so on. But when I ask him what they were, he won't tell me. He says he's got outstanding powers and nonsense like that, and he thinks a lot too much about what other people think of him and such-like rubbish. But he's good. As to Katey he jogs along with her; but I don't know so much about that. He's fond of her and she's fond of him, yet from my own experience, which, of course, is all I've got to rely upon in such a thing, I don't somehow feel she's first in his mind. He puzzles her a good deal on his queer days, and then he'll be himself and she's happy again. More like brother and sister than lovers to my eye, though of course he might be different when they're alone together. He's full determined to marry her and some days he frets and says it looks as if he'd never have enough money to marry on. And then I'm tempted to say I'll look to that and he can feel safe there; but that don't seem the right thing to do."

"Certainly not. Don't dream of it; and I hope he's too much of a man to let you in any case. You've got yourself to think about. But it's certainly true he won't be able to marry and live as he'd like to live on what he earns at the Manor. So you must face it and see Timothy's got to look elsewhere. And high time he started. As to his education, his sort is often apter to educate themselves than be educated by other people and no doubt he's doing that. The thing for a young man is to educate his conscience, Mrs. Faircloud, for conscience is the impulse and ultimate controller of our actions and probably of our fate. And conscience is a matter of education."

"He don't seem to have any temptations to go against good behaviour," declared Nelly. "I wouldn't say he'd got any vice in him, or anything his conscience might tell him was wrong and did ought to be altered. He's nice in his ways to his neighbours. I couldn't say if his conscience tells him anything he wouldn't tell me. He may not have any conscience—not that high-minded thing hid in 'em what worries such a lot of people. I never had no conscience to name myself, so it may be left out of him, Doctor."

Naylor laughed.

"That won't do," he said. "Where there's reason there's conscience. As a child's brain develops and reasoning powers begin to appear, conscience appears with them according to the environment and, out of the environment, the education of conscience, for good or evil, grows. It's not a separate endowment, but a natural product of conscious existence. At any rate that is what science would tell you. Timothy has a conscience like everybody else, including yourself. He knows right from wrong as we all do, but what is right and what is wrong depends upon such a number of side issues and opposed interests in our complex lives, that our consciences often make pretty grim mistakes no doubt. We can abandon that difficult subject and go back to your young man, Nelly. If books are going to be his joy and he honestly believes a life lived among them would be the most contented he can imagine, then we know where to begin thinking for him."

"I asked him if he felt like as if he'd enjoy to live in a book shop and sell books," said Nelly, "and he granted that was a good thought, because he'd be surrounded by books all through his working hours, but the idea of getting rid of books to customers didn't please him so well as tending books and watching over 'em. That's how his odd mind works. He'd like to be the guardian of millions of books, same as a shepherd likes to be the guardian of sheep."

"Sooner minister to books than men?"

"A lot sooner seemingly. And I wondered how you'd set about to get a young man some such task."

"He'd like to be a librarian, or something of that sort, or at any rate at present he thinks so."

"It's more than a passing fancy this time," she said. "Now you mention the word I'm reminded that I've heard him use it."

The doctor considered.

"I think his future begins to show itself," he said, "but it would mean complete translation. He'd have to leave you and take up a new existence in a town—begin in a second-hand book shop, perhaps, or something like that."

"No, Doctor, he wouldn't leave me. I'd go along with him. I'd wish to be close to him till he's married—if ever he is. Sometimes I think he never will be, though I wouldn't whisper the thought to anybody but you. If Katey found him changing—but there, we needn't to look so far forward. What's to do now is to ask you how I should get on with it and see if I could find him a beginner's job along with books. Perhaps it's beyond your power to help in a fantastic thing such as that? But you've granted it's within reason for him to break loose from the forest and turn to black-coated work."

"High time. I'll think about it and ask a booky friend of mine if any idea strikes him," promised Naylor and she thanked him gratefully.

"The friend you've been to him and me, Doctor, I never shall forget," she said. "For the minute Tim's full of Ivy Pook's wedding, because young Canniford's asked him to stand best man. He's very proud of being asked and I've got him some new clothes; but it's a bit awkward and I wish it hadn't happened."

The doctor nodded.

"So it is," he said, "but sometimes an accident of that kind will heal a breach rather than make things worse. Pook mentioned the matter to me. Of course it's nothing to do with him. Rupert can choose anybody he likes for his best man and it oughtn't to keep the Canniford and Withers folk away. They are all close friends of Paul Pook. After all a best man's not the centre of importance at a wedding."

"Paul's doubtful all the same," she said. "He's a very good friend to me and always has been and he was a very good friend to Nicholas and understood him better than anybody but me myself. He don't mind about Timothy, but when Ivy sent out her invites, all so beautifully printed, I heard from Paul there won't be no Withers there, though Rupert's mother and brother ordain to come."

"What are you going to do?" he asked.

"I'm going to the church to see the wedding and see how Timothy looks, but I'm not going to the wedding breakfast at Paul's after. He wanted for me to come, but I felt it would spoil the comfort of the Cannifords, so I shan't go. Tim's different. They can't in reason quarrel with him."

She laughed.

"Timothy's all for telling a speech to propose the health of the bride and bridegroom, Doctor!"

"Why not? A chap like him might make quite a good job of it. In that case it will do him good, too. Hope for the best."

"I'd like for no shadow to rest on him," she said, "but of course you can well understand how the Withers feel, I was always sorry for them. Katey Wish is a dear friend of Nora's; but when Katey wanted for Nora to meet Tim and see the sort he was, she wouldn't do it. She hadn't no hatred of Timothy himself, but confessed her mother would never forgive her if she went near him. And Jonathan Withers daren't know him neither. You can quite understand that."

"Yes; but there's another side," said Naylor, "a subtle side showing the interplay of character. What we often think an outrage may have served us better than we know. Demands for human action will sometimes defy conscience and take such a stand on reason and justice that no sane man can protest. The outcome and challenge of facts may produce crying need for opposition and, though conscience condemn that opposition, common sense demand it. We must be realistic and admit that blameworthy causes often confront us with praiseworthy effects. There is no universal code of morals and our values of right and wrong depend on circumstances, being subject to education and evolution, like everything else. It often takes years to see the issue of any act and show us its true and ultimate significance. Probably most of us never do learn or realise what our acts involve, or where we were hopelessly wrong, or superlatively right in this or that crisis. Others may be better able to judge such questions, but you can see the difficulty by reading the jumbled and opposite conclusions that historians arrive at. What looked at the time like a disaster of extreme magnitude, may presently reveal itself as a blessing to humanity, while in small personal affairs, a stroke of apparent good fortune may land the receiver in perdition, if his luck was greater than his wit to employ it."

"That's a lot too deep for me, Doctor," confessed Nelly, "but I've thought sometimes that for Myra Withers to hate me wasn't what you might call just hate. She reckoned I took Nicholas away from her and ruined her married life; but I never took him away, because he was gone long before he set eyes on me. He'd left her, body and soul, for years. Her nature poisoned him from the day he knew she despised him. He's told me there were times when he had to fight with himself not to strangle her, and some might go so far as to say I done Myra a good turn by taking the man off her hands where she hated him most."

"So your lack of conscience, coupled with your power to tame that aboriginal savage, may have saved Myra from a sticky death, my dear. But, as we do not know the absolute truth about anything, absolute truth being far beyond our limited wits to attain, we can only admit the possibility. However, we're adventuring on rather thin ice, Nelly, and had better leave the subject to the philosophers. I'll see what I can do about Timothy; but he would have to begin at the beginning. We'll grant the seed has appeared; we must see if the garden where it would grow is likely to suit him and can be found. It has a stuffy side to me, but the real book lover adores the very smell of a library I believe: it's meat and drink to him. There wouldn't be a fortune in that sort of work, but there might be a pension at the end of it."

"He ain't one for gathering money. He only wants it because he can't have Katey without it. He's quite orderly and old-fashioned about marriage."

"There's another career that seems to be open for him also," said Naylor. "Joe Bowring, the old organist, says Timothy has quite a good voice—a useful voice that would pay for training. He may have art in him; but, there again, he would need to work hard and patiently to make a living out of his gifts."

"He likes singing very well and I often hear him singing in a way to touch your feelings," said Nelly, "but that's just part of himself, like it is of a song bird. He don't set any store on it, Doctor, not like he does on books."

She rose to depart.

"And thank you again and again, dear man, for all your faithful kindness to the boy," she said. "And if I go from Priory with him, I'll never forget what a good friend you've been to them I cared about, and me too."

"I never pleasured anybody with better appetite," he assured her. "And nobody will be missed more than you will."

Elsewhere another mother was concerned about her son, for Mrs. Canniford, striving to awaken interest in Rupert on the subject of his wedding garments, found him wholly indifferent. Indeed, he made comments that filled her with alarm.

"Plenty of time to think about that," he said, and when Jenny explained there was not, he appalled her.

"If you ain't going to buy ready-mades, but want proper measured clothes, you ought to go to Honiton and set 'em in hand," she told him. "Such things take time."

"There's some things that don't take half a minute," he answered, "and one is for me to say if there's going to be a marriage at all."

Jenny shut her eyes and pressed her heart with both hands. She knew her son was a law to himself, in most directions; but this threat convulsed her. From the welter of her thoughts a minor tragedy came uppermost, as the trivial aspect often will before some shattering upheaval.

"And Sam Wish got the wedding cake in hand, as Katey told young Faircloud," she murmured.

"Let them that ordered it eat it then," replied Rupert. "Has Pook looked you up yet? I'm waiting to hear what he may have to say."

He asked this question every day on returning from work; but as yet, though Paul had given no sign, he was not idle. Conscious how scant leisure remained to him and fully aware that Rupert had meant what he said, the saddler wasted no indignation on the culprit himself. Indeed, in his impartial fashion, he rather admired Rupert's diplomacy and display of craft. Young Canniford revealed unguessed gifts; but had these gifts directly opposed Mr. Pook's own convictions, he had doubtless withstood their onset, defied Rupert's cunning, ignored his threats and taken the consequences. But the game-keeper's suggestions offered no actual violence to Paul's own trend of mind, and certain shadowy considerations already occupying it. He examined their implications far more closely now, and analysis of them clearly showed that Rupert's intentions, were his advice declined, appeared far more inimical than the advice itself. His desire could not be ignored however outrageous the alternative in event of Pook's refusal to gratify it. Finally Paul determined to see Jenny Canniford touching some vital aspects of the dilemma, and her replies he doubted not would make up his mind for him. Of Rupert's duplicity there could be no doubt, though what had inspired it the saddler was unable to imagine; but he felt tolerably sure that Mrs. Canniford would tell him the truth, for though capable of guile, as her recent unfortunate activities had revealed, Paul believed Jenny quite above any deliberate falsehood. 'She's not gifted to lie,' he told himself. He decided to see her and allow the outcome of the meeting to determine his actions. The position was clear and simplified by Rupert's assurance that Jenny would be found ready to marry him; but all depended upon the answer to a question, for much patient brain work now convinced Mr. Pook that to throw over both Rupert and his mother in one forthright gesture might be little better than cutting off his nose to spite his face. So he asked Jenny to tea, on an evening when his daughter was at the Manor, and she accepted his invitation and came in a tremor of deep anxiety. It was not decreased by Paul's somewhat austere and abstracted reception. In no helpful mood did he prove to be for a considerable time, and Jenny's spirit fainted while she poured out tea for him, strove to twitter cheerfully, ate and drank but little, yet spoke of the approaching wedding with resolution as an event assured. A certain unfamiliar atmosphere, as of gloomy weather, continued to brood over her old friend, and she began to fear that some unforgettable scene with Rupert still overshadowed his mind. Concerning what had really happened she knew nothing, for her son made no mention of the matter to her, and now, their tea finished and removed by Paul's handmaid, she ventured to express sorrow at the evident depression encompassing him.

"I'm put about to see you so down, Paul," she said. "Light your pipe, and don't look so grim as a ghost. It gives me the creeps to see you under the weather. You, that don't care what weather offers. But there's a lot on your shoulders I'm fearing along with the wedding and so on, and that fearful affair with Peter. But I'm praying time cures all and you'll soon be in peace and comfort again."

Mr. Pook obeyed her, stuffed his pipe and regarded her calmly. His brow lightened, but there was still a moodiness in his voice, and when he began to talk, he put a curious question which much astonished Mrs. Canniford.

"What do you know about Rupert?" he inquired, and she stared at him and considered her answer.

"All I properly know about him is that I'm his mother—more I couldn't tell you to a dead certainty. His mind's so much out of my sight as ever it was and I'd never undertake to say what's moving in it from one day to another. In the case of my Harry, what mind he's got, dear fellow, looks out of his eyes and I know what he's going to say before he says it; but Rupert's different !"

"A tolerable dark horse," suggested Paul.

"A very good name for him. He means well—I'm sure of that—but he's got a fearful contempt for how his ideas may strike anybody else."

"I marked that last time I saw him. Fearless and crafty in my opinion, and he'll sail very near the wind sometimes I find. There are things about Rupert I would have said couldn't happen, but they did happen none the less."

Jenny's soul shivered.

"Same here," she said. "Take my own case, Paul. I'd have thought little interested him less than me, but he's woke up into a fiery interest in my affairs and shown a lot of nice feeling for me, now he's leaving me, that he never showed before in his life. That proves people often have goodwill hid in 'em you never knew was there. Sometimes I wish he hadn't rose up to all this excitement on my account. But I hope he didn't say anything to disturb you when he was with you. You're always so generous to grant everybody good motives."

"I wouldn't say his motives were bad—certainly not if he was after your welfare."

"As you say, a mother's a high motive nobody could quarrel with."

"We'll even admit he wanted to do me a good turn also," replied Paul. "We'll allow that much, though surprising; but now answer me one question on your sacred word of honour, Jenny. I've a right to ask it and demand an answer to it."

"I will surely answer it if I know the answer," she said.

"You know the answer. And the question is this: Will you swear afore your God that Rupert's idea was his and not yours?"

"What was his idea, Paul?"

"That I should offer to marry you!"

Jenny turned pale and made a dramatic reply to the question. She knew that the Pook family Bible reposed upon an antimacassar mat behind her and now she rose, approached the massive volume and set both her hands upon it.

"I swear upon your Book it was no idea of mine, dear man," she said, "and may I be blotted out if it was. What my son may have said to you I don't know, but nought he spoke ever come from me, and my Maker would tell you the same."

"So far then I'm satisfied," began the other. "Because, if I'd thought you had a hidden hand in his work, I'd have took a pretty strong line. Mind you, Jenny, not for a moment did I think you could lower yourself to such an action against an old and faithful friend; but seeing the nature of his devices I couldn't rule it out. There's a hateful, cold-blooded power about Rupert I didn't know was hid in the man. And there's mysteries go along with it. And, in a manner of speaking, his gifts made him one too many for me that night. He's terrible for seeing the weak spot in another person's harness and availing himself of it. Hunting has made him cruel, but honest sport didn't ought to make you cruel. However, if I've got to choose between having Ivy in my house for evermore and another wife, cut to my own pattern so far as I know, only a lunatic would hesitate between 'em."

"If you'd begin at the beginning, Paul, and tell me what this is all about and what drives you to say such things, I'd understand better," said Mrs. Canniford; whereon the saddler set everything before her.

She heard, with fluttered comments at the more shocking details.

"Well may you have felt the world was crumbling under your feet," she said. "Devious he was bound to be, or he wouldn't be Rupert, but you might so soon be faced with a highway robber. The wickedness!"

"I'm glad you see that," declared Paul, "because there's a very ugly name for what he's done, and that's 'blackmail'; and if it wasn't for the circumstances I'd take this job to Inspector Chard and let him deal with it; but Rupert was far too clever not to count the cost and the prospect that faced me if I turned him down."

"I won't have that," said Jenny. "Never will I allow you to be put in such a position—not for a thousand sons. 'Tis past bearing and I'll never feel the same to him and I'll pray you'll exercise your manhood, Paul, and dare the man to do his worst."

"He'll do his worst at once in that case," answered Pook. "He didn't leave no doubt."

"Don't you let any living man make up your mind for you," bade Jenny, "least of all such a chap as Rupert. Who's he to drive the likes of us?"

"As to that I'm much of your mind," proceeded Paul. "I shan't feel the same to him again; but he's got a right to his own opinions, even when speaking to them older and wiser than himself, and he had a right to the opinion that you'd make me a very fine, trustworthy wife. And looking at that, though a monstrous thing coming to me from him, yet, regarded as what you might call a naked fact, I already knew the truth of it."

"I'm very proud to think you agree with him, so far, Paul. But there's a lot more to it yet. Because a woman's like to make a useful wife to a man, that's no reason on God's earth why he should marry her if he don't need a wife."

"I've held the opinion for a good many years now, that I didn't want another," he answered; "but I'll go so far as to say this, that I also felt, after your husband died, that if ever I did change my mind, I'd so soon, if not sooner, have you than any other I can call to mind. So I don't come to you as if you was a stranger woman outside my experience, and you don't feel to me as to a stranger man."

"Your friendship was my standby time and again," she answered.

"You'd be prepared to take me then?"

"How could I say different? It would be the crown of my remaining days naturally."

"I'm offering for my own sake as well as yours, mind," continued Paul. "But not for any of Rupert's plots, nor yet his plans. Up to a point you can see he was looking to the main chance."

"He would," agreed Jenny.

"Oh yes. If you come to me, mine's yours when I go to ground, or else Ivy's, so Rupert knows my money's safe—what there may be of it. But in Honeywood's case he knew that would not happen, because Peter never liked him nor yet trusted him."

"I'll come to you on one condition only: that you leave all you have to Ivy after I'm gone if I go first," directed Mrs. Canniford. "She'll hate this something awful, and I'd little like her to run about saying I'd catched you to rob her from her own. Her, or her children, must be the gainers after we're took."

Paul smiled for the first time since the beginning of the interview.

"The child of your Rupert and my Ivy would be a curious piece," he said.

"Such an infant would be like to want all the help his Maker could spare him," agreed Jenny; and then the man got up, set his pipe on the mantel shelf and caressed her.

"Queer to feel a female against my waistcoat once more after all these years," he told her. "We're going to find it a thought strange for a week or two till we're broke in to the idea; but then there's little doubt we'll warm up and show our true nature to each other and be wed round about autumn time if you're willing. For the minute I'd keep this to ourselves, however. Rupert must know, but no call for anybody else to know till the appointed time."

She supported this suggestion strongly.

"Not a word till they're married," she said. "If Ivy heard tell, her wedding day would be ruined, and you must demand silence from Rupert till you publish what you've ordained to do, Paul."

"He'll meet me there I've no doubt," promised Mr. Pook. "Silence comes very easy to Rupert most times. I lay he never talked so much in his life as he did on that night. But you can spare me in that matter, my dear. I'm a thought tired of Rupert. You can tell him to-night. He might not believe me in any case, for them that know they are untrustable themselves don't set much store on the word of other people.   He may even want it in writing."

"No more documents for me, not after the last," she said.

"Tell him next time he comes home," advised Paul.   "Then he can get on with his affairs and decide where they're going for their honeymoon. Ivy wants London, but he's for Plymouth and an excursion or two on the sea. So I expect they'll go there."

"We must be hopeful for 'em and wish 'em well, difficult as they both are."

"Yes," he agreed.   "They're our flesh and blood, fantastic though it sounds to me when I think upon 'em.   Ivy says there's things about Rupert she'll alter and quite believes it."

"Poor soul !" sighed the widow.   "She'll live and learn no doubt, like all wives."

They parted and Paul watched Jenny trip off through the dusk of a May night.   Then he went in again, relighted his pipe and speculated on the new existence he had planned.   Upon the whole it pleased him ; while, as she returned to her cottage, Mrs. Canniford was glad to meet a neighbour and distract her mind with affairs other than her own.   She found that Rupert had come home and, ignoring her son's recent activities, made her announcement.

"I can tell you something that I hope will please you, Rupert," she said after he had eaten his supper.   "Mr. Pook finds himself wishful to marry me and I don't see no reason against.   We're very addicted to each other and he feels tolerable sure we shall be happy together."

The young man admired his mother's approach, kept up the fiction she had striven to create and pretended extreme surprise.

"Fancy that now !" he said.   "Well done the pair of you !   I couldn't have heard anything to please me better, or astonish me more.   Splendid, Mother !"

She looked at him as at a doubtful stranger.

"I'm glad you're pleased," she said, "but I'll ask you, at Paul's wish and my own, not to whisper a word about our tokening, Rupert, until your wedding's out of hand and a thing of the past.   And not even to Ivy."

"Last of all to her," he said.   "You can trust me there.   This is a matter entirely for you and the saddler.   I shan't say a word to anybody whatever till you choose to blaze it out.   You ain't the sort to double-cross a simple soul like me."

"Then best you see about your new clothes so soon as you can get off to Honiton," she said and her son promised to do so.

"I'll go like a lamb to the slaughter now," he told her.   "And we've ordained to visit Plymouth for a week, or ten days.   I've got a fortnight ; but I want to spend a tidy time at the lodge before I go to work again."

"I'll be very willing to help Ivy if it lies in my power," she promised.

The wedding day arrived without further elements of doubt and though one member of the Withers' family alone took any part in the proceedings, out of regard for Paul and ancient friendship, Myra raised no objection to Jonathan's decision when he signified a wish to be there.   Mr. Pook had asked them all and was not surprised that Mrs. Withers and Nora declined to attend, setting their refusal to Rupert's doubtful operations in the past; but though these were sufficient reasons for their absence, a greater in Myra's mind appeared when she learned that Timothy Faircloud was going to support Rupert as his best man, and this might mean that Nelly would be sitting at the same table with Myra when the wedding breakfast was eaten.

"I'll pray in the same church, but I don't share the same food, nor yet sit in the same dwelling-room," declared Mrs. Withers, and she was surprised to think that Paul Pook could suggest such a possibility. Even when he assured her that Timothy's mother was not coming to the banquet, it did not modify her refusal. Jonathan, however, attended. He was much attached to Paul and pretended no quarrel with innocent Timothy. He happened also to be on good terms with the Wish family and in church sat very well contented between his Aunt Jenny and Katey Wish, who came to see her sweetheart as best man. Katey indeed enjoyed Jonathan's friendship. She often visited Pigslake to see Nora, and her tact in the matter of young Faircloud commended itself to Mrs. Withers.

The ceremony was not choral because Rupert expressed a strong desire to have everything as brief as possible. He hinted at a registry office but, finding Ivy strongly opposed to an unsacramental bond, gave way. His massive body in a suit of blue serge towered beside the bride's somewhat slighter person clad in white. She was supported by the senior housemaid from Tudor Manor, an old and valued friend, while Timothy's physical perfection made sharp contrast with the bridegroom's big-boned outlines. Mrs. Faircloud, who sat at the back of the church, gazed without emotion at her offspring, while Mr. Pook gave his daughter away with good appetite, and Jenny Canniford felt the ceremony to be a dream from which she might awaken at any moment.

"To think the pair of 'em are really united for ever and gone out in the world to look after themselves—that's very near more than I can believe," she told Paul after the service had ended.

"It'll take a bit of time to grasp," he granted. "A proper good thing is just as hard to accept at first as a proper bad one. You come back to it with renewed thankfulness every time it returns to your mind, till it's got to be an everyday blessing and part of your life, and then you heed it no more."

Timothy proposed the health of the wedded pair in a speech which he had composed and learned by heart afterwards. Already he had recited it several times in private, both to Katey and his mother, and both approved, though on Mrs. Faircloud's advice he had shortened it in certain particulars.

"You can leave that bit out, my dear," she told him, "because they'll have heard it already in church."

The young man had in truth read the marriage service carefully and incorporated certain sentiments from it in his toast.

Conscious that the wedding guests were listening with interest, Timothy delivered his remarks with increasing confidence as he reached the end of them. A few kindly people rapped on the table and their applause much heartened him.

Invited to reply Rupert declined.

"Enough's as good as a feast, folks," he said, "and we've had our feast;

and now you'd best get out of them fine feathers, Ivy, because the motor-car will be round tolerable soon."

When it did arrive, Jonathan, with Katey's aid, fastened a tell-tale trophy behind it and rice was showered upon the pair as they got in. Soon they were sped; the entertainment came to an end and the people went their way until all were gone save Jenny, who remained to lend a hand with clearing up. She found herself a little tearful after all was over, but Paul supported her, for she had never known him in better spirits.

"The house feels twice so spacious now, and twice so peaceful, too," he told her.

Jonathan and old Joseph Bowring, who was of the company, left together, while Kate and Timothy returned to Lavender Cottage that his mother might learn of the wedding feast and Tim's triumph.

"He was the leading feature of the whole affair if you ask me," said Kate. "In church he looked like something different from all the other young men, as he always does look for that matter, and at the party, after father's wedding cake, Timothy was the star turn and his speech went beautiful. To the manner born he was, Mrs. Faircloud, and his words flowed out so fluent as need be."

"I got a good laugh too," said Timothy, "and that shows I can make people laugh when I turn my mind to it."

"And Jonathan was there," added Katey. "I sat along with him and Mrs. Canniford."

"I saw him," said Nelly. "He's a smaller man than I fancied. He wasn't behaving very well I thought, Katey."

"No, he wasn't; he would be talking and saying naughty things about Ivy Pook—Ivy Canniford now."

"And Rupert's mother—did she look to stand up to it pretty well?"

"I couldn't say how she was standing up to it, but she'd got a flame new dress on," answered Katey.

"Funny what things come back in your mind, Mother," Timothy told them. "I've not been in church more than once in a way since I sang in the choir, but I caught sight of an old friend there to-day: that skull with wings on the Garland hero's monument. The funny little monster and me used to be fast friends when I was a boy, and I'd have a sort of private conversation with him when I was to church and think how fine it was to have him for a friend. I looked at him to-day out of the corner of my eye and I'll swear he remembered me and winked at me."

Timothy was in an excited and exalted mood. He talked fast, but stayed not to listen to their answers. His mother marked his elation and strove to calm it. She guessed he had drunk plenty of wine and indeed he confessed to doing so.

"Champagne we had," he told her. "First time ever Katey or I tasted it. She didn't so much care for it; but I liked it better than anything ever I drank before. Grand stuff! Sparkling cider's a fool to it."

"They've gone to Plymouth," said Kate. "That's where they'll honeymoon. And Ivy's going-away gown was a pale ginger colour trimmed with grey squirrel fur. Rupert shot two squirrels for her after she took him."

"She was properly hideous—a fearful object," said Timothy, "but Rupert didn't give a damn. He just bustled her into the motor and waved his hat to everybody and away. Power he's got."

"Little knowing what me and Jonathan Withers had stuck on behind him," laughed Katey.

"When we drive away after our marriage, we'll remember to have a look at our car, Tim."

She turned again to Mrs. Faircloud.

"And father's cake was richly praised," she said, "you felt it was cruel to crash into a beautiful masterpiece like that—pink and white icing, two tiers, and a dear little Cupid with his bow and arrow perched on top."

"Rupert crashed into it all right," said Timothy. "He likes champagne, too. He's taken it often, because at the Manor shoots, he and the other keepers wait on the guns when they feed, and what's left over they generally share between them."

Harry Canniford, his wife and eldest son, George, had also attended the wedding and entertainment.

"Mother's got a new gown I see," he said to Susan as they returned home. "How she does it I'd much like to know. And you looking so poor as a coot."

"For Rupert's wedding she'd make an effort, Harry."

George, a stolid little fellow but observant, asked a question.

"Why for did Uncle Rupert want to marry up with that higeous, long-nosed woman?" he inquired.

"There's others beside you, George, as would like to know the answer to that," replied his father. "Mystery clothes your Uncle Rupert like a garment and always have done; and what's on his lips be often told to hide what's in his head."

"You grow up like your father, George, not like your uncle," urged Susan.

"I wanted to grow up like Constable Palfrey and be a policeman," said the boy.

"Once you're to Pigslake, you'll forget about being a policeman and want to be a farmer," prophesied Susan.

At the 'Pen-in-Hand' that night talk ran on the wedding, for one or two who had attended it were present.

"And that Faircloud—lording it up there alongside your cousin !" said Ned Piper to Jonathan. "You'd have thought he was the groom."

"Yes, Ned, so you would. He made Rupert look tolerable tame for all his new clothes."

"I never see such confidence in no young man," declared the sexton.

"He swanked in church," admitted Jonathan, "but he was nervous at the feed at first. And then, after he'd drunk a good spot of sparkling wine, he was brave as a lion and got on his hind legs and made a speech—a thing you'd say might have scared him stiff to think on."

"So it did—to think on—Jonathan; but when he came to do it, then he feared nothing," explained Dr. Naylor. "A glass of champagne and the literary temperament combined."

"Very comforting to fear you're going to fail, and then find yourself a

F

success," suggested Mr. Toozey, from behind his bar. "It's generally the other way."

"A merciful law of Nature, William, and not generally the other way," declared the doctor. "We're apt to think things will be all right and if we weren't hopeful as a rule, most of us wouldn't put a hand to any useful job and might as well be monkeys."

"I'd foretell Timothy's going to be useful some day," thought the old organist. "He's got a gift worth cultivating."

"Looks to be more for books than singing now, Mr. Bowring," said Jonathan. "Full up with book learning, so his sweetheart says."

"Yes," agreed Naylor. "I doubt it will be music now, Joseph, even though he knows you think his voice good enough to train."

"Have he got the guts to train himself for anything ?" asked Mr. Piper. "I never see no man not half a century old with a mite of grit in him nowadays. Better education they may have, but what do it do ? Knocks the stuffing out of 'em. They don't stand to work like we done in our young days and they flock off the land to the towns like flies to a dead sheep—for why? Because they think there's more money and less work."

"If they was to pool their wits and build up a proper Union to fight for 'em, then they'd be putting their education to a purpose," said Christopher Banks, the head man at Pigslake. "We're all right, because Jonathan here is like his father. He works himself and he knows a man's earning powers and market value and pays what a labourer is worth; but there's a lot of farmers give the business a bad name."

"And don't know any more about their job than our Ministers of Agriculture do," added Jonathan. "My father used to say there was a million acres of Devonshire alone let run to waste, that could be turned to the nation's food if farming was put where it ought to be—our first thought instead of our last."

"Nicholas Withers would tell that education was a proper scourge to farming," said Banks. "He feared the machines for the next generation. He'd say they took the place of labour and knocked the bottom out of what man's muscles used to be worth."

"You can't deny that," agreed Toozey. "There's more oil sold and less cider now—to my certain knowledge."

"Hosses and men will soon be so rare on the land as white moles," prophesied Ned Piper. "There's coming a time when giglet wenches will run the machines and old women mind the stock and all the young men in factories, or sitting on their backsides in counting houses, and the face of the land no better than my graveyard. I shan't be here no more, thank God, but some amongst you may live to see it afore you get up in years."

"Plenty of changes coming, Ned, and plenty of need for skill and hard work too," declared the doctor. "The man that can run a machine earning twenty men's wages in a week will be worth a lot more than a day labourer."

"And anyway your job won't change," said the old organist, "and more will mine. We must have great music—more and more—while we live and grave-room afterwards."

"I don't know about music and singing, Mr. Bowring," replied the sexton; "but a grave-digger's craft may vanish yet, so sure as a thatcher's craft be vanishing. Mark me there's more and more corpses burnt up every year and less grave-room wanted in consequence, which is to deny a man his spot of earth at the end, and contrary to justice and religion in my opinion. You'll hear godless people say the ashes did ought to be saved for fertilising, so a man may eat the cream of his grandfather in his daily bread. And we call ourselves Christians !"

"A lot to be said for it, Ned," grinned Dr. Naylor.

"You think so, but parson don't, Doctor," replied Toozey. "He's very much against the practice. His reverence read in a newspaper—so he told me—that the Italian people had got it in mind to use one of their burning mountains for the purpose and calculated that the nation would save millions by so doing; and the reverend gentleman said they foreigners had disgraced themselves by such a scandalous idea."

"Not much sense in fertilising a volcano," agreed Joseph Bowring.

"But bone is lime, whatever animal it comes out of," said Jonathan Withers, "and lime is valuable to land that lacks it, like a lot of ours do, and, apart from our feelings, a graveyard's waste land in a manner of speaking."

"I'll grant there's a lot might be more useful as lime under the earth than ever they was in their own shape on it—your father included, Jonathan," replied Mr. Piper. "And women, too, for that matter : but it's a lawless thought and I'd sooner we kept in the old paths and done as our fathers done."

"If all our burying grounds was measured up over the face of the nation, I lay it would come out at a good few square miles," said Christopher Banks."

"They used to be called God's acres, Christopher," Toozey reminded him, "and it might turn out a pretty fearsome thing to touch 'em. I'm with Ned there."

"Yes, there'll be a day of reckoning, William, sure as the sparks fly upward. I shan't live to see it, but the Almighty's patience will most like be exhausted by them in their cradles at this minute."

So prophesied the sexton.

"A great satisfaction for you, to know you're going to miss such a lot of evils to come, Ned," laughed Jonathan.

Then Toozey looked at the clock.

"Closing time in five minutes, gentlemen," he said. "Name your last drinks, them that wants 'em."

At this moment Inspector Chard joined the company.

"A quick one, William," he ordered. "Just in time—the usual."

"We was talking as to burying the dead, Thomas," explained Mr. Bowring. "Are you for cremation or against ?"

"You'll find the Law to be against, sir," replied the inspector firmly, "and I don't hold with it myself neither. If it grows to be common, it will make murders easier than what they are and I'd go so far as to say they are got a lot too easy already. Undiscovered crimes gain upon us and I've heard the Superintendent confess it."

"They won't happen here while you and I are on the war-path, Tom," declared Dr. Naylor; then into the night they all cheerfully departed.

XV

Despite Dr. Naylor's confident prediction, another story was told to one astounded pair of ears upon that self-same night and a young woman under the May moon heard her sweetheart confess to murder. A starting point and genesis for this very extraordinary incident might have been traced by one familiar with its accumulation of causes; but for the recipient of the story, despite her knowledge of the teller, no grain of truth appeared; in which fact its unusual quality of interest centred.

Wandering together after their supper at the baker's, Timothy Faircloud and Kate Wish found themselves at forest edge, with the moonlight glinting through the still delicate and new-born foliage above them, and here came a culmination to the lad's day of varied experience and his little measure of personal triumph. It wanted not much at this vernal season to loosen Timothy's self-control and to-day his glasses of wine, together with his speech and consciousness of commanding attention and applause, tipped the balance at last and plunged him into a confidence he had long contemplated. So far he had defied this temptation, but unknown to himself, an urge to win Katey's still louder applause and admiration ever gained ground upon him; his increasing familiarity with literature and its vast horizons had curiously altered his perspective and created a foggy understanding of the profound difference often existing between crime and what is commonly understood as sin. He had stumbled upon the subject by chance, in a book, and instantly quickened to its significance, for it came laden with a very blaze of light into his own soul and illuminated events which he had long concealed, yet yearned to disclose for his greater glory. Little by little he had come nearer to avowal before the one companion of his life who might be trusted, and since she was the spirit dearest in all the world to his own, a thousand times had risen the impulse to tell her. For not only was Katey the solitary, safe confidante; her praise and astonishment at his secret powers would be more to him than that of any living being. He counted upon them; for months he had longed to make his revelation; yet something had held him back. Wondering what it could be, he told himself that the delight of anticipation alone delayed him; but to-night the doings of the day and a certain increased realisation of his powers combined to make him reckless, sending down the wind his old, prevenient prudence and the dictates of native reason.

So Timothy, fortified by moonlight, and deserted by caution, burst upon Katey the information that it was he who had killed Nicholas Withers and committed a perfect crime. A sense of its drama made him narrate the story as a recitation. Indeed he had rehearsed it often enough, with trees for his sole audience.

"Sit still and listen to things that happened," he said suddenly. "Pitch here alongside me, close, and I'll tell you something that nobody else but you will ever hear on this earth."

"It's always the same with a full moon," she answered. "Moonshine's got a queer power to set your inventions working. But I'm powerful sleepy to-night after such excitements, Tim."

"I'll wake you up in half a minute," he promised, "and first picture to yourself how the scene looked. Dimpsey closing down, and a big man going on two sticks, poking along behind his farm to see how work's going on at his new well. Does that bring anything to your mind?"

"Mr. Withers on the fatal night to Pigslake."

"Right so far. All quiet and peaceful. A young moon in the sky, but too early for the stars, and clouds red yet down in the west. But there wasn't only one man at the well. There were two—two men—the old devil on his sticks and a young man on his toes watching him—not five yards away! The young man—a bit of the tiger there was in him always, though none ever guessed it—the young man lived not very far off—no more than half a mile—and he hated Nicholas like hell, same as every other decent man hated him. He'd been up over to look at the well too. He was trespassing, but knew how to take care of himself very well and he got there first that eve, and when he heard Withers crawling up on his sticks, he vanished and hid himself behind a load of bricks nigh the well mouth. Up came old Nick, little guessing his tale was told and that Death stood within five yards of him ; and the young chap crouching so close didn't know himself for a minute he was going to spring. He'd come without any thought of such a deed."

Timothy broke off, licked his lips and lived the scene again.

"An owl called, just as the man was gotten to the well mouth, and thoughts rushed into the mind of the watcher in a flood, like as if the owl had sent him a message to wake the might hid in him. A most curious thing—a million thoughts crammed into ten seconds, like they say a drowning man sees his whole life stretch out before he goes down. There stood the young man hid behind that misbegotten brute's back and knew him at his mercy! And loud as a trumpet note every beat of his heart and every throb of his blood cried out 'Kill him! Wipe out the hateful dog once for all and clean the world of him!' That was the voice the young man heard. No time to argue, or doubt. It was a job calling for a brain to work like lightning. It meant such a lot and such a upheaval all round the country side. But all was took in by the avenger—the tiger waiting there. Yes, he took it all in and girt himself and sprang like an arrow from a bow, leapt at the enemy from behind his back, set his strength to it and struck his victim down head first into the well as you'd strike a wasp on a window pane. There was nerve and pluck and brain power all working to a perfection! No hangman ever cast off a murderer quicker than Withers was cast down to his death, and he didn't know no more who had torn his life out of him, than the hawk, hovering in the sky, knows who's shot him. A marvel of vengeance and slaughter was the death of Nicholas Withers, with a mort of mastery hid behind it—brain power that reached out, far beyond the old devil's death, to make the killer safe himself after, so he could stand by and hear the people babbling and the police searching, and everybody well content to believe it was all an accident. But I lay a good few—his family included—well knew he was murdered and blessed the unknown killer who had swept him out of their path for evermore. And there you are, Katey—a crime in the grand style, worthy to set beside the crimes in history—like when brave men killed Julius Cæsar and many another tyrant. But not a sin you understand—not a sin to make the people hate the murderer's name, nor make him sorry he done it, but just the opposite of that: a great act of bravery to make him proud of himself. Never a pang of sorrow nor yet what they call remorse did that avenger feel—never a pang! He'd done his duty swift and sure, and he'd done it so well that he was safe himself and beyond all suspicions. Not that he'd have felt fear to proclaim what he'd done in a free world, but there was good reasons against that, because the Law must have hanged him. All men of good will would have forgiven him, but that wouldn't have saved him from the Law. Besides, there were two women he cared about—one tokened to be his wife and the other his own mother; and for his mother's sake he needed to bide dumb, her being the only creature on God's earth to care a mite for the dead man."

Timothy ceased and did not look at Katey, but kept his eyes fixed on the moon. His arm was round her where they sat and he had felt her body shiver once or twice; but now she drew away from him a little and there was silence for a few moments.

Then Katey reached a stage in her riot of mental emotion when she could laugh; and she did laugh while Timothy stared at her, amazed in his turn.

"You can find it amuse you?" he asked.

"Yes, I can," she answered. "Your moony nights often make you funny, like you was funny when you let down that wine. But this don't sound too funny on second thoughts, darling. You're dreaming, and you'd best to wake up. You—you, who've told me how that even now, in the heart of the woods, you'll sometimes get a queer feeling when the dark comes down and you see things that only the dark can show you—you, that hates death and could never lift a finger to kill a man for a million pounds—whatever will you invent about yourself next? Drop it, Tim. Be sensible and say it's meant for a joke."

"Are you telling me you don't believe the greatest thing ever I did?" he asked—his face all eyes in the moonlight.

"No more than I believe lots else you've told me, my lovely. Where would I be if I did? For God's sake don't ask me to believe it. Can't you see what it means if I was fool enough to?"

Timothy felt puzzled.

"Are you telling me I never knew you all these years?" he asked. "Are you telling me I was mistook in her I fell in love with and count to marry? Are you telling me it means different to you from what it means to me and you haven't got no better wits than to laugh at such a tremendous thing and doubt it?"

"Yes," she answered, "I'm telling you that, and for your peace you'd best believe me, though never, never will I believe you. You're always one to mix up your dreams and realities till often I can't tell one from t'other; but I'm just ordinary and never mix 'em. And I won't now. Listen to me, my precious chap. If there was one thing ever you feared and felt timid about, it was your fellow-creatures. I've marked it scores of times. Storms and floods and thunder and lightning you never feared and, if there'd been wild beasts in the forest, you'd never have feared them, but men you mistrusted and I well know you feared Nicholas Withers—same as most other people."

"It was him from my youth up that taught me to fear men, because he was treacherous and cruel. Before I knew anything about other men

I thought they must all be like him, and I felt it was better to die young than grow up into a thing like him. But I soon got to see he weren't the only pattern of man, but a rare monster different from most of 'em. And then I got to hate him and sometimes I'd even hate my mother for not hating him too. I don't fear one living man now, because I've got more power than most of 'em and a deeper mind. All I'd own to fearing is unknown things— not men—that I'll feel watching me in the deep woods now and again. But not men. I'm fearless of men. I killed him, and if you don't believe me, or else pretend you don't, then God's my judge, I'll use my craft again and kill somebody else and get away with it and show you !"

Timothy looked marble white and rather mad under the moon, but Kate had never feared him in his most extravagant moments and did not do so now. She stuck to the argument.

"You'll never be one too many for me, darling," she said, "whatever you tell me, because I love you and know there's wonders hid in you; but well I know there's things you never could do. And murder's such a thing. Such a story as this was never your work. Some one may have done just what you tell; but it wasn't you. I grant I don't know all that's hid in you, no more than you do yourself yet. You and me are going to find out all them fine things together some day and glory in 'em; but there's lots of dark things that never homed nor harboured in your heart and couldn't if they would. If angels told me you'd killed Nicholas Withers, I wouldn't believe 'em and if you but think for a minute and look all around such an awful job as that, you'll be glad and thank God I don't believe it and won't rest nor feel one mite of peace till you don't believe it either."

"And haven't I looked all round it ? Haven't I thought, above all else, that you were bound to see it with my eyes ? You talk about an awful thing; then think all round it yourself and see it was a grand, powerful thing, only to be done by an outstanding man. Are you telling me I mistook you ? Are you telling me that you are the common-place, go-by-the-ground sort you often pretended to be ? Are you blind to what I did while you see me safe and free, like any other conqueror ? Was I right in everything else, and only wrong because I loved you well enough to trust you ?"

Kate, still calm, though her heart beat fast, kissed the face he bent down to her.

"No, my dear heart," she said. "You wasn't wrong to trust me. I hope not anyway. You must be patient, because there's need to be. I'm built on an everyday pattern, but I'm bright enough where you're concerned. You've lived with this ugly dream a long time I reckon and let it get a firm hold on your mind. I've only heard it this moment and it haven't got any grip on my mind yet and never shall if I can prevent it. I won't let it get on my mind and I'll never rest day nor yet night till I get it out of your mind, because I see a lot more what it means than you do. I'm not blind to what you think you did—far from it; but I see sides to such a fearful deed you haven't seen. And when you have seen 'em, I hope you'll laugh, same as I did, and say it was all a maggot boring in your brain—just another dream that never could be."

Timothy's surprise began to verge on anger.

"If you're fancying any foolery like that," he said, "then best we drop it now and I'll tell you again by daylight, when you're not sleepy and yor mind's clear. It's your mind that's clouded, not mine. I'll tell you again and rub in some more fine things about it—above all the cleverness. A crime it was and done so skilled, down to the least detail, that it amazes me yet looking back. Such safety after a murder was never known before. I never plotted for it— there wasn't time; but not one slip did I make. I slew him and went my way, and death closed down on him and not one fellow-creature, nor yet the doomed man himself, ever suspected me. Never a soul on earth could have found a clue to link me with it. That's what they call genius—the genius of a great mind put to do murder. And so perfect that, let alone other people, if I wanted to confess to the world I couldn't prove I killed him myself! There would only be my word behind it with no support. If I was to walk into the police station to-morrow and tell Chard I'd killed Nicholas Withers, would he believe me? He'd laugh at me."

"Yes he would: same as I did," declared Kate, "same as everybody else would. And don't that make you think, darling? If everybody that ever knew a thing about you would laugh at the thought of you taking a lame man off his guard and killing him dead behind his back, then can't you see they was more likely to be right about it than you yourself? And if the people would never believe a word of it, why the mischief should I, of all people?"

"You've got to believe it," he said. "If you're trying to tell me I'm lying to my future wife—then we're up against something, Katey, that even I don't see how we can get round. You'll need to think pretty deep about this. Other men may lie—not me. I never lied in my life."

Chill struck to the heart beating so near him and the girl did not immediately answer; but her mind contrived to concentrate and she felt in dim fashion that, so far, she held her own.

Timothy spoke again.

"I've thought upon that fine point: that there's no evidence," he continued. "Nothing can touch me. Never was a man safer. I've asked myself how I could prove I done it and win the fame I deserved for it, even if they chose to hang me, or put me away for life. I've asked myself, but there's no answer. It's hid for evermore. Only you and me will ever know it; but that's enough for me. What you've got to do is to believe it also and measure up the results and see my stroke has made Priory a better place for everybody that lives in it."

"Do you think your tokened wife cares two pins for Priory, or anybody else but you?" she asked. "This is between you and me and none else but us in the world. And we think different and I know you never done it and thank God I know it. Again and again you hear how weak-minded people have said they'd done awful things—just to get in the news, without a pinch of truth in them—a fearful deed to do."

"And impossible to such as me," he answered. "Am I the sort could sink to that—with a brain like mine? You know better if you know anything at all. It's properly damnable that, knowing me and the power hid in me, you can't rejoice to welcome how I've used that power and done a mighty thing. Instead seemingly your one wish and hope is to hear I never done it, and you try to pretend I couldn't have done it. Pitiful and mean that is! Here was a man that commanded the hate and fear of a score of people and did evil and flourished afore the nation; and now he's gone and forgot, like the log of wood you threw on the fire yesterday. And I did that grand piece of work; I banished him off the earth, and you want to believe I didn't! What's come to you? I let in a flood of light upon myself and you blink at me, like a stupid owl woke out of sleep, instead of rejoicing same as I thought to see you."

"I wish I was asleep and this no worse than a nightmare," said Katey. "I'm fighting not to take it serious and praying you're having a bad joke with me; because, if you aren't, then I'm up against it, Timothy. True or false I'm up against it good and hard. And you've got to take your mind off yourself for five minutes now and think of me. If we don't make too much of this and you own up you're fooling, that will lighten its shape to me and I'll try to forget it; but if you cleave to it and say it's true—can't you see where I am?"

"Where are you, except to know a bit more of the man you're going to marry? Is it too big a thing for your wits to take in?" he asked.

"But if my wits take it in, then were are you?" she answered. "I'm a thinking creature, just as much as you are, and can look further forward seemingly. If you don't know where you stand, I'll tell you. Either you're a liar, or else you're a murderer, and a murder's a murder however grand you thought it was. You're always panting to be different from everybody else, but what sort of fearful difference is this? Don't you feel nothing but pride? Aren't you sorry to know what a hideous thing you say you've done when you look at it from outside?"

"I'm sorry," he said, "but not for killing Withers. Sorrow won't undo that. Sorrow won't bring his filthy life back again. I'm only sorry because I was fool enough to misread you."

"And cruel enough—cruel enough to burst this horror on me that loved you so well. What have you done to me? For God's sake go back on it, Timothy, while there's time and own up you're just trying me out to see how much I can believe. And look at it my side. This savage tale don't make me think higher of you as you say it ought: it makes me think lower of you if I'd let myself believe it for one moment. Can't you see that? Can't you see, now you've tried this out on me, that being what I am, I properly hate it, same as everybody else would properly hate it? Such things, if others heard 'em, don't mean you'd be the village hero, darling—they mean that you'd be parlous near to the village idiot. Because not a living soul is going to believe you done it, so you'd only be held a harmless liar and no worse and no better. And where am I then—tokened to a harmless liar!"

"Take the lie back," he shouted at her, and echo whispered it over the woods. "I never lied and never will. 'Tis you that look like a mad one— not me. Can a man show he loves a woman better than by putting his life in her hands same as I have? That's a test for his love and a test for hers; and you wilt under it—you're long ways short of what I thought. You can't face up to a real live thing, so you cry to me to say it's false—else you won't love me no more. That's your look out, not mine."

"Don't say it, Timothy," she begged. "Keep off all that. We ain't reached to that. I love you yet, as I always shall love you, and I'll stick to you so long as you leave it in my power. But I tell you I don't believe this and I won't believe it. Every scrap of my soul and body cries out against believing it."

"You must," he answered. "You must believe it, else your love's dead. If you don't believe it, then that's all your love's worth, or else your wicked way of casting me off, because who would marry a woman that says he's false ?"

"No—no, Timothy, I'm trying to show you the only hope that's left to us. If I don't believe you, then we may yet keep together : but if I do, then we never shall, because I wouldn't marry a murderer for anything on earth. I'll love you as I remember you. I'll love the memory of you—all—all till to-night. But if you hold to this, I won't marry you—never will I do it."

Timothy broke off moved by trivial thoughts.

"When I go to work of a morning," he said, "and pass your door on my way, I whistle, and sometimes you hear and peep out of your dormer window and I get a glance of you; and then I go refreshed to the forest. But other mornings, when you're still sleeping and don't hear—then how long is the working day, Katey."

She felt tears in her eyes.

"Come close, come close again, Timothy. Put your arm round me. I'll never be afraid of you. Who could fear a lover that talks like that ?"

"You're tired," he said. "Go home and sleep and you'll see all clear by daylight and mark there's nought so grand as truth. It may be terrible, but it's always grand. Our minds have grown up together and you're open-minded for a girl. There's come a pinch of fear on you—that's all. I'm not pretending. I was never built to pretend. I've come to this night gradual and often told you things to help you to stand up to this, and I reckoned you'd reached a pitch when I could tell you. To doubt me now is to go back on yourself and heed a lot of stuff your mother taught you when you was a child. Truth is better than pious frauds they cram into us when we're young. A good, brave murder is worth a wilderness of paltry little good deeds inside the law. All that parts us is because you don't see it big enough, but when you do——"

"Don't fiddle about like that," she implored. "No natter how I see it, or don't see it. The blessed thing for you is that I don't believe it and never will believe it; and if you praised yourself for doing it from now till Doom, I wouldn't believe you'd done it. I'm not built to believe it, any more than I believe in the knights killing the dragons you've often told about. And that's the truth of me anyhow, and if the truth is grand, then the truth of me is just as grand as the truth of you. I say you've got mixed up in a fairy story, as I've often known you to do before, and I pray you to break loose out of it and let your love for me and your hope for the future tell you I'm right. If you can make yourself see it is just a mad dream—got into your mind and grown up, little by little to look like truth, Timothy—if you can make yourself see——"

"If I'm lying, then I'm mad," he said very solemnly. "Have you thought of that ? You can marry a brave man who did the world a service, same as Brutus wiped out Cæsar. You can be proud to marry a wonder, but you can't marry a village idiot, only left to wander the streets free because he's harmless. That's the mess you'll be in if you don't believe me, Katey."

She moved away from him again and a wave of indignation rose in her young heart.

"And what must you be to have put me in such a mess?" she asked. "If you'd really done this wicked deed, you'd have been strong enough afterwards to keep it to yourself for evermore. You'd never have squeaked—least of all to the woman you was going to marry."

"What they call the parting of the ways between you and me then," he answered. "You're the cruel one to punish me like that. But drop it for to-night and come home now—else they'll think we're lost."

"We ain't lost—not to each other anyhow—not yet," she cried. "Don't, don't say it, Tim! There must be a way yet—oh, my dear life, there must be a way."

They rose and walked together silently, and he held her hand as he was wont to do.

"It's like this," she began again presently. "If you bring it down to the very fewest words, it's like this. You believe you did a certain act long ago—you quite believe it and you've nursed it—hid away like a mother nurses her baby—and have seen it grow. Then you've told me and, feeling deadly sure the only chance in my life is not to believe, and driven by every drop of blood in my body, I won't believe it. Nought you say can change you and nought will ever change me. So how would it be if we put it before another person—a wise person who'd hear us and we could trust? And how would it be if we agreed to abide by what that wise person decided to decree, which ever way it went? Somebody older than us you'd be willing to trust—somebody not going to be influenced by anything except what they thought was the truth?"

"There's no such outside person," he answered. "No such person in reach of us anyway."

"There is one such person—your mother's friend, Mercy Grepe. Well known for a wise woman. We'd have to go to her together, because only together we'd make it clear. I couldn't go without you, because this is a sacred thing and I wouldn't tell a word you wasn't there to hear. She could list to us both; it would be easy enough to see her and she'd never speak a word to a soul after about it; but the hard thing is to know if we'd agree to go by what she said. You'd need to give me your solemn promise on that, same as I'd give you mine."

Thus the distressed young people distracted each other. Timothy, staggered by an attitude so unexpected, tried to imagine how things would be with him if he accepted Katey's theory and confessed to a delusion on his part; while she lost heart and saw how the best that could now happen must be bad and destroy their unity for ever. He did not answer her last words and she spoke again.

"You'll be going away to other work before very long now. I've made up my mind to that, sad as 'twill be; but I'll know, if the right work offers, how you'll love it and better yourself every day and bringing us closer together presently. That's how I've made myself look at your going, hard though it was; but this—we can't part like this and feel there's a dreadful horror come between us. We can't part and never come together again. We ain't built to suffer anything so foul as that."

"You never know what you can stand up to till it comes," he said. "I don't see how 'Mother Forty Cats' can help us, and I don't see myself going to an ignorant old woman like her for any advice. If you believe in me, same as you always said you did, you wouldn't think such a mean thought as to want another opinion upon me. I ain't a sick cat, to be took to old Grepe and doctored. How can I trust her? I was a damned fool to trust one woman and I don't feel much like trusting another."

"You can trust her. Everything folk take to her is sacred—just so sacred to her as what you've told me to-night is sacred to me. If I believed you, I'd be just so dumb as I am now not believing you."

"And if she believes I've dreamed it, then we go on same as we're going; and if she believes me and not you, then what?"

"Then I'll believe it too."

"And what'll you do then?"

"Time to face that if I have to come to it," she answered, "and better not you press for any more from me to-night. I'm cruel tired and feel awful. You've knocked the bottom out of my little world and I'd best to think more and talk less. You can tell me when you decide if I shall ask Mercy Grepe to see us, or if you'd sooner not. It looks to me all one now anyway."

They were at her door and she left him then and went in; while he, in a maze of astonishment, anger and grief, passed upon his way.

But next morning he did not whistle nor yet lift his eyes to her window, and she would not have heard him had he done so, for dawn lighted Katey's casement before she slept and he was gone to work before she wakened. She tossed and turned, wept awhile, then dried her eyes, told herself she must be brave, then, drowned in the medley of her thoughts, wept again. Alternatives there were, but only a choice of evils and now one appeared the more dreadful, now the other. She mourned her lack of brains to discover any third channel through which some kindly light might beckon; but no such way of escape could offer now. Then came thoughts of wonder and resentment and a new and crushing doubt—thoughts that she strove to resist, for they asked a very terrible question. What fashion of love was that which had made Timothy tell her these things and, knowing her as he did, was it possible he could in truth suppose she would feel increased admiration for him on hearing them? He knew better; he must have known better; and that surely meant his love for her was not the conquering, triumphant, all-knowing, all understanding magic she had believed it to be. He loved the awful thing he thought that he had done, better than he loved her. He loved it so well that he could not hide it any longer and had apparently believed that she must welcome this evidence of his power as proudly as he did himself. Which meant that she had never penetrated to the inner haunts of Timothy's mind, that dreaming she was the very altar-piece of his inner soul, in truth a very different idol had long since reigned there and won his devotion. And now he demanded her to be the worshipper instead of the worshipped, expected her to join him at a shrine created by himself, wherein evil was the divinity. Katey had plenty of common sense though little imagination. These things only dimly she sensed, while lacking words for them; but they were clear in outline and she could only fear that they meant a mind deranged. Rising anger against him perished before such a thought, for who should hate a stricken brain ? 'I'll love him to my dying day ; I'll never let anything in the wide world stop me from loving him—not starvation, nor yet torments, nor nothing——' she told herself, 'but which ever way it is now—whether he's wicked or mad—I'll love to think on him and all the beautiful things he'd say to me.'

And when Timothy went home that night his mother, who was working with her needle, saw that he had returned in no happy mood.   He looked pale and agitated and she bade him go to bed.

"You're tired and you'll be late to work to-morrow, Tim, if you don't get your sleep.   A big, exciting time you've had and you'd best be off.   No, don't drink no more—I'd say you'd had enough and to spare to-day."

He was going to drink from a spirit bottle, rarely touched and kept as physic, but he desisted.

"Exciting all right, though not so pleasant as you seem to fancy," he said. "It may be exciting to find out faults where you thought there were none ; but it's not particular pleasant."

Nelly smiled.

"Don't you tell me you have quarrelled with Katey," she answered, "because I won't believe it.   We shall be moving away to a town for your sake soon ; but don't do nothing foolish and wilful to weaken the link between you and her when you live further apart."

"There's things weaken the links a lot worse than distance," he told her. "There's gaps between our senses, and when you find 'em, they shake you up, Mother.   You can't make women understand."

"Men have always found that a difficult thing to do," she agreed ; but still he played with his wrongs and let her know a little more.

"I've told her an almighty fine secret kept to myself this longful time—told her, so she could share it and all it meant.   And what's happened ?   She don't think it's fine at all and hates me for telling her and—worse—won't believe it !"

Nelly felt a pinch of anxiety.   Her son, as she had noticed ere now, was not an amorous type and sex found no deep place in his interests thus far.   She had for a moment suspected another reason for his trouble and pictured advances declined by Katey in the moonlight ; but the girl could be trusted there and he would certainly have mentioned no such reverse.   It seemed that he spoke of some secret from long ago, at last confided to his sweetheart and met with a chill reception.

"I don't want to know what you told her and have hid from all else," Mrs. Faircloud said, "but if she can't share your pride about it, no doubt there's good cause she don't, Tim.   You must agree to disagree.   She is a bright girl and have a right to her opinions I expect.   Go to bed now and things will come suent again next time you see her."

"They'll never come suent again," he answered, "and the sooner we've quit Priory the better for me.   Give me books : there's more life in them than in people that think they're alive, but might be better dead."

XVI

SATISFIED that the time had come to proclaim their intentions, Paul Pook and Jenny Canniford chose the day to do so, and she announced her engagement to an astonished sister one morning, while at a later hour, the saddler mentioned the matter before a full bar at the 'Pen-in-Hand.' He dropped in for his evening drink, listened to some excellent singing and then, assured that Peter Honeywood was not of the company, addressed Mr. Toozey.

"You'll be interested to hear, William, that after all these years, I've changed my mind and ordain to marry again," he said, and the innkeeper beamed upon him, while others who had grasped his words signified applause.

Toozey stretched over the counter and shook Paul's hand very cordially.

"Best news ever ! And now I see why you've gone so light on your toes of late and took on good spirits we explained different. We thought 'twas the marriage of your only one had lifted you, Paul, but never did we count on the good news of another wife for you."

"Name your drinks, souls," replied Pook. "A round on me, William. Yes, I've had the good fortune to meet with a fine woman who sees her way to wed. Mrs. Jenny Canniford she is—one of an old Priory family that was always well thought upon—mother of Harry and my son-in-law, Rupert, and sister of Myra Withers."

Again they applauded and presently drank the health of the engaged couple.

"That's one in the eye for somebody who shall be nameless," squeaked Ned Piper. "I know, William—no politics; but I'm damned glad the market gardener's missed that market any way. Jenny Canniford was always a darned sight too good for him."

"When's it to be, Mr. Pook ?" asked Christopher Banks. "Great news, sure enough, because you'll link up with Pigslake now and you was always first favourite there."

"That's for my future wife to determine, Chris," replied Paul. "I'd say tolerable soon. But Mrs. Canniford's run her eye over my place since the coast was clear and counts on a few things to be done to suit her. She don't want much room for her own property, not having much in any case. Harry and Rupert will take most of her stuff, but we need a few yards of fresh wallpaper and such like at my house, though it's well up-to-date and full of additions that Ivy bargained for when she came home."

"Do she and Rupert know the great news, Paul ?" asked old Mr. Bowring.

"He knows, Joe, and mighty pleased he was to hear it. Now his wife will come to know, because I've wrote to him to tell her. Both me and Mrs. Canniford have had a picture post-card or two from Plymouth, and Jenny's got a fancy for us to follow their example and go down to the sea for a bit after we're married. There, or else maybe Cornwall. She hasn't decided so far."

They continued to discuss the good news; then entered Peter Honeywood with the doctor. Peter ceased to know Paul after the painful incidents of the past; but of late peace had returned to him and an increasing sense of lone-liness. For several weeks any thought of Jenny was sufficient to awaken his anger but, as the days passed, he hated her less and missed her more. The widow's abrupt disappearance from his life had created a blank that Peter found himself powerless to fill, though he made several efforts and strove to better his acquaintance in Priory. But those whom he endeavoured to cul-tivate either disappointed him, or let it be perceived they were not interested in these sudden tokens of friendship. Jenny stood unique and elevated above them as a statue on its pedestal, and though pride supported him while he continued to resist the temptation, the strain this effort entailed grew too severe and the conviction at last dawned that he might yet regain what he had lost. Peter, however, did not deceive himself. He recognised that only through one channel could any hope of reconciliation exist and he felt sure that, did he now return, the sole apology that Jenny was likely to accept would be a speedy offer of marriage. In other words this must mean that she, with base assistance from the saddler, had triumphed over him; and this ugly fact suffered to delay action a little longer; but he had now reached firm ground again. He was prepared to suffer some indignities in view of the return they might be expected to bring. He told himself that he would stoop to conquer and guessed that Jenny's good sense and fine feelings could be counted upon to make his passage easy. Against Paul also his animosity began to weaken and he found himself growing more tolerant. Then a bright idea dawned. Jenny had used her friend to good purpose and it occurred to Peter that he might do the like, compose their quarrel, admit his own errors of judgment and learn privately from Pook how things now stood in the vital quarter and whether the time could be considered ripe for pacifica-tion and forgiveness. Peter in truth found his Irish blood grown cool again and, seeing the immense stake involved, was prepared to lift a handsome olive branch. Baser instincts still whispered that he would have opportuni-ties for getting some of his own back again after marriage; but he did not encourage these reflections. Rather he let hope wax to a conviction that out of evil would come good, and his long dalliance reach a happy ending.

As he entered the inn an opportunity for some days sought confronted him. Here was Paul, evidently in the best of good tempers, and Peter saluted him with utmost amiability as though no cloud had ever dimmed their ancient intercourse.

"The very man I wanted to see !" he said. "Fetch your glass along into this corner and give me five minutes, Pook. I'll have a port to-night, William, please."

Silence fell on a dozen tongues, then Toozey raised some other theme, talked loudly and strove to distract his clients from this dramatic happening; while Paul, himself, struck dumb for the moment and disposed to set down his own glass and fly, took hold upon his nerves, nodded and repaired to a corner beyond earshot of the bar. Toozey followed with a glass of port, and when they were within reach of their own voices alone, Honeywood spoke. Paul knew that many eyes were fixed upon them, but his companion was unaware of it.

"Here's luck," began Peter, sipping his port and drawing a pipe from his pocket. "I'm one that can't bear no malice for long, my friend. Malice is a load hurts no back but your own in the long run and, before I speak, I'm wishful for you to understand that our difference of opinion in the past is gone out of my mind like a bad dream. I've put it out of my memory; I'm sorry I said things I didn't ought to say and I'll go much further than that. I'll admit that you were right and I was mistook, and that it was a neighbourly and a Christian act for you to help Mrs. Canniford open my eyes to a line of conduct I pursued too far along with her. The details I don't know and don't want to know. I'm a bachelor and ignorant of the feminine mind; but I'll say this: that her document, though it caused me to be very angry with you and her too, showed me in course of time where I'd failed her. In a word, my dear man, I was wrong and I suffered my caution to outrun my good manners. Hard though it is to own it, I'm ready and willing to do so this minute. So we'll clear that out of the way first and I'll make so bold as to believe you'll accept the hand of friendship and be as we were."

"Certainly I will," agreed Paul, "and now, Honeywood, you'd best to hear me."

"Glad to; but I haven't done yet. We've got so far that you can let the past bury the past, and very pleased I am to think so. But that being out of the road and us on a firm footing again, thank God, then we come to the much more delicate matter of Mrs. Canniford."

Peter finished his port at one gulp, picked up his unlighted pipe from the little table before them, put it down again and spoke, before Paul had framed his reply.

"Where a lady's concerned, no doubt the proper way is to approach her in your own person and scorn go-betweens, however well-intending," he continued, dancing the trinkets on his watch chain with a nervous hand. "And if you agree, then I'll go before her in a very different spirit from when I met her last and pray to find her in a different spirit too. But you was in the core of this business from the start and, most like, have seen her since and compared notes as to the situation. You may have reckoned your well-meant plot had failed, little knowing that it was far from a failure but opened my eyes to my shortcomings. And so I'll ask you to befriend me once more and tell me how I'd stand in that quarter if I was to look in and pour oil on the troubled waters? Something tells me, Paul, I shouldn't knock in vain, and God, He knows, I wouldn't waste no more time. If she'll calm her mind to listen, the first word she'll hear is an offer of marriage the instant moment she's ready and willing."

For half-a-minute Pook was silent while voices and laughter droned from the bar and Mr. Bowring sang a few notes to illustrate a musical problem.

"I'm much afraid I've got to disappoint you there," he said at last. "A good deal has happened since that painful affair, Peter, and by strange chance I'd just told Toozey and the chaps here what has fallen out before you came in the bar. You see it's like this. Jennie Canniford and I were old friends and after we thought we'd failed, as you truly said, we came together in misfortune and found a lot of ways to support each other, as them in like misfortune often can. And, to cut it short, she's going to marry me now once for all. And very sorry I am for you, though very well content for myself. It was an ill-convenient thing to fall out for you, I'm fearing, but you never know what's coming to you, and I hope presently you'll find another to take her place in your affection. You'd make a powerful good husband for any woman—none doubts that. And you'll have learnt by now the vital need to be quick in action."

"Took you !"

"She has, Honeywood."

The other leapt to his feet and shouted aloud.

"Then you're a damned traitor—a damned, shifty scoundrel and a dirty dog and an underground snake," he cried. "If you was a younger man, I'd take you by the throat and scrag the beastly life out of you—and her too !"

Every word reached the silent but attentive spectators; but while Peter ignored his audience, Paul was fully conscious of it and, as became a victor, kept calm.

"I'm sorry you feel so bad," he said, when Honeywood stayed to get his breath. "The fortunes of war went against you, and I'd push home now if I was you, because it ain't worthy to let yourself go this way before the people."

"To hell with the people, and to hell with you and her ! And never you, nor that false cat, dare to cross my path again, else I won't answer for my actions !"

Peter, forgetting his pipe, stormed out of the bar, but hearing the laughter that followed him, turned before the cool night air had brought any reaction and, quite beside himself, bawled at Toozey.

"And never again do I come in your pot-house—a nest of drunkards and fools and traitors that it is !"

The unfortunate man departed and Toozey looked somewhat ruefully after him.

"He'll keep his word and I'm sorry to lose him. Gone mad by the look of it, Paul."

Pook mopped his brow.

"Didn't take it very dignified," he answered. "A nasty thing to happen in your bar, William. But he'll come back when he recovers."

"He'd chucked Jenny Canniford weeks ago for good and all," said Ned Piper; "all the world was well acquaint with that story. My wife got it from Mary Ann Chard, and Alice was very pleased to hear it. So why did he want to rip out like that when he found a better man than him had got her ? Was she to wait till Doom for a vain ape like Honeywood ?"

"It was his manhood rising up against his disappointment, Ned," explained Paul Pook. "The poor chap has come to heel and is cruel sorry for what he did and wanted to know if my future wife would let bygones be bygones and give him another chance."

"Been building on it no doubt," said the old organist. "He may know the right time for onions and potatoes, but he never learned the right time to gather a woman."

"I told him I'd won her and his chance was passed," continued Paul, "but full of renewed hope as he was, the ugly fact proved too much for him."

"You might have him up for calling you a damned traitor," suggested Christopher Banks. "I'd say it was actionable to call a man that."

"What them in a passion says is no odds," declared Toozey. "Best to laugh it off and leave him to come round, if he can, and be sorry. The sort that's quick to anger soon burns out and feels themselves no better than a pile of ashes after. He'll suffer for this—not only for what he's lost, but also for what he's said here in the public eye. Such words may be forgiven, but ain't quickly forgot."

"Funny how small things amuse you even in the midst of big things happening," said Mr. Bowring. "As Honeywood rose up in his wrath and rage, the jewels on his watch chain all seemed to chatter and clink in a furious key as if they were angry too."

"And never paid for his port wine, Bill," reminded Banks.

"I'll pay for that," promised Paul. "The least I can do for the poor soul."

Toozey nodded.

"You speak as a conqueror," he answered, "and now you must have a round along with us."

But on the morning of that day, Jenny had announced her engagement at Pigslake, and Paul now left his companions to learn her reception.

Mrs. Canniford had eaten mid-day dinner with Myra and, when they were alone afterwards, declared her news.

"You'll be glad I hope at what I've got to tell," she began. "We've kept it very quiet for the minute, because he wished it, but now the time has come and them that may feel interested will hear we're tokened."

Myra, quite ignorant of the truth, guessed that Jenny's market-gardener had spoken at last.

"I've been waiting a longful time to learn he'd rose to the scratch and wondering, off and on, why you wanted him; but I suppose you did, so I ought to say I'm glad, my dear."

Jenny laughed.

"That was all off a good bit ago. I didn't tell you, because I hate to bother them I care about with my surprises unless they hap to be pleasant, which they seldom are; but this is a grand and beautiful surprise—not Peter Honeywood, but our dear old family friend, Paul Pook."

"I never ! That's a lot better news anyway, since you was set on another husband."

"I wouldn't say I was set on another, Myra, but he came at a convenient moment and I don't deny I'm very fond of him."

"So am I for that matter," admitted Mrs. Withers. "A good, high-minded man and I've cause to be fond of him, for he befriended me in the past when he could and was the only one ever Withers would listen to. I'm glad you took his fancy."

Jenny sighed with relief.

"I've been through a good bit lately," she said, "and my future looked more dark than usual till Paul came to the rescue. I didn't tell you, but Honeywood fell out very bad with me and cast me off in a most shameful manner. There's a nasty side to him and I'm glad now he showed it before it was too late."

"Often enough," declared Myra, "the only saving clause to marriage is the children. So it was in my case, though I had to pay a bitter price for 'em. We're both mothers, and many other mothers would tell us the same."

Jenny agreed.

"They come—our childer—oft enough like stars shining out of a stormy night," she said. "Anyway it was so in your case; and a more blessed boy and girl than Jonathan and Nora no woman could wish for. And I've got my two sons—not so successful as your pair, but well-meaning."

"Harry ain't exactly a star on a stormy night," admitted Myra, "and you know my opinion of Rupert without me telling you again. However, I won't say nothing about nobody but you and I'm very pleased to think you'll be lifted up to a good position with a good man to look after you and a lot of anxiety took off your mind. Not that I'd ever have let you want, Jenny, because you've always been a faithful sister to me; but now you'll be in a safe position and, if you had to commit marriage again, you couldn't have found a better."

"So I feel it and thank God for watching over me I'm sure, just when I'd grown a thought faint-hearted too," said Jenny.

"I'll advise you about one thing," added Myra. "I know what your mother's heart is, but watch out that you always put Paul first and your eldest second in future. Don't you cram Harry and his family down Paul's throat, because that would be a mistake. You can help Susan a bit behind the scenes, same as I used to help you; but never you let Paul think Harry's first in your mind and more precious than what he is, because he's a sensitive man and got tender nerves, though he hides 'em very clever. But if he thought anything like that he'd suffer."

"I'll bear it in mind," promised Jenny. "Very good advice I'd say. Paul's getting to understand Rupert, so far as a fellow creature can understand him, and his view of my youngest will depend a lot on how Rupert serves Ivy. He was thunderstruck, like us all, when Rupert took her; but he's not one to worry over mysteries and he's hopeful. He says they are both queer, and very often queerness will cleave to queerness and make a success where you might dread a failure if not worse. But there's no doubt Rupert likes her so far. He's enjoying his honeymoon to Plymouth and sent me a big flat fish he'd catched in the sea down there. It was too tired for me to eat, but I took it to Mercy Grepe for her cats. And Rupert said the weather was fine and they were having some fun on the water. That meant he is I expect, and having it alone, because Ivy's no sailor and owned to it before they decided for Plymouth; but he overruled her there."

"He would," answered Myra. "I don't want to hear no more about him. When do you ordain to take Paul?"

"Autumn time."

"Does Ivy know?"

"Paul's writing to tell her. I wanted him to wait till they were home, because, so far, she hasn't took to me and when she hears this it's like to mar her honeymoon; but though I warned her father, he didn't take no odds of it. He says she's got what she wants, and did ought to rejoice to hear he's got what he wants, too."

But Mr. Pook's letter, which reached Rupert's wife on the following morning, could not be said to mar her honeymoon after Rupert had uttered his comment. She enjoyed her altered state and found that the initial embarrassments and complications of married life might be considered compensated by its dignities and importance. Henceforward she would be called 'Missis' instead of 'Miss'; henceforward she would stand with the wives of

Priory and enjoy that implicit measure of respect accorded to them. Rupert had gone upon his way with complete indifference, making no effort to modify his manners, or change his mode of life. He proceeded as usual and found his principal pleasure in going on the water with fishermen, and leaving Ivy to spend her time ashore. The lodging-house keeper with whom they resided, supposed them an old married couple, and felt much surprised to learn that she was entertaining honeymooners. But Rupert appeared so unaware of his lapses, and so often declared his pleasure and contentment, that Ivy found no cause for reproach. He went his way, but was always delighted to see her when he came back.

Then came her father's announcement, and Ivy handed the letter to Rupert without any expression of pleasure.

"What d'you make of that?" she asked frowning.

He read it and laughed.

"Cunning old birds!" he said. "When the cat's away—meaning you—the mice can play; but you needn't look so frosty. Nothing could surprise me more—I'll own to that; but when you come to size it up, I doubt we could have planned anything better for 'em."

"Where do I stand? That's what matters to me," explained Ivy.

"You're all right—so am I for that matter. Now, whichever one of 'em goes first, when the money's finally cut up, it's ours; because it comes to you if your father outlives my mother, and to me if she outlives him and lasts longest. And what's mine's yours. It's safe now, which old Honeywood's money never would have been. How Peter got that scrap of paper and what enemy sent it to him we shall never know, but he did us a very good turn whoever it was."

"I'd dearly like to hear who found it and sent it to the man," said Ivy, and Rupert agreed with her.

"So would I, if it was only to shake his hand," he replied.

"Her hand more like," she thought. "It's just a sort of trick some nasty woman might have hit on."

XVII.

MELANCHOLY days were spent by Timothy and Kate after their difference of opinion concerning his tragic news. Nelly Faircloud and the girl's parents found it easy to see that some serious quarrel had arisen, for a week passed and the lovers did not meet, and while his mother grew anxious at her son's persistent gloom, Mrs. Wish and her husband observed their daughter much under the weather, though inquiry furnished no reason. For many a morning on his way to work Timothy had ceased to whistle and passed the baker's in silence, while, though Kate peeped from her window aloft, unseen, and thus gained fleeting glimpses of him, she gave no sign and waited day after day to learn from him whether he would agree to suggestion and let one older and doubtless wiser than themselves listen to his story—to judge whether it was true, or spun of some bygone dream that the dreamer had come to regard as truth. Convinced, from her knowledge of Timothy's many excursions into romance, that this must be so, and equally positive that he ought to welcome such a solution, both for her sake and his own, Kate felt assured that old Mercy would agree with her and liberate the young man from his dreadful incubus; but as time passed and he gave no sign to show he would abide by such a test, or even permit it, her spirits sank and no amount of fortitude could conceal the fact.

Then, in a dawn when she was not peeping to see him pass to work, Timothy chose to break his long silence and she heard his voice again.

Not for a moment had he considered her suggestion, while puzzling his brains as to what alternative course might be pursued to restore their understanding. Her point of view had staggered him. That she would fail to approve his heroic homicide, or realise the immense amount of human satisfaction and relief occasioned by it, he had never feared. He imagined that intercourse with himself and his liberal outlook upon life had turned her mind ere now to larger issues and cleared it from commonplace opinions and conventional moral values. He knew she was clever and swift to see that his judgments were sound, yet ready to oppose them and argue against if prompted to do so. Then it had been his masculine rôle to solve her difficulties and prove himself right, usually succeeding, though sometimes failing to do so; but failure in such a tremendous matter as his confession, he never bargained for, and the catastrophe was doubled by Katey's line of opposition. His massive arguments in his own support apparently counted as nothing with her. She had never so much as troubled to consider them. To his recital, despite its wealth of detail and realism, she had retorted with crushing and absolute disbelief. Argument he was prepared for and felt assurance that he could meet; but to be discredited once and for all and accused of saying the thing that was not—this attitude bewildered Timothy and angered him no little. His self-esteem smarted and time failed to cure his resentment, for the more he thought upon her response to the greatest event in his life, the less he liked it. Followed to its source, her capacity to disbelieve shook him very gravely, for it argued something far different from the admiration and trust that he imagined accompanied her devotion, and that she could decline to give credence to any statement of fact from him, presented a vision of Katey's mind striking to the very root of his own affection. It was a revelation of infirmity he had never suspected, while her suggestion that they should unfold the story in other ears only served to hasten his disillusionment. In twenty-four hours she had suffered a complete change of value and he was horrified to find his old estimates so utterly confounded. He considered what must be his immediate response and for a while dreaded to think upon the future. Then his dread diminished and he had reached the stage of contemplating life without Katey, before he allowed himself to see her again. Once determined as to what he must do, he thought to write to her. He wrote a good hand and was proud of it, but something told him it would be better to speak than set down any written words, and he knew that the morning hour before she was up would ensure absolute privacy. It was a grey, peaceful dawn as he passed on his way to the forest, stopped, picked up some small stones, flung them against her window and wakened her. She leapt up guessing that it was Timothy, came to the window and leaned out.

"Oh, Tim," she said, "I knew it could only be you. Shall I don something and come down ?"

"No need," he answered. "I only want a word and you can hear it where you are."

She knew by his voice that he came in no forgiving spirit.

"I've wondered what you was thinking all these dark days," she said, "and wondered how June month could hold such dark days. More like winter it's been for me."

"We make our own weather, or so I mostly find it," he answered. "Listen. I won't have my affairs bleated out to that old woman and, thinking on it, I wondered how you could belittle yourself to utter such a feeble thought. Who do you think I am to let my actions be put before 'Mother Forty Cats' for her to judge 'em? But, since you won't believe me, and God forgive you for that—since my solemn word, given in trust to your ear only, makes you think I'm weak in my head and a man not trustworthy, I'll do this. I'll tell a third party. A monstrous, wicked thing that ever you should demand a third opinion on any act of mine and it will never be the same between us no more; but that's your work, not mine. That's your answer to the honour I paid you when I told you my secret. And now I don't care a damn who knows it, or what haps to me when they do. I'll tell one other and that other's a woman, who knows me better than ever you did, or will. I'll tell my mother and chance her hate to hear it. I'll say that I've told you and you don't believe it, and I'll say that all I demand from her is to know if she believes it, or if she don't. And, according to what she says, I'll plan the time to come."

"Think, think before you do that," she begged. "Don't chance her hate, Timothy, else you'll be left all alone in the world, without one left to care for you. You can fare without me, not without her. True or false, the thought of such a thing will be frightful for her. She's gentle and tender-hearted. She cared for Nicholas—cared dearly for him—the only one that ever did."

"No matter for that," he answered. "Let her do as she's got a mind to, and when you hear that she believes it, you'll know whatever may fall on me is your work. You go on disbelieving one that was always the soul of truth. Doubt a man's dreams and you doubt all else about him, though his dreams may be a darned sight finer than the realities of common men, and if I will to get out of a beastly world by my own hand and will power, then no doubt you won't believe that either."

These alarming words did not oppress Katey. She, too, had been reflecting pretty deeply since their last meeting and while still convinced of Timothy's innocence, duly weighed the implications of his confession. His present attitude afflicted her, but she was only thinking for him now and not herself.

"Whatever you do, don't take that story to your mother, Tim," she begged again. "For the sake of the past, when we were so proud of each other and so happy together, don't tell her. Don't tell anybody. I don't want you to tell anybody at all now. You're right about old Mercy. Keep it to yourself for evermore and I'll keep it to myself for evermore, and I'll go on loving you for evermore, even if we never meet again."

"Too late," he said. "Your love's a different pattern from mine. I never doubted one word you said to me. You shall hear what my mother thinks if you want to. In any case no matter now. And another thing:

it's fixed up that I leave Priory; but whether mother goes with me I'm not certain now. Most likely not."

Looked down upon from above, Timothy's fine figure was foreshortened and seemed to have lost a little of its beauty, as his spirit had also perceptibly shrunk in Katey's mind during this brief interchange. She looked after him as he strode away, then went in, shut her window and began to dress. She felt very sad and deeply perturbed for him; but she did not weep: she even smiled a little at a sudden thought.

'Perhaps that's all nonsense too,' she told herself. 'Perhaps he invented he'd tell his mother to fright me. Which he surely did do; but I doubt he meant it. Mrs. Faircloud would never have another day's peace on earth if she believed him.'

But Timothy kept his word and brought the story to his mother. With a mind that had lost equilibrium and in a temper poisoned by Katey's refusal to believe him, he turned to Mrs. Faircloud, sat beside her on a June night in the little garden of 'Lavender Cottage' and once more told his tale.

"Most like you've seen that I'm put about, Mother," he said, "and thought perhaps it was because I'm leaving Tudor Manor plantations and going to work indoors and far ways from my old home. But I'm glad as to that. It had to come and the work will put my brains higher than my body in future, and lead where I want to go."

Already the tiny lines of thought were beginning to trail over his beauty, but none knew that save Nelly herself. He cared nothing for his appearance, and the sedentary life awaiting him, though it would stamp its mark upon his face, was now inevitable. A friend of Naylor's had reported that a second-hand bookseller in Redchester needed an assistant and Timothy was going to make trial and dwell in the city.

"No, that's all right," he continued. "What's all wrong is Katey Wish. I've told her something of immense importance bearing on my character and my powers. I've honoured her by letting her into the secret of my life."

Timothy would often open his mind in this flamboyant fashion and his mother felt no great interest thus far.

"And Kate don't think it an honour perhaps," she suggested. "Often you'll find what's dear and wonderful to us leaves other people quite cool, Tim."

"It didn't leave her cool," he answered. "When I throw out a challenge it don't leave people cool—not if they've got the sense to see my meaning. And when I say or do a thing, it's been well thought out and got rhyme and reason behind it."

"Well, Katey's reasonable enough. A very quick mind I'd say, with love to sharpen it."

"So I thought. I told her what I'd done long since—and why I'd done it —brought it before her, same as I'm going to bring it before you. And what happened? She neither praised nor blamed. She simply refused to believe it, and that's where we stand now."

Nelly laughed.

"Sure that's nothing to make such a fuss about," she said. "She had a right to disbelieve if she chose. On your wild days you oft say things folk can't believe, and you're often the first to admit it was just a flight of fancy after you've calmed down. You were always given to such nonsense from a child, and I daresay the habit sticks when you're with her sometimes."

"No matter for that. I told her a truth—the greatest and best thing ever I did—and she said I never did it and it couldn't be so. Then she made a proper shocking plan and asked me to tell somebody else with an open mind and see if they would believe it, or side with her and refuse to believe it. I declined any such folly as that, and then I thought on you and, though you're the last person ever I meant to tell, she's put me in a fix now and I'm going to tell you. So the one of all others to be relied upon and trustworthy above all else, will hear it. And when you do, then Kate will find she was wickedly wrong to disbelieve, because you will believe."

Mrs. Faircloud followed this rambling introduction as best she could.

"Talk slower," she begged, "and think twice before you talk at all Timothy. If I understand you right, you think I'm safe to credit something that Katey won't. And what follows? Have you told her you're going to tell me?"

"I have," he answered. "If a third party's got to come in, though I never counted on such a thing, then you're the only one on earth that shall come in. When I told her, she didn't want me to tell you and said it couldn't come to no good, and very like it won't; but I'm going to tell you and it may hurt you a lot, and that's her fault, not mine."

"Wait a minute. Don't be in no great haste," said Nelly. "If it's only to hurt me, what's the sense of that?"

"To convince Katey she's wrong and let her see anything that may happen after is her fault, not mine."

It took much to disturb the placid spirit of Timothy's mother. She had even faced the need to leave Priory on his account and make a home for him near his work without regret, yet hoping to come back to the country again some day, when they separated on his marriage.

"Be calm about it and think before you speak. You say your going to hurt me, and that's no matter if I can help to heal you. But look all round it and always weigh the cost if you're out to hurt anybody," she told him. "Say I believe you. Does that mean Katey will come round and believe you too?"

"If it don't, then I've done with her."

"I see. And suppose I'm on her side and don't believe a word of what you're going to say, Tim, does that mean you've done with me too? You see there's things to be thought on before you open your mouth."

"I've thought of everything that can be thought on and I'll take the consequences, and if you don't believe me I'll—I'll. No matter to you what I'll do."

Nelly debated for half a minute.

"Lovers are very apt to quarrel over straws and then think the whole stack's in danger," she said. "To get another point of view don't often occur to 'em, because they generally come to see they was both in fault and tumble over each other to make it up again. But as you and she haven't done so seemingly, there's no harm in trying it out on somebody else and agreeing to abide by their ruling. All the same I don't feel in no hurry to be that somebody else, Tim. Couldn't you have another talk with her first ?"

"There's nothing left to talk about. You can't talk to a person who tells you they don't believe you."

"Haven't you got any proofs to convince her ? If a thing happened by your act, you must have proofs to show you was the reason it happened."

"If I had proofs I wouldn't show them to her now. If a woman loves you she don't want proofs when you say a thing is so. To want 'em is to insult me. As a matter of fact there are no proofs but my spoken word, and what's the love worth that doubts your word ?"

"As for that," said Nelly, "a woman can love a liar just as well as any other sort of man, and because she doubts that you're mistook over this affair, whatever it may be, that isn't to say she don't love you as dear as ever. Tell me what's the matter. I'd be very sorry if anything cruel was to come between you and that girl."

"Something cruel it may be," he said. "Something cruel it is. The strong have to be cruel to be kind now and again, and what looks cruel close at hand may take its true shape and look a merciful stroke on a longer view."

"No call to talk out of your books to me, my dear, that's wasting time. Tell what you've got to tell—something you say you've done and your future wife don't believe you ever did."

Once more Timothy recited the story of his crime. It followed the course of his narration to Katey but he added a few dramatic touches inspired by repetition of the narrative as he proceeded. He lived through the scene again and with unconscious art reached his climax.

"And mark you this, Mother," he concluded. "There's sins and there's crimes. A man like me don't recognise petty things like sins. He looks ahead to the big reasons for what he may do and scorns the two-penny halfpenny talk of sins. And now you know all there is to know and that's God's truth, whatever you please to feel about it."

His mother's expression had changed as he told his tale, but she never interrupted or, by sound or gesture, indicated any emotion whatever. She did not once take her eyes off him and, in the silence that followed when he finished, they were still upon his face ; but they were no longer linked with what they mirrored, for her mind had retreated into the past. She revealed none of the shock or mental confusion that sudden tragedy is apt to bring. Her intellect strove to create a mental picture of Timothy's attitude to life at the time her protector had died; but her memory was never strong, and no salient features of what her son did or said after the sudden end of Nicholas Withers, returned to her. She only recollected that he was unmoved by the accident and had expressed satisfaction at her great bequest. Now the young man waited for his mother to speak and at last she did so in her usual quiet voice.

"So that's what buoyed you up and made you feel on better terms with yourself," she said. "I always thought it was because of the money he willed to leave me."

"So it was: one of the many good things that followed when he had gone, Mother."

"You knew what he was to me and you had no call to hate him, because he always bore with you for my sake; yet you say you killed him in cold blood and felt proud to do it."

"I knew what he was to the world—a greater thing than what he was to you. My thoughts ran far above you. And the chance came to put him out and I was the tool to do it and I was protected afterwards, as a faithful tool should be, and no suspicion ever turned my way. And if you believe in Providence, there was Providence at work. That's how any fair mind must read it."

"Hear me now," she said. "Hear what I'd have done if they had catched you and proved it against you and put you away for a life-time, because they would most like have thought you too young to be hanged. I shouldn't have shed a tear for you, Timothy; I'd have only wept for myself, because I was the mother of a boy who could sink to murder and be lost to every human thought."

"I didn't sink to murder, I rose to it," he said.

"No, Timothy. Nought but a filthy, cowardly murder it would have been for a young man, strong as a lion, to leap from behind his back in the gloaming upon a cripple just off his sick bed and going on two sticks," she said quietly. "A thing to break a mother's heart if she'd got a heart to break. I didn't sorrow overmuch for him, because I never sorrow much for them that are dead; but I'd have sorrowed for the living—for you and for myself, that brought you into the world."

"What matters that now? No use looking back; look forward. I only want one word from you, Mother, and you know what it is. Think as you will, and blame me if you like; but you've got to speak that word no matter what comes of it."

"You shall hear it," she answered. "Yes, I know what that word is and, if there's a God that cares one straw for you and me, I'm thankful to Him that I do know what it is. I'd say that Katey was dead right not to believe this horrible stuff you've told to her and me. And I don't believe it neither and never, never shall. She knows you inside out, because she loves you and her love don't blind a girl like her; and I know you and did know you from the day I started to learn all about you after you was born. And if Kate and me agree out of all we know and feel to you that you're mistook in your imagination, and building fancied truth on evil dreams, then better far you trust us to know we're right and be thankful to find yourself wrong. I'd hoped you'd grown beyond your old itch for telling tales wove out of fancy, because they was always apt to be bloody and painful, and I'm a lot fretted to think such a pitiful maggot as this had come to life in your mind. I'll grant that you believe it yourself for the moment, worse luck, same as you often did of old; but you can't sweep this out of your mind, nor let it die too quick, Timothy, and come to see that we women are right. You ain't built, nor never will be built, to shed a fellow's creature's blood. Too much part of me ever to do such a hateful deed; and I hope your powers of hoodwinking yourself with your nightmare dreams won't reach to such a hideous pitch no more."

"What would you make of me?" he asked.

"You're a man now—old enough to set about making yourself," she answered. "And you have set about it. You've declared yourself for a scholar and ordain to live your life along with books and make them your business. But for God's love let 'em stuff your head with wisdom and good guidance, not beastliness. Then they'll be more than the joy of your life; they'll help you to run your life in a good pattern. Let 'em clear your mind if they can, not cloud it, my dear."

"Then I know where I stand," he told her. "You've chose to build up a barrier between me and you, same as Kate has chose to build up a barrier between me and her. Well and good. I won't try and break down that barrier—too proud for that. I won't waste time trying to make you see you ain't large-minded enough to face a thing like this. You can't even understand it. A man might; some women might, but not women built same as you are. I'll go to Redchester, and I'll go alone. I'll take a brace of rooms and I'll face up to life and most like you and her will live to see what's in me and what I shall make of it; but I won't neighbour with you any more, Mother, and I won't neighbour with her any more. You've cut yourselves off from me for ever more now, because you ain't big enough to stand up to great deeds, nor yet hear about 'em. Do a man like me knuckle under to a brace of women who think he's weak in his head and agrees they're right and he's wrong?"

"You shall do as you wish," she said. "At your age you can look after yourself very well if you give your mind to it. But let time pass and try to think of a brace of women for a while and forget yourself. I matter nothing and, if you don't want me, then I'll be very well content to stop here with my neighbours and at your call if you feel to need me again any time. Mothers are used to be dropped when their childer grow up. But Katey's different. She's serious. You've promised to marry her and if you break with her, it will lose you a lot of well wishers, because you may be sure she'll never tell the reason. However that's not like to trouble you if your love's dead and she'll get over it."

He leapt up and prepared to leave her.

"You tell me to forget myself for a while; and I tell you to remember me for a while, and try to imagine what it must be for such as me to hear his solemn and tremendous words scorned and his oath flouted. Who am I to suffer it? What have I done that my word —— ? But little you can measure me and I was a fool to think you could."

Upon this tame conclusion he left her, in doubt whether to seek Katey, inform her of his experience and sever all connections, or take his agitation to the 'Pen in Hand' and drink. He decided on the latter course, and when he was gone his mother sat on in her garden, watched the summer stars emerge and considered the situation that her offspring had created. It was too dark to see her work and she left it on her lap and allowed her thoughts to estimate these things from varied standpoints. Her pulse did not quicken and her temper remained unruffled. One minor aspect of the future contented her and determined an issue. She had long decided to go with the young man into his new life and exercise her old watchful care, while more friends than one advised against this course and begged her to stop at Priory. They had pointed out that it would be a wise experience for her son to live independent as most men of his age desire to be, and she had seen the force of the argument and only proceeded against it on the plea of Timothy's unstable nature. She had expected that, alone in a new environment among town dwellers, he would be lost and welcome her as a link between the old life and the new. But now, learning his own resolves for the future and his desire to part from her, she perceived that it might be wiser for him to make the experiment and leave time to report upon it. She loved him in a temperate fashion and had been a faithful mother to him, but there was no passion of maternal devotion in Nelly's nature and his hard words did not distress her over much. So far she was content and glad to remain in her own home, serving perhaps as a second home for Timothy, whither he might return from time to time when leisure served him. She had uttered her genuine convictions and found herself quite honestly of opinion that his confession contained no spark of reality. It echoed many a sanguinary myth of his earlier years and in her opinion directly contradicted his capabilities. The very drama of the story seemed full of artifice to her ears and on a par with boyhood nonsense declared in the same fashion with smaller command of words. But the old flights of imagination had contained their own denial and were capable of disproof. Indeed he would often laugh when, waiting for time to pass, she would return to some freakish avowal to prove that his performances were a romance. To do so was not possible before this confession of murder. She puzzled to find some refutation yet, though not a shadow of truth supported it in her own opinion, she could think of no argument or fact that absolutely contradicted the possibility. She felt little fear for his fate, since he could furnish no proofs to substantiate his story. Had he possessed such, he must have advanced them when Katey refused to believe him. Then continued reflection brought Mrs. Faircloud into a frame of mind where, like his sweetheart before her, she began to wonder whether another opinion might be taken and Timothy's avowal set before an impartial intelligence. She thought upon Dr. Naylor, yet shrank from him as the confidant of a story so tremendous. He had been exceedingly kind in the matter of Timothy, always taken a sanguine view of his future and was frankly hopeful. Already he foretold success for the young man and believed that, through the channel of books, he must come into his own. She remembered that, thus far, only women had heard these things, and that night before she slept decided yet another woman should hear them. Her mind turned to Mercy Grepe, even as Katey's had done, and she determined upon a secret consultation in that quarter, quite ignorant of the fact that this was the arbiter whom Timothy had already declined. 'It's very simple,' thought his mother. 'Only to tell her the tale and see if her view jumps with mine and she don't believe it, or if she sides with him and does believe it.' Nelly felt tolerably sure that the wise woman would share her own opinion, yet her last unanswered question before she slumbered was to wonder what Mercy might counsel if she took the opposite view.

She heard Timothy come home and go to bed and he bade her good night as usual when he passed her door. The next morning he was calm, though very silent, took his meal and at six o'clock went to work.

Then Nelly set out for her ancient friend and found her eating a breakfast of oatmeal porridge with cats and kittens about her feet.

"Come in," she cried, "whoever it may be," as the visitor knocked. "Shameful late to my food this morning, but I slept bad and the birds couldn't wake me as they mostly do."

"Cruel not to sleep," admitted Nelly, "and I'm always sorry for myself when I've had a bad night. Not that I often do. You look a thought tired I'm fearing, Mercy."

"Folk over eighty be apt to look tired," said the old woman. "You must be thankful for small mercies by that time."

"You ought to have a girl to help you and run your errands."

"I don't want help yet, but soon shall," confessed Mercy Grepe. "Little by little the flesh shrinks off your bones and your bones can't do no work by themselves if your flesh is gone. But I'd say my mind was clear and I still can see tolerable clear. I'll get mixed up among my cats now and again, because the tabbies run so alike."

" 'Tis your mind I want, my dear, if you can spare a bit of time to listen. I've come to a pass with my boy and something out of the common from him over-got me last night and it looked to me as I'd much wish to hear how it sounded to you."

"I was very glad when Timothy ordained to put his gifts to a purpose at last," said Mercy. "I'd say he'll fare well along the road of books."

"That's what I count on and hope for, and I was going with him to Redchester; but I don't go now by his own wish. We've fallen out, so to say, because he's told me a curious thing. He abounded in fancical ideas when he was young, but I'd hoped he was past all that now."

"He's puzzled you before to-day and may again," said the elder.

"He has. If you don't chance to know for certain who your child's father was, you can't know him so well as you would otherwise. But he's mine—my only one—and I've tried to do my duty by him and stand up to his funny nature. No doubt I was liking his father very well for the time being, before Timothy came in the world, but I can't mind who 'twas now."

Nothing shocked Mercy.

"He don't remind you of nobody twenty years ago?" she asked. "If you could see one of your friends from your Valley Farm days reflected in your son, it might help you to understand him."

Nelly smiled her still entrancing smile.

"I couldn't tell you with no certainty after all these years and it don't matter in any case," she answered. "But I needs must go back to Nicholas Withers, because it is to do with him what Tim told to me last night. I've never felt no discomforts about Nick myself. He'd left his wife, body and soul, long before he came to me. Some might even go so far as to say I done Myra a pretty good turn by taking the man off her hands; but, of course, she wouldn't go so far as to grant that. He treated her badly because she openly despised him and he was the sort of man that didn't mind being hated, but couldn't stand no contempt. And now we come to Timothy. When he was young he went in fear of Nicholas, but hadn't no great need to. Withers thought nothing of him, because he was the type of nervous, fidgety lad the farmer felt to be useless, but he knew I cared for the boy and Withers would no doubt have served him and helped him into some better job of work if he had lived. So that's how it was till last night, when this is what Timothy confessed to me. You've got to think all round it Mercy, before you can measure up for or against, and you've got to know him as well as I do to feel sure. And before I tell you there's one more thing to take into your account. I wasn't the first to hear it. He told one other before he told me, and that was his sweetheart. And because of the way she took it, which disappointed him a lot, he decided to tell me—you may say for his own credit's sake."

Having cleared the air to her own satisfaction, Nelly proceeded and, with attention to exact truth, told Timothy's story.

"It don't sound quite the same as how he told it," she concluded, "because his heart was in it and he liked to act it as he went along, and gave all sorts of little touches. He always acted his tales of old and he made this sound so real and ruthless as he knew how. But the point that looked most tremendous to me wasn't what he said he'd done nor yet how he said he'd done it. The point that over-topped the story was that he rejoiced in it and plumed himself for a fine, powerful character that made other men look small compared with him. He claimed he'd done a most valuable murder, Mercy, and wanted to show how he'd put all Priory in his debt for a valiant deed none but him had the pluck to perform. No remorse, no thought of himself as a dirty coward, to kill a sick man by stealth —nothing like that. Just pride to have done it and got away with it. Hadn't even enough sense to see that being what Nicholas was to me, I shouldn't love him no better for killing the man; but counted I'd take the larger view, and forgive him because of the good he'd done to everybody else ! And that's how it is, my dear, and I'm terrible wishful to hear what you may think as to the truth or falsehood of it."

Mercy had finished her porridge and set down two saucers of lukewarm milk for her cats while she listened. She did not answer immediately and the visitor made a suggestion.

"If you feel it's too big a thing to decide upon out of hand, I'll give you what time you might feel to want, my dear, before hearing you upon the subject," she said.

"No need, Nelly. I'll ask a question or two—that's all; then I'll say how I think about it," replied Mercy. 'You say he told Katey Wish first, and then he was disappointed and came to you. Do you know why he felt to be disappointed with how Katey took it ?"

"Yes, he told me. She heard it and denied every word of it. Wouldn't believe him, and he was so sore that he parted from her in anger I understood."

"Couldn't bear to be denied ?"

"Not for a moment."

"And what did you tell him, Nelly ?"

"Exactly the same. I said he was ever one to dream and imagine things so vivid till at last he'd get to believe they was real. I said this was the ugliest and fearfulest dream ever he'd had, and I told him I didn't credit a word of it, and never would."

"And what's the result of that ?" asked Mercy.

"The result is he's making up to fling over Katey and has decided he'll go to Redchester and live alone there without me. I'm not sorry for that, because he's quite capable to look after himself and very nice in his attention to his body and his clothes. That means I can bide at 'Lavender Cottage,' which I am glad to do, and shall always be in reach of him if he wants me. But Katey's different. It will make a lot of sorrow for Katey, and her folk will turn against him—naturally."

"As to that you may be mistook," said Mercy. "Kate's a sensible piece and practical and would stand up to it after the shock was over. You've told everything very clear and I'm glad you came to me."

"The jar for him was to find his future wife and his mother thought alike. He didn't expect that."

"Wait and I'll try to see what moved him to tell this tale and where his mind stands between you two women now," answered Mercy Grepe. "It turns on his mind and whether other stronger minds have power to influence it."

"I don't feel much fear myself," declared Nelly, "because he's a great one to look after himself, and finding we won't believe him, he may come to believe us, don't you think?"

"No. He won't do that for shame. Some day perhaps, after he's calmed down, but not while he's proud of the thought and smarting to hear you scoff at it. He'll be wanting to find somebody willing to believe it; but better he don't tell no such thing to any other pair of ears, because, if some man heard and did believe it, he'd be in that man's power."

"He's safe enough. He couldn't furnish a mite of proof he did it. If he could, he'd have showed it to me."

"Let me think, my dear."

Quiet fell for a while between them and when a big cat jumped to Mercy's lap, she appeared to consult it and thoughtfully scratched its throat.

"I'd say he's done with Katey. You can take that for granted, if it helps you to get any ideas," said Mrs. Faircloud, presently.

The elder preserved silence a little longer, and then spoke.

" 'Tis a case for holding the tongue if ever there was one, Nelly," she began, "because, true or false, if it got out there's going to be a mort of trouble. If this reached so far as the police, they'd most likely disbelieve same as you do, but where does that leave 'em? A man such as Thomas Chard would feel it his duty to report what he'd heard, and doctors would be called to Timothy and might prove very apt to explain the matter by saying he was weak-minded. And if they did, even if they didn't order for him to go in an asylum, the world would know what they had found and the boy would be done for. Either he really did it, or else he's worked himself up to think he did and his yearning—to be somebody out of the common order—has helped him to decide that he did do it and so become famous, if only in a left-handed fashion. Some itch so cruel to be heroes that they'll do evil to become so, when they can't find no other way, and wickedness is a lot easier than virtue. But we've got to mind that he don't grant he did evil and the murder, if murder there was, looked all to the good for him. If you grant he done it, then he's not mad and have all his wits about him. But the urge that drove him to tell anybody, looks like his mind's wandering."

"Yet, knowing him as I do, I'd never say there was right down bats in the belfry," declared Nelly. "Wild and fanciful and baffling to the orderly mind but, between his flights, clever and steady. Decent in his habits and respectable and good to his work. It's a throw-back for him to come out with this murderous story, and that's why I'd fight to disbelieve it anyway."

"You disbelieve it and don't allow it points to him being touched, but is as you say, just a throw-back to his childish ways of telling stories to make him look grand?"

"Exactly so, Mercy."

The old woman nodded.

"I wouldn't say but that's the right and proper way for you to look at him."

"And now tell me what you think is the truth," begged Nelly. "That's why I came—to get your straight opinion. You've told me I'm right to take the line I've took and no doubt you reckon Kate was right to do the same, even if it meant losing him; but now tell me if that's what you honestly think yourself, my dear woman."

Mercy made no immediate reply and regretted the direct question.

"It's like this," she answered. "If nobody in the world can prove a thing happened, then there's a tolerable fair likelihood it never did happen. In this case you've got one man's word that he done a thing that looked out of his bent and inclinations, which were peaceful and on the timid side, as I've often heard you say. We've got his word, but no proof that he's telling true, and his own character and record to argue very strong he is not. I might grant that there's no more proof he didn't do it than there's proof he did; but you'd say that there is more proof he did not, knowing his character so well as you do. And for his future hopes and good credit, and for your own sake and Katey's, if she's still in a frame of mind to marry him, I'd say carry on as you've begun. Stick to your point of view and don't budge an inch from it. Show him what might come out of it if anybody else got to hear about it. Be firm and don't argue and let him go to Redchester and fill his mind with a new healthy manner of life. If he wants to say any more on the subject, tell him he's nursing a serpent in his heart and, if he ever hopes to shine in the world, he'd best to cast it out. Tell him the mother-wit of women has confounded the wisdom of men time and again, and will so continue. Speak strong with all your faith behind the words, Nelly, and promise him that, so sure as he's born, a time will come when he'll look back and thank his God you was right about it and he'd been misled by the devil to fancy things that never happened, and never could happen."

"And leave it at that," said Nelly.

"Leave it at that. And let Katey leave it at that. But don't let her do more than take her stand. Don't let her fret him worse than she must. If he raises the question, you can both tell him, it's never going no further on a mortal ear, because I don't count and no word will ever go out from me."

"That will do to go on with," declared Mercy's client. "Other things is like to arise out of it, but we can leave them till they do.   If his betrothal is broken off, which looks to be tolerable certain, her people will want to know the reason why; but we can leave that for the minute. Katey's one to be trusted, in any case, and she may make it quite simple by dropping him and refusing to give a reason to anybody. A girl can do that easier than what a man can."

She rose and fetched out her purse.

"And thank you very much indeed, my dear. I'd say, whatever you think yourself, that your advice to me is very good and I'm a lot beholden to you. I'll let you know where I am presently, and I'll tell you another thing. Now I'm going to stop at Priory, I shall look after you a bit and seek out a nice girl to come and run your errands and watch over you."

"Bless your heart. No call to worry about me, Nelly; but very like you to think of it. I'll take your money because I know you'd wish me to do that and there's none I'd pleasure sooner. Things will work together for good I hope; then his mind will come back to peace through his books."

"I expect so," answered Nelly. "I was never much a one for books myself, but to dote on books ain't no sign of a weak mind, is it ?"

"Certainly not," agreed Mercy. "I'm no reader either, but a passion for book-learning ain't a vice, same as so many other passions will come to be. There's no more orderly folk than reading people and like enough, if the truth could come to be known, you'd find that books do more good than harm."

She asked a question as Mrs. Faircloud went her way.

"One thing, Nelly. Your boy's never threatened to take his own life or any rash deed like that ?"

The younger shook her head.

"Not serious—only now and again he's said that he'd never wanted to be alive and was brought into the world from no wish of his own; but he was free to go out of the world if he chose and nobody could stop him. Just to shake me up. He'll try all he knows in some of his moods to see me go off the rails; but he never has, and he never will, poor dear boy. He couldn't kill himself, no more than he could kill anybody else."

XVIII

WHEN Timothy learned from his mother, who had gathered the fact through Katey's parents, that they regarded his engagement as at an end, he declared satisfaction.

"She's kept her mouth close shut as to her reasons for breaking it off," explained Nelly, "and told her mother and father that the particular cause don't signify. She feels your future life in a township would make against her love of the country and open air, and doubts as you get more learned and wrapped up in your books and seek out for clever friends and supporters and so on, whether she wouldn't find herself a good bit in the way. All very natural and proper, and Milly and Sam Wish haven't took it to heart over much, because as soon as they heard what you were going to do, they felt doubts for the future. So you can say 'Goodbye' to her without any shame, and the folk will understand that you were both sensible to break it off and go your different roads."

"I'd ordained to see her and let her know my will," said Timothy, "but she's been mostly up to Pigslake with her friend, Norah Withers, of late and, now I know it's finished, there's no call to see her again. Some day perhaps, when I come down from town to spend a week-end with you, I'll look her up on a new footing. After all we've felt for each other and all she's expressed as to her worship of me and her looking to a great future with me and so on—after all that—it's funny to think my fine deed frightened her away from me and she took the same pitiful line you did yourself, Mother. I'd reckoned I'd tuned her up to rise to what I did, but she lacked the mind I fancied she'd got and was just ordinary. That's where love fooled me and I'll waste no time that way in the future."

His attitude had obviously cooled to his mother and he never again returned to the subject of his confession and its reception until many months were past. His exodus from Priory created no comment but many were gratified that Mrs. Faircloud had decided to remain. More important incidents demanded attention and the approaching nuptials of Paul and Jenny won general applause. Mrs. Canniford lived in a whirl of excitement, and her friends agreed that she and Saddler Pook had done wisely and must both be gainers by their union.

The return of Rupert and his partner passed practically unnoticed, but impartial observers in a position to judge, reported that already signs of increased amenity began to appear in Ivy. At the 'Pen-in-Hand' it was thought that long days, in sole company of Rupert, might well make her greet the world at large with welcome. Jenny took much heart from such beneficent changes for she had feared that better knowledge of her son was unlikely to increase her daughter-in-law's good will—always at low ebb. She dreaded, too, what Rupert's bride might say and think on hearing of the approaching marriage. But her alarm was allayed when the honeymooners returned.

"How he's done it I couldn't tell you," she confided to Paul, "but already he's employed his gifts on Ivy and she's come home in a frame of mind I'd never have thought was within her reach."

"She's beamed on me too," repeated Paul. "I was like you and rather feared a hot reception, but, no; butter wouldn't have melted in her mouth. It's a most puzzling fact that you never can tell how anybody's going to take anything. You think you know 'em and you feel sure how they'll shape up to a bit of news; and then when the time comes, those you expect to weep surprise you by laughing, and others again that you feel positive will rejoice, howl their heads off."

"Rupert's work on her," declared Jenny. "Deep as a well he always was and always will be."

"He looks to be standing up to Ivy all right so far, and her to him," said Paul. "There don't seem to be a cloud between 'em as yet. He wouldn't show it if there was, but she couldn't hide it. She's come home more cheerful and human than I can ever remember her to be and even her voice sounds a bit less bleak."

"She kissed me," said Jenny, "not just her usual frosty peck, but as if she wanted to."

Marriage, it seemed, had created these transformations, and longed-for wifehood's increased importance, brought complete satisfaction to Ivy's limited but acute intelligence. She was exceedingly proud of being married to a powerful and forcible man, and his indifference to all the small niceties of life that she had fostered, did not depress her, since he made no effort to interfere with any of her arrangements which failed to affect his own. She swiftly found that his method of life was never going to be changed by her, and that, in matters of habitude and the conduct of his own leisure, she could expect no voice; but he exacted nothing save close attention to such details, put no restraint of any sort upon her and in truth manifested scanty interest in her household affairs. She found him a very handy man, always ready and willing to pleasure her and capable of carrying out every sort of task her new home demanded.

"You'll find," he told her, when they arrived to dwell at a Manor lodge, "that I can do a score of things you'd need to pay for, if I couldn't do 'em. I've always made it a cast-iron rule never to pay any man a bean for a job I can do myself, and I've saved tons of money that way and learned knowledge of other crafts than my own. The more you know how to do things, instead of getting 'em done for you, the cheaper life is, and the easier it grows to save money. If we was cast away on a desert island, Ivy, so long as I had the tools, I'd make shift to carry on."

"God forbid," she said, "but I'm with you there and I admire you for it, Rupert. I'm the same. What I saved Lady Garland in sempstress work, in my maiden days, only she and me knew."

Ivy was fond of referring to her maiden days with a pitying smile. They now looked to her much as its empty chrysalis might be supposed to appear in a butterfly's eyes.

"I've come to see marriage is worth while," she confessed to her old friends at Tudor Manor. "I always felt it might be and was disposed to give it a try, and I find I was right. If both parties bring patience and long suffering to married life, then they'll find union is strength. In my case Canniford's one who will have his own way, I grant you: I knew he would before I married him; but against that he never questions my way. He may not follow it here and there; but he never questions it. Free as air I am, and he's got the sense never to come between me and my religious convictions and rules of good conduct and good manners, though he don't share 'em. Not one of them arguing men, so you can save your time haggling where you differ, and that means peace. If he wants a thing to happen, it's got to happen and there's an end of the matter. And if I want a thing to happen, most times he'll raise no objections whatever; but if he don't want it to happen, it won't. Reliable, that's what my husband is, and I'd say the sense of security such as he breeds is worth a lot."

"Just the opposite of his brother Harry," suggested one who knew the hedger and ditcher.

"Just the living opposite," agreed Rupert's wife. "Harry bleats his way through life like a lost lamb, and I often wonder what the mischief Susan could find in the poor soul."

At saving, Ivy also saw with her husband's eyes, and shared thrift created a very real bond of fellowship between them, for she praised Rupert's remarkable gifts in this sort, while his own infrequent words of direct approbation were generally won by some triumph of economy on her part. She had come now to approve her father's marriage.

"I should always have had him on my conscience a bit, because, though at work on him before you found me and took me, Rupert, there was a lot wanted altering in his way of life; but now I feel my duty in that quarter's ended."

"He'll be a darned sight happier with my mother than ever he found himself with you," said the gamekeeper, "same as I'm better content with you than I was with my mother. She won't get on his nerves nor yet spend his money. She knows the value of money, same as only them can do who never had none. He's a thought too prone to be open-handed; but I shall rub it into mother to head him off from that."

"In a manner of speaking it's her duty to me to see he don't waste his substance," agreed Ivy.

Myra Withers had taken charge of Jenny when the approaching translation of her sister became known.

"You must go to him befitting," said Myra. "You can't provide your additions and your eldest can't help you and you may lay your life your youngest won't. But a proper set-out and proper clothes are called for and I ordain to do that. You shan't go to him in rags, or little better."

"I was never one for rich garments," confessed Jenny, "but I'll be thankful for a few new clothes worthy of the man."

She spent a good deal of her time at Pigslake now, for not only Myra, but her nephew and niece were much attached to her. Mention of Rupert, however, found them cold and none at the farm pretended any renewed interest in him or his bride.

"I thought, so like as not, Ivy would kill him before the honeymoon was over," said Myra.

"Or else he'd lay her out," added Jonathan.

"No," declared Jenny, "far from it. They suffer each other gladly so far as Paul and me can tell. It looks like a case where two people, famous for rubbing their neighbours the wrong way, have found their salvation in each other. Early days yet, of course. Harry says there's much hidden from his knowledge on the subject, but there's such a cruel lot hidden from his knowledge on every subject, poor dear."

"How does Cousin Harry like you marrying Mr. Pook, Aunt Jenny?" asked Norah.

"He's pleased for my happiness," declared Mrs. Canniford, "but he don't feel I shall have much time and thought to spare on him and his family now. He says that it's a common thing for a poor man to be hemmed round by a lot of rich relations—all no more wishful to succour him than the rest of the world."

"Generally the other way," suggested Jonathan. "'Tis the rich man gets choked up with the other sort most times."

"In the matter of Harry and Susan, my deepest affections go out more to their childer than themselves," confessed Jenny. "It may be wrong and I'd never name it in no ears but yours, but I get more private happiness along with George and Percy and Emmeline than ever I do from their parents."

"More hopeful you find 'em?" suggested Myra.

"A lot. You can please them and win their undying gratitude for a slice of bread and jam; but it's cruel hard to make Harry uplifted."

"Yet he's always in good work," said Jonathan, "what more does any industrious man want than good work and plenty of it?"

"He can't help taking his dark views," explained Myra. "He's built so. If he had a thousand a year and a park, he'd always be envying them that had ten thousand a year and a parish."

"He's poor at figures," confessed Harry's mother. "I doubt if more money wouldn't confuse him."

"Thank God, his boy, George, looks to be a cheerful nipper," said Jonathan.

"Very cheerful indeed you'll find him," promised Jenny. "I'd go so far as to say that George is a truer Canniford than what his father is. George reminds me of my dear first. My John hoped on, hoped ever. Hoped to better us while he lived and hoped to better himself when he died."

"Paul Pook always thought well of Canniford," Myra reminded her sister.

"He did then—thought very well of him—and I shall be able to chat now and again about dear John to Paul, because he'll have the patience to listen."

"That's a bright thought for you, Aunt Jenny," declared Norah.

"Where are you going to be married from?" asked Mrs. Withers.

"Nowhere in particular, my dear. We've planned it out. There won't be no upstore, nor party, nor anything to call attention. With the young it's different. In our case just a private wedding and dignity, and then off we go—to Plymouth for a week. Both Rupert and Ivy was so full of praise for Plymouth that Paul feels, since manners ordain that we clear out for a few days, we might so well go there and take the sea air as any other place. No odds to me of course, though strangely enough I went to the sea with John on my first honeymoon."

"To Lyme Regis, and didn't like it, I remember," said Myra. "You can come here and have a spread after the marriage in church if you was so minded, Jenny; but I guess Paul would sooner just go through with it, as you say, and fade out quick after it was over."

"Like you to think of it, my dear, but I'm with him. We both want for it to be obscure and no fuss. He's so well thought upon that they was wishful at the 'Pen-in-Hand' to have some singing and a presentation of a pony-trap they've bought; but 'no' he said, 'let it be peace with honour, but no fireworks.'"

"A nice little second-hand governess car they've got, so you'll be able to drive up and see us when you mind to," said Jonathan, "and if we come to your wedding, you'll have to promise to come to mine and Norah's—when they happen."

"Please God I shall witness both of 'em," declared his aunt with fervour.

"You must have the bells, Aunt Jenny," said Norah. "You can't have a proper wedding without the bells."

"Nought blazes such a thing abroad like bells, and Paul was against, but the ringers would have it so and bells there's going to be," admitted Mrs. Canniford. "But no singing or other delays in church. We just pop in, do the holy deed and then off in Godfrey's motor car to the railway."

"Be Harry going to give you away?" asked Jonathan.

"No—nor yet Rupert," answered Mrs. Canniford.

"You can't see Rupert giving anything away—not even his mother," granted her nephew.

"No complications like that—just us and his reverence at the altar rails," explained Jenny, "and the fewer in church, the better we shall like it. We both want it to be as different as can be from our first marriages in the full bloom of our youth."

"There's one won't be there, and that's Peter Honeywood," said Myra. "For the rest, who can tell?"

In the event a great many friends assembled to see the ceremony and shout good wishes after the vanishing car when all was over. Every member of the uniting families was present and the bells rang a peal of grandsire triples to mark the glad occasion; but a greater event than Paul Pook's wedding occurred within a few hours afterwards and, as the sun set and evening descended, tenor bell sounded once more, this time alone. It told of death and Priory learned that the lady of the Manor was sped at last. Her passing swept the earlier incident out of men's and women's minds and speculations as to the nature of the new order were on every tongue.

In one quarter the subject opened very intimate and personal problems between a man and his wife, for a secret, in possession of the husband alone, must now appear and he had always determined to bring it before his partner before any other body should do so.

Ivy, who had spent most of the day after her father's wedding at Tudor Manor, where the rumour of Lady Garland's approaching end was now three days' old, returned to the keeper's lodge when all was over, and after Rupert joined her during the evening, she proved tearful and full of memories. He bore with her for a while, making no comment on the varied incidents she summoned from the past, and then he took up the conversation and gave her something more cheerful to think about. It involved his own confession of private knowledge uttered with curt frankness, yet modified by a certain tact and consideration for Ivy's feelings, scarcely to have been expected from him.

"Alfred Bodkin, the butler, tells me she made all arrangements for her funeral long before she lost her mind and went off her head," he began. "Her ladyship willed to be took to the grave in one of the farm wains and to be drawed by two white hosses and no more. And for pall-bearers, her nephew and his brother, along with Jacob Townley, the head keeper,

Bodkin himself and the land agent. They want three more and I'm going to be one of 'em. Godfrey does the funeral. An oaken coffin, and he's had the timber by him for some years, since that big tree fell in the huge storm three winters ago."

Having sketched the immediate future, Rupert delayed a little, refilled his pipe, and turned to the past.

"So much for that," he said, "and the funeral's this day week. She herself ordered a week to pass under her will, because she wasn't going to be hustled into her grave before she was cold, which is the modern fashion when folk die. A week above ground she demanded and a week she'll get. And now there's one or two other things you don't know, that's like to help you bear up."

"I am bearing up," answered Ivy, "but you can't but look back over all those years of her affection and kindness, Rupert. They come back on you now she's gone, because they was so unusual between a mistress and a maid."

"She was an unusual mistress and you were an unusual maiden," he said, "and a lucky thing for both of you, you come together. I ain't sorry she's gone myself, because you can't wish the mad ones to linger. They make a deuce of a lot of work for the sane ones, and call for a lot of money and don't get no true pleasure from being alive themselves. But I'm just and I never under-valued what she did for me and gave me my chance when nobody else would. So I'm glad to remember she didn't go dotty before she heard I'd made good, and I'll be very well pleased to stand with the pall-bearers."

"I must see to your black," said Ivy. "I've warned you time and again, Rupert, that you'd be caught napping by a sudden death some day."

"So long as it ain't your sudden death, no odds," he answered. "And now listen, because I'm going over to Priory to-night with a message for Toozey. Your father wouldn't have no singing at his wedding this morning; but there's to be singing at the funeral, because her ladyship always wanted it to be took more or less joyous."

"Being of opinion that when a true Christian goes home, we ought to go into exultations and not whimper about it: I've heard her say so," declared Ivy.

"No doubt. Now give heed," he said. "A word or two for your ear first, before the parish hears 'em."

"If I have a quarrel with you, Rupert," she answered, "it's because I don't hear your voice so often as I ought."

"That's all right. You're going to hear it now. Least said, soonest mended most times. Such a lot of folk say they're sorry they opened their mouths too wide about one thing or another, that you can't but mark most mouths are safest shut. But there's going to be a lot of chatter over you, before very long, and you'll see it's bound to be, because you're going to find yourself in the news as they say. And you'll have your friends, if you've got any, purring over you and I'll have my enemies—quite a lot—pointing their fingers at me."

Ivy stared at him in amazement; then she spoke.

"What madness are you telling, Rupert?" she asked. "What have you done now?"

"Don't be striking in. Listen. It's like this. Everybody knows the Garlands are awful rich and will so continue till there's a Labour government comes in to knock the stuffing out of them; and Lady Garland was a tremendous wealthy woman and there's no doubt when her will's opened, it will be found that out of her hundreds of thousands of pounds she's made some bequests to her people much over and above what's to be expected. Her interests were with us, not her own class, and I happen to know through a secret channel, Ivy, that she let herself go in that matter where she felt like it. All told, no doubt, it's but a fleabite to the riches of the Manor; but from the point of view of the folk, she's dispensed a lot of cash."

"They used to count up there that she'd got more than half a million," said Ivy. "Alfred Bodkin—her butler and her husband's butler before her—always said the estates bring in a huge fortune—or so it seemed to work-people."

"That's right. And Alfred will lick his lips when he hears what's coming to him. And not only Alfred I expect. And now I'm coming to you. Also a word about myself and I hope you won't get up in the air when you hear it. I never hid the fact that I wanted a spot of money with my wife, when I took one. And why not? There's nothing I can see to be shocked at in that. Right or wrong that was my intention and that's what turned my attention to you in the beginning. If you'd misliked me, or felt I wasn't up to your standards, then you'd have turned me down and no harm done; but what happened? I found you a most likeable woman and suitable to my requirements in every way and, what mattered more, you sized me up and came to consider I was pretty much what you could do with as a partner. We unfolded our feelings and found common sense was our strong suit, along with proper respect for money and contempt for the opinions of most other people except ourselves. I never should have found any female to hold a candle to you, even if I'd looked for another, but though no doubt you could easily have found a better man than me, and I wasn't worth a lot, except to be trustworthy and saving and very much at your service once you took me, still you reckoned it was good enough."

"Get on to what's coming," said Ivy. "All what you say is true, Rupert. I felt you was agreeable to my feelings for a husband and time's proved it, because a more understanding pair than us you wouldn't find. Complete in ourselves you might say. But go on with your news."

"Well, the next thing is how I came to know such a secret," he explained— "how I, of all men, and an outdoor man at that, should hear you was down in her ladyship's will and what you was down for."

"She told me once I wasn't forgot," said Ivy. "The saintly woman never forgot anybody that was worthy to be remembered, and a lot that wasn't I expect."

"You was remembered all right. So was Alfred Bodkin, so was the housekeeper—all in the grand style. Old Alf will get his lodging-house at Redchester now. And a lot of lesser indoor ones have cause to be tolerable joyful too. A year's wages for half a score of 'em."

"How you hang fire, Rupert !"

"Bodkin's got five thousand pounds for his lifetime of faithful service, and you—you're in for three thousand, Ivy !"

"Three thousand pounds !"

His wife grew a little faint, turned very pale and fanned herself.

"You ain't trying to be funny, are you ?" she asked.

"Never tried to be funny in my life and never shall," he answered. "It's true and must be true in Lady Garland's case, because she made her will when she was sane and couldn't alter it after she went silly, even if she'd wanted to. And now you'll be asking a lot of questions and I'll answer two of 'em, which is all that's like to matter."

"Three thousand pounds !" sighed Ivy.

"A drop in the bucket out of three hundred thousand."

"And why, knowing about this by some tricky miracle, could you have the heart to keep me from the pleasure of knowing ?" she asked.

"That was the first question you was dead sure to put," he replied, "I heard it last autumn, at a big shoot when the new lord of the manor and another chap were talking rather loud at lunch and I was pouring out sparkling wine for them. The other chap was the family lawyer and a great friend of Captain Garland. Intimate and talking about the will her ladyship had made a year before. Joking over it and the lawyer, who's an elderly chap and must be a damn bad lawyer but was a very good shot, prattled about the wondrous generosity of the Captain's aunt. They didn't pay no more heed to me than if I was a plate on the table and were talking aside together. And I heard the lawyer, who knew Bodkin very well, say that he was in for five thousand; and then he asked who 'Ivy Pook' might be, because he'd never heard tell of her, but she'd got three thousand. And the Captain knew who you were and said you was his aunt's lady's maid and she thought a deuce of a lot about you, and felt much in your debt. After that I faded off, and next time I came round they was talking of other things."

Ivy had grown calmer.

"And you stored it up, then turned your attention to me ?" she asked.

"I did—what they call cause and effect, my lamb; and the reason why I kept it under my hat was that if I'd told you, you would have instantly thought the money was the cause of my affection. Knowing about your hugeous legacy, you might have turned me down out of hand and looked round for something better-class; and even after I'd took you and made good, the news might have shook you off me. Just common sense and I wasn't running any risks with my chosen wife in the balance. After I came to know what you were, I'd have been a born fool to chance losing you."

Ivy considered.

"It's a devious story, Rupert, but I don't know I've any great cause to quarrel about it," she said. "Of course I'd have got a lot of pleasure from knowing a secret like that; but I can see your point of view."

"If she'd lived, I was going to tell you next Christmas for a Christmas

G*

box," he answered. "That was the idea in my mind, Ivy; and while we're on the subject I'll say one thing. I never want to put a finger to a penny of that money. It's yours and if you wish to please me you'll let it bide and never touch a penny but only use the dividenders when they come in. And save a bit of them too. Save and let the stuff grow same as I do with my small money."

She was reflecting.

"Very much to the good, Rupert," she said. "That's just the same as I see it for the minute; but big money like this may enlarge our ideas come presently."

"It may," he agreed. "You may not want to hide up the money in a napkin for evermore, of course, but I wouldn't be in any haste to mess about with it. A come-by-chance like this must be taken mighty serious—same as I took it from the moment I heard tell about. And don't you whisper a word to a soul till the will's made known. I might lose my job if it ever got out I'd heard them men talking and made a note of it."

"Not a word," promised Ivy, "except in my prayers to thank God for His mercies. And if it was heard how you knew this before you courted me there'd be a lot of nasty things said about you."

"That's right," he agreed. "They wouldn't matter to me, but naturally you wouldn't like 'em. I heard something nobody had any right to hear, but the only one to blame is that chattering lawyer."

"This will put me in a class by myself you might almost say," mused Ivy and Rupert gave one of his rare laughs.

"Oh yes; there's always something that makes the people cringe a bit before big money," he agreed.

"I remember Alfred Bodkin saying how wealth meant security or danger, according as you were wise or foolish," said Ivy. "Thank the Lord we're the wise ones."

"I must seek for old Joe Bowring now," he told her, "because the church organist is on his holiday and parson's wishful for Bowring to plan the music at the funeral and wants to know if he's game to carry it out. He'll be at the pub most like."

Ivy asked him a question as he departed.

"Would you say I ought to get a bit more dressy now, Rupert?" she inquired.

"Waste of money in your case," he answered, "but no doubt you'll want to show a new feather or two."

XIX

TIME sped and another harvest occupied the prime attention of Priory. Great events were duly acclaimed and took their places in the past, to be remembered a little while, then absorbed gradually and forgotten. A new lord of the manor was greeted as hopeful and understanding. The people had known him for a long time and approved both him and his wife. Paul Pook did not hesitate to declare that marriage had largely added to his measure of contentment and might quite possibly lengthen his life; while Jenny was frankly happy with him.

"You can see envy looking out of the eyes of some of 'em," Ivy told her mother-in-law on one occasion, "but the respect is there, because they well know such a thing wouldn't have overtook me unless I'd been an outstanding woman."

"True by this hand," declared Jenny, "and a nest egg that your father says ought to double your husband's wages; but you've got the blessing to know money's sacred in Rupert's eyes, so you won't feel no anxiety in that quarter."

At Pigslake life proceeded with reasonable prosperity and a wedding was predicted for the coming year; while Nelly Faircloud at 'Lavender Cottage' followed her uneventful path and began to feel satisfied that all was well with Timothy and his new existence had not disappointed him. He spent an occasional week-end at Priory, but did not seek the village gathering, choosing rather to walk in the woods and renew acquaintance with trees and his old companions of the forest. There he sometimes met with Rupert; but for the most part he kept to himself, his mind occupied with his own affairs. He did not visit the baker on these occasions, and his mother never mentioned Katey or her family until he should care to do so. But he never alluded to the past, or the cause that had dislocated his former plans for the future. He was full of his books and all that they meant to him.

"My intention now," he said, "is some day to have a book shop of my own and, as my employer is pretty old and has taken to me and sees the rare sort of booky stuff I'm made of, in the future he may retire and leave me to carry on. He's a most brilliant bookman himself and very willing to teach me."

Of his daily life and new friends he said but little, but he declared great interest in Redchester Cathedral and its history. His bent began to reveal itself and he spoke of joining the Devonshire Association and studying its various historic interests. Nelly marked his diction, new words and niceties of speech. He showed no great anxiety on her account but invited her to spend a week-end with him, see famous edifices and hear the singing at the cathedral. Twice she did this, and on his birthday sent him a present of twenty pounds. For such a gift he was greatly obliged and thanked her heartily. She saw that his physical beauty began to lose its youthful quality and take a more delicate distinction. To her ear his voice was pitched in a lower key than of old.

'The difference between an indoor man and an outdoor man,' thought Mrs. Faircloud, 'and was sure to overtake him soon or late.'

She felt no increased maternal attachment for the young man, but was glad in her placid fashion to know that he had set out upon his life's adventure with every prospect of success. And then, nearly two years after he had left her, Timothy wrote a very remarkable letter that revived the past most unexpectedly, and gave her something to think about. She had not seen him for six months when his long communication arrived, with its considerable challenge for thought.

Thus he had written.

"*My Dear Mother,*

"*It is a long time since I sent you a letter, but a good deal of correspondence, regarding old libraries and such-like, is part of my work now and I have not much time to waste on private writing. I can now inform you of some matters of interest which you will be glad to learn. I have had a rise and my employer says I am making up into a first-class expert and to the manner born. I have corrected him once or twice by a sort of instinct. I am more naturally gifted than he is. As he says, 'a man born with a soul for the book trade.' But I know myself to be a great deal more than that and already I feel a time will come to show I have a deeper understanding of literature than he has. I couldn't know more about books than what he does, after a life-time at them; but I know more about literature than him, owing to my great love for reading. I am now a student and a scholar, and making up for the years I spent hacking the trees though, even in those days, I was one for the inner meaning of things and saw a lot more in the scenes of my work than a common woodman could. Looking back at the past, I see that I was always shaping for a very different kind of life than looked to be my lot; but now all the wisdom and wonder stored up in books is within my reach and I cannot help feeling surprised sometimes how it is, with such a lot of valuable information set down by deep thinkers in the past, the bulk of men and women continue to be such utter fools. I plunge into philosophy as well as history sometimes, and am a good deal drawn to it, because the ancient sages make you think a lot, and it's most astonishing to read books by men dead and forgot for centuries, and yet full of sense and well up to date for wisdom and a lot wiser than many who are writing books to-day. Only students, or scholars, or schoolmasters ever open a page of these things now, and there's very little great literature wrote by living men to-day. Only what we call 'tripe'—stuff like story-books and such that's dead to the world a month after it's published.*

"I find that I despise the things most people seem to want in Redchester; but only now and again do you meet anybody, outside our regular customers, who get their peace and pleasure out of the richness of good books. And I have now decided that in a few years' time I shall set about writing a book myself, to make people think, and point out to the general public what a fine thing it would be for their minds if they read grand old books more and gave rubbishy new books a miss. But not yet—not until I have soaked myself deeper in fine writings and made thousands of notes on the subject.

"You will be interested to know I have now quite decided that the pen is greater than the sword; and when I'd decided about that, it followed how a good many of my ideas about power and greatness in general were changed. What I thought was power in my young days I now see didn't amount to real power at all and I can now tell you a most interesting event, which I rather think will give you and one other a lot of satisfaction to know. Looking back I have often studied my own make-up and my gift of imagination and seen what grotesque shapes it used to take in childhood; and then, seeing how it changed with gathering knowledge, I found myself facing some very striking facts. You wouldn't understand about psychology, but I am beginning to study this also and, applying it to myself, I realize it means a lot.

"But what will wake you up is this: that I clearly see now, I carried on a fault of youth into my manhood, and really believed I'd done a mad thing that I never did do. And when I tell you it was the thing that separated me

from you and Katey Wish, then you'll quickly understand what a great discovery I have made. The truth is that you evidently saw clearer in that little matter than I did, at the time, and my convictions about the death of Nicholas Withers were only the last example of my old gift of imagining things so vividly that I got wrapped up in them, and so at last came to believe them. I made my dreams come true, in a manner of speaking, and I always resented it, even in my tender youth, when I let out some wonderful, fancied deed and nobody would believe it. But psychology shows that is what happened in that stupid business. It had come to be my fancied, master secret and I hugged it to my soul. It was far more true to me than any other truth in the world so, when firstly Kate and secondly you refused to believe it, I suffered hell, because such a refusal showed your contempt for me and your belief I was only a liar, and a bad liar at that. My brain rocked for a day or two and I felt that the quicker I got away from both of you the better. Then I licked my wounds and learned wisdom and kept hold on my growing intellect, and now I'm rewarded. It's always the truest greatness to own up when you find you are in the wrong, and now I'm schooled to own up frankly, that you were right and I was wrong, and that your knowledge of my nature in the past was deeper than my own. I had built up my belief that I killed Withers by brooding it into such a solid thing that it grew to be actual truth ; but you, coming to the news without any preparation, felt it ring false from the moment you heard it, and nothing would convince you to the contrary. And you were right. No such horrid event could have happened and it all looks very petty and silly to me as I turn back my thoughts upon it from where I stand now. So, to say the last on the subject, I was wrong and you and Kate were right.

"I don't think any more of the past these days, but only of the future and you will see in a moment that this discovery has to do with the future. I am very glad to have made it, but I can't get away from the fact that it has a bearing on my duty ; because, if we all go back two years and more, and consider where we stood, we must all see that, knowing what I know now, I should have taken a very different line. Now I agree that you were both right and, if I had grasped your rightness, of course I should have buried my pride, and admitted it, and things would have taken their proper course. In that case I should have been thinking about my marriage to Katey by now. And so I put myself in that position and my thoughts turn to her. We never met again after our difference and you never named her name and I never wanted to hear it for that matter. But now she'll be as glad as yourself to know that the clouds have rolled by, and I can come before her next time I visit Priory. Then she can welcome me back in her life again ; but not the green boy I was that she will remember, but something a lot better worth her attention ; and I'll help her to catch up with me as soon as she likes to set about trying. That's my duty as well as my inclination, and you can tell her so and ask her to write to me, and also that I still have the ring she sent back to me when we parted.

"No more at present, but I shall be glad to hear that all is well.

"Your affectionate son,

"Timothy."

His mother reflected dispassionately over this long letter and was in no great haste to reply. He had showered facts upon her, for the most part satisfying; but what he appeared to take for granted, as a result of his own convictions, could never happen. She pondered long upon this sudden change of front, arising, so he declared, from his larger experience of himself and broader views. So broad indeed had they become that he could dismiss the whole business as a silly myth with which none need be longer concerned. 'It may look like a bad dream to him now,' thought Nelly; 'it may seem something to pass off with a high hand; but surely he can't imagine everything is going to be just the same after a break-up like that, just because he's wishful to get back to the old starting point and go on where he left off? Life don't stand still with everybody else, while it goes on with him.'

Two days later she answered Timothy, after having read his letter several times. The doubt that affected her most deeply she reserved for discussion with another; but meanwhile she traversed his news to the best of her power.

Thus wrote Nelly Faircloud:—

" *My Dear Son,*

"*I was very glad to hear the news that you are making good with the gentleman at the Bookshop and proving to him that you were the very one to suit him. And I was gladder still to hear you feel you are in just the job you find best suited to your needs, because, if you properly like your work and go to it with good willing, that's half the way to doing it. And if you've had your wages put up, that's a sure sign your master thinks highly of your cleverness. It will be very wonderful if you rise to write a book yourself and I shall be a lot interested to hear tell what it is going to be about. And if you can prove to the people the pen is mightier than the sword, then no doubt you'll have done a fine job of work and get your name well thought upon by the bettermost.*

"*It is a great pleasure to me to hear that, along of your studies and learning, you now believe that Katey Wish and me were right when we withstood you about that fearful affair, and I only feel sorry we hadn't got the words to show you how badly you'd got off the rails about poor Mr. Nicholas Withers. Mayhap, if you'd took that tale to dear Dr. Naylor, he'd have had the brain to put you right and make a lot of difference to your future plans of action and brought you back to your senses before it was too late. But, of course, the great thing is that the light have broke at last and you can feel and believe you never took a fellow-creature's life. And by now I guess you feel very thankful that you was mistook, because all your deep reading and wisdom must long since have shown you that such a horrible deed was nought to be proud about but far ways different. Now, thank God, you can feel for evermore there's no millstone like that hanging round your neck, which is a lot to the good, Timothy, because, if you had gone on believing yourself a murderer, it would have got home on you soon or late, and most like ruined your life.*

"*Now I come to Katey ; but I must tell you I can't give her your message, because she's tokened to Jonathan Withers and they count to marry after corn harvest. She was such a one for the open air and the country in general that I doubt she would have been properly happy in a bookshop, but, come presently, I expect you will meet with some clever young woman to suit you*

*and share in your work and make you a proper home, because there's no
book ever was wrote could serve you so well as a partner, who watched after
you and loved you, and took joy to see you get up in the world.*

"When you mind to come I shall be glad to see you, as I always am.

"Your affectionate

"Mother."

A few days after she had written her letter, Nelly, desiring another
opinion upon Timothy's, consulted the only source possible. Mercy
Grepe alone might learn of his avowal, or be permitted to comment upon
it. Moreover Mrs. Faircloud remembered the support accorded to her
own opinions in the past and felt glad to think the wise woman would
welcome such a conclusion. Mercy was as usual with her cats in her garden,
and she and Mrs. Faircloud sat upon a seat together while she read the
letter slowly and her visitor watched a kitten playing with its tail and thought
of Tim's childhood.

"What d'you think of that, my dear?" she asked when the letter was
handed back to her.

"There's a lot of different ways you can read it and a lot of different
roads you can follow the workings of his mind before he came to write
it," answered Mercy, looking down thoughtfully upon her small friends.
"Some might read nought but an eye to the future and what he would like
to happen; and some might say it was a kindly letter aiming to make them
who cared about him the happier for what he tells."

"I had it in me very strong to show it to you, because you always upheld
me when I said he never could have done it," explained Nelly, "and, so far,
I am a lot the happier, and reckoned that you would be also, to know that
we were all in the right and he has lived to grant it. You can see, through
his high and mighty learning, that he knows what we women saw at the
time was true enough; but it all looks quite small to him now, like a man
laughing when his mother tells him what he was used to do when a little
boy. So that's that, and all to the good; but when he turns to Katey, of
course, it ain't so good. My feeling is not to say a word to Katey and,
then again, she being the only one who knew how it was with him, I ask
myself whether in justice to her memory of him, she ought to hear he's come
round and seen sense. But it looks too late."

Mercy considered.

"There again there's more roads than one that a body might take,
according as they read this letter," she said. "Have you answered it?"

"I have and told him Katey's going to wed Jonathan Withers. That's
all that matters to him; but do anything more matter to Kate?"

"No," declared Mercy. "I'd leave it at that. To my certain knowledge
Milly Wish's daughter had a bad time over that job and faced up to it pretty
well and got her reward. It wouldn't make a pin of difference to her,
nor yet set her in two minds about Timothy, to hear he was wishful to have
her back. She's a girl with a very clear turn of intellects and she acted
straight. Her mother told me Kate decided that she and your boy didn't
see alike on matters of importance; but she put no name to 'em and never
queaked a syllable about the truth of it. You leave her alone, Nelly—that's

my advice. And don't cherish no hopes—mother-like and for Timothy's sake—that she would ever go back to him now. She wouldn't."

"I am glad to hear you say that," declared the younger, "because I feel the same. A bit too good for Timothy she is—to say it kindly. I told him in my letter that he'll live to find a town-dwelling girl some day to make a home for him and take pride in his cleverness. And maybe some day, when Katey's married, and if she's allowed to see me again in the future and willing to talk about the past, then I'll be able to drop in her ear that Timothy went back on it and has confessed we were right to disbelieve him."

Mercy nodded her head without speaking and Nelly changed the subject.

"Do Mary Piper—Alice Piper's niece—serve you well?"

"Very well, my dear, and like your good-willing to find her for me. A nice maid and saves my old bones a deal of weariness."

"Take care of yourself and don't be delving too much in your garden, nor let your cats martyr you," begged Nelly. Then they kissed and she went her way.

The old woman watched her depart and turned her mind into the past. Many strange memories were hidden there with which she was wont to occupy her thoughts, summoning into the light deeds done aforetime and the men and women who did them. She went in presently, put on the kettle and made herself some tea. She sat down to drink it and a yellow cat jumped upon her lean lap, padded, purred, and looked into her face with his steady, orange-coloured eyes. It was a cat that Mercy always declared to possess that rarest feline attribute: personal affection for an individual other than himself.

She stroked him and spoke to him, confiding, as she sometimes did to an unconscious creature, facts that no fellow being had ever learned or would learn.

"I can talk to you, 'Sandy,'" she said, "because it won't go no further and you keep my secrets so close as what I do myself. And I can tell you when I, that cleave to truth like my second self, told lies and said the thing that was not. I said 'em to that dear woman what have just left me. I said 'em for her peace, but they weren't the truth of what I thought. Yet much that looks like chance to us be doubtless planned careful enough in the council chambers of Providence, or so I believe, and if the outcome's good, it ain't for we to quarrel with the ordination. And so, when I heard that tale, how the woman's son had put away Nicholas Withers, I agreed her line was best and her peace could only come by denying it. Yes, I agreed with her, 'Sandy,' my lad, and said she was in the right, well knowing that man's mother and his sweetheart to be in the wrong. Would he have raged same as he did if it was a dream? Would he have cast the pair of 'em off and hated 'em in his heart if they hadn't robbed him of the praises he thought he'd earned? Not on your life! And remember the one that died. Would Nicholas Withers, a man so quick and keen and so much in love with his life, have played that foolish, clumsy part and fallen down a well like a kitten or a puppy? Never. He was put down same as Timothy told 'em. He was catched like a stroke of lightning from behind his back, and all that happened after everybody can see; but only young Fairclough knew who was responsible for the good that befell.

He done it and he kept his secret so long as he could hold it in, and then his queer wits went back on him and he blabbed it out where it was safest in his thoughts to do so. And fate served him handsome to the end, for he's got all he wants but his girl, and he's better without her; and his mother believes surer than ever now that he's innocent, so out of his evil good comes—so far as human eyes can see. And you and me will bide dumb on that, 'Sandy,' for 'tis a secret would be no service to living or dead no more."

*   *   *   *   *   *

A thousand, thousand Priories jog upon their immemorial way, with the old melodies and dissonances, the old echoes of joy and tribulation, sounding their notes of hope and fear, as familiar as those of the thrush and blackbird that haunt them. Eternal recurrence and sleepless change go hand in hand to speed the tide of affairs for ever ebbing and flowing in every human home—currents from which may be captured but passing ripples—leaves of history torn from their context in past and future. For beginning and end alike are hidden from mortal prescience, since events arise out of causes unrecorded and in their turn become the cause of effects to come. The fabric of our existence is woven from one generation to another by those who know no more of its pattern and purpose than the particles of moisture that create a cloud can guess its significance and vast design; but all men and women of goodwill must admit that, though the object of our creation remains a mystery, our power to justify it shines clear enough; for none shall deny mankind's endowment: to write nobler pages in the book of human life than any yet recorded. At least that is one living truth about our little selves.

THE END